Dugan & Diamond

Carnival
1909 – 1931
Glass

Identification & Value Guide

Carl O. Burns

COLLECTOR BOOKS
A Division of Schroeder Publishing Co., Inc.

The current values in this book should be used only as a guide. They are not intended to set prices, which vary from one section of the country to another. Auction prices as well as dealer prices vary greatly and are affected by condition as well as demand. Neither the author nor the publisher assumes responsibility for any losses that might be incurred as a result of consulting this guide.

Searching For A Publisher?

We are always looking for knowledgeable people considered to be experts within their fields. If you feel that there is a real need for a book on your collectible subject and have a large comprehensive collection, contact Collector Books.

Front cover: Amethyst Butterfly & Tulip Square ruffled bowl, $2,350.00; sapphire blue Big Basketweave 8" vase, $375.00; amethyst S Repeat banquet-size punch set, $6,500.00.

Cover photo credits: Carl O. Burns, David Doty, and John Muehlbauer
Cover design by Michelle Dowling
Book design by Terri Stalions

COLLECTOR BOOKS
P.O. Box 3009
Paducah, Kentucky 42002-3009

Copyright © 1999 by Carl O. Burns

Contents

Dedication

To my dearest Marsha, my loving and supportive partner in life, a Pennsylvania native, who has trod many times on the very ground where the Dugan/Diamond factory once stood. Your understanding, during the long hours I spent apart from you preparing this book and the last one, your patience with the phone calls and correspondence at all hours of the day and night, and the inspiration and support you gave to me when I needed it most, have forever impressed within my soul the truest meaning of the word "love."

About the Author

Carl Owen Burns has spent 29 years as an active carnival glass collector and full-time antique dealer. This is his third book on the subject of carnival glass. His first, *The Collector's Guide to Northwood's Carnival Glass*, was published in 1994, and his second, *Imperial Carnival Glass – Identification and Values,* was released in 1996. His educational articles have appeared in the bulletins of "The Heart of American Carnival Glass Association," "The Lincoln-Land Carnival Glass Club," and "The San Diego Carnival Glass Club." He is also a member of The National Imperial Glass Collector's Society and was one of the founding members of The New England Carnival Glass Association.

In addition to old carnival glass, he also collects Imperial slag glass, which was produced from 1959 to 1976, and is an avid record collector with an impressive collection of blues and rock and roll albums. He is also a full-time antique dealer and his business, Minnah's Antiques, is well known throughout the country.

When not engaged in the above pursuits, he can often be found casting for trout on the many rivers, streams, and lakes in the mountains of western Maine, where he lives with his wife Marsha.

Acknowledgments

Books such as this are not possible without the participation, aid, and encouragement of a great many people. As the author, I am really just a reporter. My job is to sort through and correlate information that comes to me through the vast network of carnival glass collectors all over the world. This would not be possible if people were not eager to share their knowledge and to promote the hobby of carnival glass collecting. And I have yet to meet a carnival glass collector who is not! Nowhere else in the field of antiques and collectibles is there found such a willingness to share information. In this respect, every person who has ever had interest in carnival glass has contributed to this effort.

And, there are some who have gone that extra mile in their participation in this project. They truly deserve far more applause and praise than space permits here, and they shall always have my heartfelt thanks and deepest appreciation.

A very special note of thanks goes to David Doty who came to my rescue at the eleventh hour, providing beautiful photographs of some extremely rare and unique Dugan/Diamond carnival pieces, that otherwise would not have been included in this book. David, I owe you one…big time!

Likewise, a very special thanks goes out to John and Lucile Britt for their eagerness and willingness to share from their vast carnival glass photo library.

My thanks goes out to my dear friends Robert and Darlene Hurst, for entrusting to my care nearly 50 pieces of Dugan carnival glass while photography was in progress.

And a special "tip of the hat" to John Muehlbauer, for sharing with me his extensive research notes on the Farmyard Bowls and for the many photographs that he provided.

My deepest appreciation to Steve Jennings for his kind permission to reproduce portions of the only known Dugan Factory catalog, and to all the members of the San Diego County Carnival Glass Club and the Southern California Carnival Glass Club for their permission to reproduce selected assortments from their book of Butler Brothers Wholesale Catalogs, entitled *Catalogs Selling Carnival*.

Likewise, a note of thanks to James Measell for his kind assistance in helping locate some crucial sources of information.

My sincere thanks goes out to all of the following wonderful people who provided information and photographs and/or opened their homes to me and allowed me to photograph glass from their collections:

Susan Aguiar
Rich Brazel
Mike Carwile
Greg Dilian
Richard and Cathy Fenton
David Ayers
Richard Burke
Kevin and April Clark
Rob Cooper
Tom Dryden
Gregory and Helen Ferguson
Dean and Diane Fry
Rick and Debbie Graham
Mary Hadzima
Elton and Irma Kilmartin

Mr. and Mrs. Robert Leonard
George Loescher
Jeri Sue Lucas
Lee Markley
Tom and Sharon Mordini
Gloria Pfeiffer
Alan and Loraine Pickup
Jackie and Randy Poucher
Marvin and Doris Quick
Casy Rich
Heidi Ritterbush
Diane Rosington
Edward C. Stalder
Tom and Joan Steskal

Introduction

When I first became interested in carnival glass back in 1969, the hobby was very different from what it is today. The glass was really just emerging onto the collectors' market and prices were very low. There were probably no more than a few hundred collectors nationwide. The first couple of carnival glass clubs were still in their infancy and there was precious little reference material. Pioneer researcher Rose Preznick had published a series of four small books containing carnival pattern drawings. Marion Hartung's 10-book series was only up to book number eight, while Sherman Hand was undertaking the monumental task of completing the first series of carnival books to contain actual color photographs of the glass. At that time, most research efforts centered around "The Big Four." This was the term that we used in reference to the four known major producers of carnival glass: Northwood, Fenton, Imperial, and Millersburg. Few of us had ever heard of the Dugan or Diamond Glass Companies of Indiana, Pennsylvania.

Yet, the very first reference book on iridescent glass made specific mention of the Diamond Glass Company as a producer of the glass we call carnival. The book was entitled simply *Iridescent Glass*. It was written by Larry Freeman and was published way back in 1956. It would be nearly 20 years before anyone "picked up" on this passing mention of a then obscure glasshouse and made the effort to find out more about it.

Of course, the citizens of the town of Indiana, Pennsylvania, knew full well that a major glasshouse had once operated there. It was on a five-acre plot sandwiched between the railroad line and the old fairgrounds. From 1892 to 1896, the factory was home to the Indiana Glass Company. Harry Northwood operated here as the Northwood Company from 1896 to 1901. Thomas Dugan, Harry Northwood's cousin, took over operation of the plant in 1901, and in 1904 it became The Dugan Glass Company. The ownership would change hands one more time, in 1913, and it would become the Diamond Glass Company until the plant was destroyed by fire in 1931. This was all well known by the people of Indiana, Pennsylvania; what was not known in early carnival collecting circles, was that as much as 20 to 25% of all our beloved carnival glass had, in fact, been made here! This lack of knowledge was soon to change, and The Big Four would become The Big Five.

During 1975 and 1976, construction was underway on some improvements to an athletic stadium in Indiana, Pennsylvania. This stadium sat on a tract of land that had, at one time, been bordered by the old railroad line and the old fairgrounds. Among the improvements being made were several large planting beds for flowers, trees, and shrubs. During these excavations, workers became intrigued with the numerous, colorful glass fragments that kept turning up in their diggings. Unbeknownst to them, these planting beds were being dug at the exact site of the old Dugan/Diamond Factory dump! Three men, Harry A. Helman, his son Del, and George McMillan spent countless hours sifting through these diggings, filling box after box with fragments of glass. Their efforts were to forever change the face of glass collecting, for included in these shards were dozens and dozens of fragments of the beautiful glass that we call carnival.

The boxes of shards were sent to William Heacock, the author of the best selling series of books entitled *The Encyclopedia of Victorian Colored Pattern Glass*. Bill was just getting involved in carnival glass research at the time. He contacted Bill Edwards and arrangements were made for the two men to work together, cataloging and identifying the numerous carnival glass fragments. What they found proved to be quite a shock. The vast majority of these carnival fragments were of patterns long credited to Northwood! Clearly, something was very wrong here. Granted, Harry Northwood had once operated here, but had left the site to open his new plant at Wheeling, West Virginia, a full six years before carnival glass was introduced to the market. So, what were all these fragments doing here? There could only be one answer: these carnival glass patterns had to have been made here! And, they had not been made by Harry Northwood! A new door in the history of American glassmaking had been opened. A "sleeping giant" awoke.

By a strange twist of fate, at this very time, I was preparing to photograph a previously unlisted piece of Northwood glass: a non-iridized crystal Memphis handled whiskey decanter. I had met Bill Heacock just a few months earlier and he had requested that I send him documentation of any unusual glass "finds" that I might uncover. At the precise moment that I attempted to photograph this decanter, my trusty, but aging Nikon F decided to "give up the ghost," and began its long journey to that great photo studio in the sky. The cost of repairing it was prohibitive, so with four years of high school drafting classes under my belt, I turned to the next best thing to a photograph. I made a detailed, to-scale drawing of the piece and sent it off to Bill.

A few nights later, the phone rang. It was Bill and he seemed very excited. The whiskey decanter was certainly a nice find, but he was more interested in the drawing itself. Would I consider doing several carnival glass pattern drawings for him? I agreed to give it my best shot and he read off a list of pattern names. It seemed to me to be a rather odd assortment of seldom discussed patterns, so I inquired as to the purpose of the drawings. After a slight pause, Bill swore me to absolute secrecy. He then told me about the shards and what was going on. Thus, I became one of the first few people to know about the whole affair. Bill was preparing what would surely be a landmark article, for *The Antique Trader Weekly*, concerning the carnival glass now known to have been made at the Indiana, Pennsylvania, factory. Some of the drawings would be used in the article and in a future series of articles that would appear in his new bi-monthly publication *Pattern Glass Preview*.

Over the course of the next few weeks, I sent over 20 pattern drawings to Bill and several of them did indeed appear in his research articles. It has always been most gratifying to know that I was able, even in this small way, to be a part of the unfolding story of carnival glass production at Indiana, Pennsylvania. For me, it marked a turning point in my carnival glass collecting. I would no longer be content to merely collect the glass. I knew that someday I wanted to write about it and share with others what I had learned along the way. I began to seek out not only the glass itself, but also virtually anything to do with the making, marketing, and distribution of it. My home began to fill up with old catalogs, trade journals, advertising, and just about any other related materials that I could lay my hands on. Over the years, I have probably spent as much money on them as I have for the glass itself.

It would be 16 more years before I felt that I had gained sufficient knowledge to begin putting down on paper what I had learned. My first book, *The Collector's Guide to Northwood's Carnival Glass*, was published in 1994. It was followed by my second on Imperial carnival glass, in 1996. You now hold in your hands the third, (but not the last), book in this series about carnival glass. This one is a particular "labor of love" for me, because it was my small involvement in the initial unveiling of the story of carnival glass production at the Dugan and Diamond Glass companies, of Indiana, Pennsylvania, that sent me down this road.

The Bombshell

When the late William Heacock's article introducing the world to the carnival glass made at Indiana, Pennsylvania, appeared in *The Antique Trader Weekly* in 1981, it exploded like an atomic bomb in carnival collecting circles. There are, I'm sure, many of you reading this who well remember that article and all of the ensuing controversy. There were those who refused to accept it and publicly denounced the whole thing. For some reason they just couldn't grasp the fact that some of their beloved glass did not come from where they had long believed it had. Many of the patterns that were found in the Helman shards had long been credited to either Northwood or Fenton. A couple were even believed to be Millersburg!

Change can be a funny thing. It happens to all things, both living and innate. It is, in fact, the very essence of all things. Nothing stays the same forever. The very earth we walk upon; the nightly display in the heavens that we gaze upon; the clothes we wear; even the way we think and communicate are never constant. They are always changing. Without change, we would not even be here. Yet, for some dark, obscure reason, we humans tend to resist it and perhaps even fear it. It seems to make us uncomfortable. We want things to stay as they are, but the reality is that they never do.

It took quite a few years for some people to accept the changes in the carnival collecting hobby that came about as a result of that article. I think a lot of them feared that it would have a negative effect on the value of some of their glass. And, for a short time, it did! During the early 1980s, some of the pieces in question did experience a "leveling off," and even a drop in price. Rarities like the Farmyard Bowl and the Christmas Compote, long believed to be Northwood creations, were affected. But, this did not last for long. Values not only rebounded, but surged far above the pre-1981 levels, as more and more people began to accept these changes in the hobby. Eventually they realized that a whole new door in the carnival collecting hobby had been opened. The carnival glass made by the Dugan and Diamond Glass Companies is now eagerly sought, and often highly praised, as some of the most beautiful carnival ever produced. The "sleeping giant" is alive and well, and it has taken its rightful place in the history books of American glassmaking.

The Shards

The quantity of carnival glass fragments unearthed by the Helmans at the factory site in Indiana, Pennsylvania, was quite impressive. From them we have been able to establish many designs as Dugan or Diamond products. A large quantity of shards in non-iridized colored, opalescent, and custard was also found there and these too have helped to establish a Dugan or Diamond origin for many additional patterns.

Fragments of all the following carnival glass patterns were found at the factory site in Indiana, Pennsylvania.

Apple Blossoms	Jewelled Heart	Vintage Perfume
Beaded Panels	Lattice & Daisy	Windflower
Bells & Beads	Many Fruits	Wreath of Roses
Butterfly & Tulip	Nautilus	Apple Blossom Twigs
Crackle Car Vase	Persian Garden	Beaded Shell
Dogwood Sprays	Quill	Big Basketweave
Fishnet Epergne	Sea Gull	Circle Scroll
Garden Path	Soutache	Dahlia
Grape Arbor Bowl	Strawberry Epergne	Double Stemmed Rose

Inverted Fan & Feather	Vintage Powder Jar	Leaf Rays
Golden Harvest	Waterlily & Cattails	Malaga
Heavy Web	Wreathed Cherry	Mary Ann Vase
Keyhole	Beaded Basket	Pulled Loop
Lined Lattice	Beauty Bud	Pony
Maple Leaf	Dugan's Cherry	Raindrops
Peacock at the Fountain	Coin Spot	Single Flower
Question Marks	Fanciful	Target
Rambler Rose	Fan	Victorian
Single Flower Framed	Floral & Grape	Vineyard
Stork in the Rushes	Heavy Iris	Woodpecker
Swan Novelty	Holly & Berry	Wide Rib

The identification of these shards further opened the door for additional pattern attributions. Because all these patterns could now be established as either Dugan or Diamond products, other designs that appeared in company with them, in the wholesale catalog assortments, could now be credited to these two firms as well. In addition, several of the above patterns, like Jewelled Heart, Keyhole, and Inverted Fan & Feather, were used as exterior designs in combination with other interior motifs. Thus, we can now firmly establish all of the following patterns as either Dugan or Diamond creations.

Stippled Petals	Compass	Long Leaf
Four Flowers	Ski-Star	Grapevine Lattice
S Repeat	Constellation	Golden Grapes
Stippled Estate	Farmyard	Puzzle
Floral & Wheat	Georgia Belle	Honeycomb
Petal & Fan	Round-Up	Vining Twigs
Wishbone & Spades	Spiralex	Fishscale & Beads

During the 1980s, another important discovery surfaced. Steve Jennings was presented with a 1907 Dugan factory catalog! It had survived the 1931 fire, and had been exposed to the elements for 10 years before anyone found it. That it survived at all is miraculous. Along with it were found several original pattern mold drawings. It is the only known Dugan catalog in existence! With meticulous care, Steve preserved all of this and had copies made. I was fortunate to obtain one of the copies in 1988. A lot of questions and mysteries were cleared up by this catalog. Likewise, many others were created by it, some of which remain unanswered to this day. Still, it is a priceless document. Perhaps one day others will be found. My only hope is that whoever finds them will have the good sense to preserve and share them with others.

Thomas Ernest Alfred Dugan (1865 – 1944)

It is my intent neither to involve the reader in a detailed biography of Thomas Dugan nor to present a lengthy history of his years in the glass-making industry. That has already been done in the excellent work entitled *Dugan/Diamond — The Story of Indiana, Pennsylvania Glass* by William Heacock, James Measell, and Berry Wiggins. I highly recommend that you read it. My focus here is to provide today's collector with a source of reference concerning the collectibility of the carnival glass produced by the factory that bore his name and that was produced by its successor, the Diamond Glass Company. However, in order to do that and to give the reader some sense of perspective regarding the carnival glass produced at Indiana, Pennsylvania, brief outlines of both the man and the factory are necessary.

In March of 1881, just eight months prior to the arrival of his soon-to-be-famous cousin, Harry Northwood, 16-year-old Thomas Ernest Alfred Dugan set foot on the shores of America, in company with his parents and his younger brothers, Alfred and Samuel, Jr. His father, Samuel Dugan, had been a glassworker in England, likely in the area of Kingswinford, where the family had lived.

The following year found young Thomas and "Cousin Harry" living at a boarding house on Jacob St. in Wheeling, West Virginia. Both had obtained employment as glass etchers at the Hobbs-Brockunier plant.

In November of 1887, Harry Northwood formed the Northwood Glass Co., at Martins Ferry, Ohio, the first of four plants that would bear his name. Samuel Dugan and his sons, Thomas, Alfred, and Samuel, Jr., were all employed there, in various capacities. It was during this time that Thomas met and married Emily Dorsett. Their Washington Street home would soon be blessed with two daughters, Verna May and Pearl Elizabeth.

When Harry Northwood moved his operation to Ellwood City, Pennsylvania in 1892, the Dugan clan moved with him. Samuel, Alfred, and Samuel, Jr. were employed as glass blowers, while Thomas was appointed as the plant foreman. It was during his four years spent here, in Ellwood City, that Thomas Dugan began to experiment in earnest with his own glassmaking techniques. He was no doubt responsible, at least in part, for several of the innovative "Northwood" creations that emerged from this plant. A third daughter, Emily Roberta, was born to Thomas and Emily Dugan on July 7, 1893.

Problems plagued the Ellwood City plant right from the start and in 1896 both the Northwoods and the Dugans moved again. This time, the Northwood Glass Company took up residency in the vacant factory in Indiana, Pennsylvania, that had once housed the Indiana Glass Company. It would be here that Thomas Dugan would finally move out from under the shadow of his famous cousin Harry and establish his own identity in the history of American glassmaking. In fact, when one examines many of the glassware lines later created by Thomas Dugan, and many of the wares which emerged earlier from this plant under the Northwood name, the influence of Thomas Dugan's hand in many of Northwood's earlier lines becomes quite apparent.

In 1899, the Northwood Glass company was purchased by the National Glass Company, a combine of several different glass factories. It retained its name, but all of Harry Northwood's molds became National Glass Company property. This is a key factor in understanding the events surrounding the production of glass that occurred there in the years to come. Harry Northwood was appointed as National's London sales manager and he soon departed with his family to England. Thomas Dugan was appointed factory manager and superintendent, while younger brother Alfred took over as plant foreman.

Things did not progress smoothly for the National Glass Company. By 1901, Harry Northwood had severed his ties with them, and moved on to establish H. Northwood & Company, in the old factory in Wheeling, West Virginia, that had once housed Hobbs-Brockunier. Thomas and Alfred Dugan remained in charge of the Indiana, Pennsylvania, factory that operated as the Northwood Works of The National Glass Company through 1903. One of the most innovative and unusual lines introduced by the Dugans during this period has been erroneously dubbed "Pink Slag" by today's collectors. Made in the Inverted Fan & Feather (Feather Scroll) molds that were left behind by Harry Northwood, this shaded, opaque pink glass is not true slag glass. It was made from a single heat sensitive batch of glass that changed color when "warmed in." It was likely produced for a very short period of time, as examples are rarely found and eagerly sought today.

In 1904, the Dugans, in company with several other investors, purchased the plant and all of its assets (including Harry Northwood's molds) from National, and the Dugan Glass Company of Indiana, Pennsylvania, was born. The firm adopted a trademark, consisting of a diamond with extended sides enclosing a capital letter "D", although comparatively few items from Dugan bear this mark.

From 1904 through 1908, Thomas and Alfred Dugan enjoyed considerable success with their new venture, introducing a wide variety of lines to the trade. Some were made in molds left behind by Harry Northwood, but many others were of their own creation. Mold blown, decorated water sets, and wine sets proved to be very popular items, as were their lines of flint, blue, and green opalescent pieces. The 1907 Dugan factory catalog is dominated by these lines. Their Intaglio line, what we call goofus glass today, also proved a popular seller. The Filigree line, in rich colors of emerald green, cobalt blue, ruby, and opaque ivory, all with either silver or gold decorations, proved a winner as well. Perhaps the most significant, yet often overlooked lines by today's collectors, were Dugan's Venetian, Japanese, and Pompeian art glass lines. While made from a completely different process than the glass we call carnival, they hold the distinction of being some of the very first inexpensive, iridescent wares offered to the public.

The pressed, iridescent glass that we now call carnival was introduced to the trade by the Fenton Art Glass company during the winter of 1907 – 1908. It took the market by storm, and like the bulk of their competitors, the Dugans were producing it by early in 1909. These new iridescent lines would become the backbone of the firm's production for the next four years. Thomas Dugan's dedication to quality and artistry was expressed to maximum levels in many of the iridescent patterns and shapes to emerge from the plant between 1909 and 1913. Designs such as the famous Farmyard bowls and the Christmas compotes are masterpieces of the glassmaker's art, as are many examples of Dugan's peach opalescent carnival glass, an innovative color that was surely a Thomas Dugan creation.

The exact circumstances that led to the departure of both Thomas and Alfred Dugan from Indiana, Pennsylvania, are still unclear to this day. Yet in January of 1913, depart they did, and in July of that year the plant's name was changed to the Diamond Glass Company. For the next year, Thomas was the New York representative of the Cambridge Glass Company and may well have been involved in the marketing of that firm's iridescent glass lines. In mid 1914, both he and his brother Alfred had started a new venture, the Dugan Glass Company of Lonaconing, Maryland, in association with, of all people, the National Glass Company. After only five months, Thomas Dugan resigned, reportedly due to "friction in the directorate of the company," and the firm was renamed the Lonaconing Glass Company. (Strangely, no iridescent glass is known to have been made by the Dugans while they were at Lonaconing.)

After the failure of the Dugans' venture at Lonaconing, Alfred Dugan returned to Indiana, Pennsylvania, where he became factory manager at the Diamond Glass Company. There is some evidence to indicate that he may have had a hand in the development of some of Diamond's later iridescent colors, such as ruby. He remained in the employ of the Diamond Glass Company until his death, in July of 1928.

Thomas Dugan eventually settled into the position of production supervisor at the Hocking Glass Company in Lancaster, Ohio. During the 1920s and 1930s, Hocking produced several iridescent glass lines, primarily of the utility ware type, and Thomas Dugan may well have played a role in their development and production. He remained with Hocking until his retirement in the 1930s. He passed away on February 22, 1944.

The Diamond Glass Company, 1913 - 1931

The Indiana, Pennsylvania, factory operated as the Dugan Glass Company for six months after the departure of Thomas and Alfred Dugan. In July of 1913 it was decided to change the name to the Diamond Glass Company. John P. Elkin was named the new company president and Edward J. Rowland became the general manager.

Iridescent ware continued to be a mainstay of the firm's production, much of it being made in molds that Thomas Dugan, like his cousin Harry Northwood before him, had been obliged to leave behind. This was augmented by the creation of many new patterns, specifically designed for iridescent production. Apparently Diamond enjoyed great success with their iridescent lines, many of which remained in production right up until the factory closed in 1931.

By the mid teens the firm began to develop new colors and shapes as the styles, tastes and demands of consumers changed. Softer, pastel colors in more simple shapes and patterns were "in," and by 1916 the era of the glass known today as "stretch" was underway. It, too, would remain in production, in varying degrees, until 1931.

The firm also enjoyed considerable success with a variety of other glassware lines. Of particular note were their mold blown, decorated crystal lines called Bluebird, Butterfly, and Wild Duck. Wholesale catalogs from the 1917 – 1918 period offer huge assortments of this ware, so they were likely very popular sellers. Equally popular were their mold blown crystal lines featuring delicately cut fruit, floral, and star designs. In 1925, Diamond introduced its #900 line, popularly known today as Adam's Rib. It was made in a tremendous variety of shapes in a wide range of iridescent and non-iridescent colors. This proved to be one of Diamond's most successful lines and it is eagerly sought by today's collectors. Among the last lines developed was one called After Glow, which was introduced in 1928. This line was comprised of novelty items in delicate shades of pink and green. Many of these pieces were made in molds revived from the earlier carnival glass era. While this was primarily made as a non-iridescent line, some iridized examples are known.

Between 1928 and 1930, Diamond experienced some "rough waters," as the effects of the great depression began to grip the nation. In addition, a gas explosion interrupted operations for a time, there were problems with working conditions, and "half-time" shifts for the workers had become the rule. However, all of these problems seem to have been resolved, and by mid to late 1930, the plant was once again operating at near full capacity.

Then, on June 27, 1931, disaster struck. A massive fire, of undetermined origin, swept the plant, leaving over $100,000 worth of damage in its wake. While the main production area of the factory remained relatively intact, the office area, stockrooms, decorating rooms, and the packing areas were totally destroyed.

For a time, rumors circulated concerning the rebuilding of the plant, but it was not to be. The economic conditions of the 1930s would simply not allow such a rebirth. The company was forced into receivership; the plant was dismantled and sold for taxes. Many of the company's molds were purchased by other glasshouses. The era of glassmaking in Indiana, Pennsylvania, had come to an end.

Carnival Glass Production at Indiana, Pennsylvania

One thing became clear to me very early in the preparation of this book. For many years, we have generically referred to all the carnival glass produced at Indiana, Pennsylvania, as "Dugan." We can no longer do this! We are dealing with a unique situation here. There was a major change in the plant's operation "mid stream" in the carnival production era, and Thomas Dugan is really responsible for only a portion of the carnival glass made there. We are really dealing with two distinct companies, under two distinct managements, each of which produced distinctly different carnival glass. The carnival glass produced by Thomas Dugan, from 1909 to 1913, is, in many ways, very different from that made by the Diamond Glass Company between 1913 and 1931. There are considerable differences in pattern design, color, and iridescent quality.

In order to fully appreciate and understand these differences, it is essential to look at each firm's production separately. To do so requires a fairly lengthy text and a good deal of thought and concentration on the part of the reader. I apologize for that, but some things simply cannot be adequately explained in a few words.

Dugan's Carnival Glass Production, 1909 - 1913

Thomas Dugan had apparently been experimenting with iridescent glass, in one form or another, for several years prior to the introduction of what we consider true carnival glass. As early as 1904 he was producing several mold blown, iridescent art glass lines called Venetian, Pompeian, and Japanese. These lines consisted primarily of vases and various novelty items, most of which were fashioned after ancient Roman and Oriental shapes. Many of them have a faint silver/gold iridescent lustre. However, the process by which this was achieved is not the same as that used to make what we call carnival glass. The molten glass was collected on the gathering rod and then rolled in "frit," very finely crushed glass. The frit became embedded in the molten glass. When the piece was hand shaped and "warmed in," this frit would oxidize, resulting in the silver/gold iridescence.

Between 1904 and 1909, many assortments of this ware appear in the wholesale catalogs. Often they were included in the same assortments with opalescent glass novelties. Shown at right an example of Dugan's Venetian art glass in green, circa 1904 – 1905. On the left is an assortment of opalescent and Venetian novelties, from the October 1905 Butler Brothers Wholesale Catalog.

The Fenton Art Glass Company introduced the first iridescent glass to qualify as true carnival during the fall and winter of 1907 – 1908. Naturally, all of that firm's competitors wasted no time in trying to gain a share of the market and Thomas Dugan was no exception. From existing trade journal reports and wholesale catalogs, we know that the Dugan Glass Company was producing carnival glass by sometime in early 1909. The earliest documented assortment of

OUR VENETIAN AND OPALESCENT NOVELTY ASST.

An incomparable group of 10 and 15 cent leaders.

C882—Big new fancy shape pieces in the rich opalescent and Venetian glass, most of which are actually worth double the price here named. Asst. comprises 12 articles, each one in asstd. colors such as blue, green, canary, amethyst, etc. ¼ doz. each of the following:

9½ in. fancy footed opalescent salad dish.	Large nut or rose bowl on 3 fancy feet.
6 in. fancy shape Venetian vase.	9 in. fancy footed salad dish.
8½ in. fancy footed comport or card tray.	6½ in. twisted Venetian vase.
6½ in. fancy Venetian vase.	8½ in. diamond cut table dish.
8 in. deep flaring fruit bowl.	10 in. extra large opalescent vase.
Large size, fancy shape Venetian rose bowl.	Per dozen, **80c**
8¼ in. tall ear of corn vase.	Total 6 doz. in bbl., (bbl. 35c)

Dugan's carnival glass appeared in the Mid Spring 1909 Butler Bros. Wholesale Catalog. Two vases, the Target and Wide Rib offered in marigold, currently hold this distinction.

In the rush to gain a share of this rapidly expanding new market, many existing molds already in use for making non-iridized colored and opalescent ware were rushed into iridescent production. Some of these earliest Dugan carnival patterns included.

Beaded Panels	Jewelled Heart	Pulled Loop
Quill	Daisy & Plume	Compass
Spiralex	Vineyard	Target
Keyhole	Tiny Twigs	Stippled Estate
Flower & Beads	Swan Novelty	Pinched Swirl
Honeycomb	Nautilus	Fan

Many of these designs appear in the 1907 Dugan Factory catalog, which of course, dates just prior to the carnival era. Some, like the Vineyard Water Set and Nautilus, were made in molds left behind by Harry Northwood. By late in 1909 to early 1910, new designs, created specifically for iridescent production, began to appear. Patterns like Stippled Petals, Ski-Star, Dugan's Cherry, Petal & Fan, and the Fishnet Epergne all date from this time.

At this point, it becomes crucial to closely examine two aspects of Dugan's carnival production: the patterns he created exclusively for iridescent production, and the colors in which he chose to make them. Both are very important, for herein lie some critical clues to the vast differences between Dugan's carnival glass and that made later under Diamond Glass Company management.

The following list is a representative sample of some of the carnival glass patterns that were definitely made during Thomas Dugan's tenure at Indiana, Pennsylvania, circa 1909 – 1913:

Farmyard	Heavy Iris	Four Flowers
Persian Gardens	Many Fruits	Wreathed Cherry
Christmas Compote	Wishbone & Spades	Dugan's Cherry
Apple Blossom Twigs	Fanciful	Round-Up
Heavy Grape	Butterfly & Tulip	Border Plants
Dogwood Sprays	Grape Delight	Victorian

All of these patterns show many similarities. All of them are beautifully executed: flowing, graceful patterns that are aesthetically pleasing to the eye, with great attention paid to pattern detail and molding quality. They are quite obviously products of a man totally devoted to a quality rather than quantity ethic. As we shall later see, there is a marked difference between designs such as these and those produced after 1913 by the Diamond Glass Company.

This quality ethic becomes even more evident when we look at the surprisingly limited variety of carnival colors that Thomas Dugan produced. The bulk of his iridescent production centered around four colors: marigold, amethyst, peach opalescent, and white. A fifth color, called oxblood by many collectors, could also be included. Even though it is a variation of the amethyst color, it was marketed as a color unto itself. Production of some of these colors continued under Diamond management, but here again, there is a marked difference in tone and iridescence.

Peach Opalescent: Without any question, Thomas Dugan was the largest producer of peach opalescent carnival glass. In fact, I am convinced that he created the color. This popular and beautiful color was created by combining two different forms of glassmaking to produce a single product. First, a piece of conventional clear to white opalescent (flint) glass was made. It was molded, shaped, and then sprayed with the iridizing solution (in this case, ferric chloride), resulting in the beautiful marigold iridescent overlay. Because of this double process, peach opalescent carnival was far more costly to produce than were many of the other carnival colors. Of course, this cost was passed along to the consumer. The prices for peach opalescent assortments in the wholesale catalogs reflect this. They are often two to three times that of the assortments of other carnival colors. This explains why we find so few large, multiple piece "sets," like punch sets and water sets, in this color. The cost was simply prohibitive, especially to the consumer.

There is also virtually no doubt that peach opalescent was one of the earliest carnival colors developed by Thomas Dugan. This is confirmed by its early appearance in the wholesale catalogs. Various 1910 Butler Brothers' issues are loaded with assortments of Dugan's peach opalescent that offered such patterns as Caroline, Ski-Star, Stippled Petals, Jewelled Heart, Petal & Fan, Cherry, and the Fishnet Epergne. These same assortments also confirm that the enamel, floral decorated pieces of peach opalescent that are sometimes found were indeed done at the Dugan factory. Several examples of these items appear in the Fall 1910 Butler Brothers catalog. While Thomas Dugan called this color Pearl Iris, it was often marketed under the trade name Mexican Aurora. Northwood, Fenton, and Westmoreland also produced very limited amounts of this color. However, at this early stage (1910), there were virtually no assortments of this color, by any of these firms, in any of the existing wholesale catalogs. So there is no doubt in my mind that this unique carnival color was indeed, Thomas Dugan's "baby."

In both iridescent and opalescent quality, Dugan's peach opalescent carnival is unsurpassed. Often the marigold color is of a deep, rich, pumpkin-like tone, and the opalescence is especially heavy. On some examples the entire exterior surface is heavily opalized. Here again, we will see a considerable difference in the peach opalescent made later by the Diamond Glass Company.

White: The introduction of Dugan's white carnival line coincides roughly with Northwood's introduction of the color. However, Dugan's white carnival may actually pre-date Northwood's, if only by a matter of weeks. Northwood's white carnival was introduced in January of 1912. A December 1911 trade journal describes a new Dugan iridescent line "of a much softer and delicate tone," called "Alba Lustre." Lustre is a term often used to describe iridescent ware; "alba" is the Latin word for white. Literally translated, this name means white iridescent.

Thomas Dugan was certainly one of the most prolific makers of white carnival glass. He was, at the very least, on par with Northwood's production of the color. As far as the actual number of patterns made in this color, Dugan may have even surpassed Northwood. Most examples show a good, heavy translucent frost, with excellent pastel, multicolor iridescence. An occasional weak example is sometimes found; however, I am becoming more and more convinced that these may be examples of continued production by Diamond.

Amethyst: With only a handful of exceptions, nearly all of Thomas Dugan's carnival patterns can be found in this color. And, what a color it is! It is an exceptionally dark, rich, deep shade of purple, and is usually quite heavily iridized. A quick glance at just about any example will serve to make even the most diehard skeptic realize that Thomas Dugan was anything but stingy with his iridizing sprays. Dugan's amethyst carnival is among the most heavily iridized of all amethyst carnival glass. The richness and blended depth of iridescent colors is often a sight to behold. It is a true testament to Thomas Dugan's dedication to quality. I have even seen, and owned, examples with such a heavy, solid "electric blue" iridescence that virtually no other iridescent color was visible on them! At the opposite end of the iridescent spectrum is Dugan's amethyst carnival with the gun metal iridescent treatment. This is a rather dull, silver/gray iridescence. It was marketed by Dugan as a separate iridescent line that was introduced in January of 1911. Items in the Maple Leaf pattern are often found with this iridescent treatment.

This is probably beginning to sound like a broken record, but we will see a big difference between Dugan's amethyst carnival and that produced later by Diamond.

Oxblood: This is a term used by today's collectors to describe Dugan's entry in the "black amethyst" field. This color was introduced in March of 1910 and was marketed by Dugan under the name African Iridescent. This base glass color appears nearly opaque unless held to a strong light source. It will then appear as an exceptionally deep purple with a strong red tone. Hence, the name "oxblood." Here again, most examples exhibit a rich iridescent blend, often highlighted by a brilliant gold tone. Patterns like Wreathed Cherry, Heavy Iris, and Many Fruits are often found in this color.

Marigold: We have a major surprise here! While huge amounts of marigold carnival were produced at Indiana, Pennsylvania, the vast majority of it was made after 1913, under Diamond Glass Company management, Thomas Dugan made comparatively little marigold carnival. The carnival patterns that he produced in full lines (berry set, table set, water set, etc.) are often found in marigold. However, when we look at the novelty type of shapes (bowls, compotes, plates, nappies, etc.) which made up the bulk of his carnival production, we see a very different picture.

Perhaps we can best illustrate this by first listing the major full line Dugan patterns. These were all designs that are primarily found in water sets, table sets, berry sets, and/or punch sets.

Beaded Shell	Maple Leaf	Quill
Circle Scroll	Wreathed Cherry	Many Fruits
Dahlia	Heavy Iris	Jewelled Heart

All of these patterns, which originated during the Dugan years at Indiana, are often found in marigold. Now, let's do the same thing with a representative sampling of some Dugan carnival designs produced primarily in novelty shapes.

Farmyard	Dogwood Sprays	Nautilus
Heavy Grape	Victorian	Petal & Fan
Raindrops	Border Plants	Ski-Star
Soutache	Apple Blossom Twigs	Fan
Starfish	Wishbone & Spades	Fishnet Epergne

Most of these novelty patterns are either very rarely seen in marigold or virtually non-existent in that color. Most of them are primarily found in peach opalescent, white, or amethyst. Thomas Dugan simply did not make all that much marigold carnival glass! As we shall see, only in the Dugan patterns carried over into production by Diamond, or in those designs that are strictly Diamond creations, do we find a proliferation of marigold production.

About 90% of Dugan's carnival production centered around the above-described colors. Only on rare occasion did he venture outside this five-color realm.

A mere handful of green carnival Dugan pieces is known to exist in a few patterns. In most cases, only one to three examples of each are known. A couple of assortments in the 1911 – 1912 wholesale catalogs do offer Target, Wide Rib and Pulled Loop vases in green carnival, but these are the only ones that I could document in green from the wholesale catalogs. Three known examples of the Farmyard bowl exist in green, along with a handful of pieces in a few other Dugan patterns, but that's about it. Here again, it is primarily the patterns introduced by Diamond after 1913 that are found in green.

It was apparently only during his last few months at Indiana that Thomas Dugan began to produce cobalt blue carnival glass. The wholesale catalogs seem to confirm this. No assortments of Dugan carnival are offered in cobalt blue until the spring of 1912. At that time, the Floral and Grape water set, Grapevine Lattice water set, and the Grape Delight rose and nut bowls first appeared, offered in "Royal" iridescent, which was the trade name used to market cobalt blue. As Thomas Dugan is known to have departed within a year of this date, he could not possibly have been responsible for very much of the cobalt blue carnival made there. The bulk of it was made by Diamond, after 1913.

Only a handful of Dugan carnival pieces have surfaced in other colors, such as vaseline opalescent and blue opalescent. A few patterns like Pulled Loop, Target, and Dogwood Sprays have turned up in those colors, but these are so rare that they must be classed as experimental.

Virtually all the other carnival colors made at Indiana, Pennsylvania, such as aqua, olive green, celeste blue, ice blue, sapphire blue, ice green, and true red, were developed after 1913 by the Diamond Glass Company.

Disaster and Change, 1912

The year 1912 did not begin well for Thomas Dugan. On February 5, the citizens of Indiana, Pennsylvania, must have been stunned by the headline that appeared in *The Indiana Evening Gazette*:

FIRE CAUSES $20,000 LOSS
Early Morning Blaze Devoured The Mold Shop And Large Quantity Of Expensive Molds
At The Dugan Factory

The newspaper went on to report that the fire almost completely destroyed the machine shop at the plant. This was the portion of the plant where the molds were not only created but also stored. By today's monetary standards, a $20,000 fire would not be considered all that bad. By the standards of 1912, it must have been catastrophic! Fortunately, the fire did not affect the main production area of the plant. Thomas Dugan stated in the article that they had been fortunate in that many molds had been in use on the main production floor at the time of the fire, and thus had been saved. It was also stated that the firm did have duplicate molds for a few patterns and that these, too, had been saved. However, it is obvious from these accounts that a great many molds were lost in the fire.

This tragic fire could certainly explain some long-standing mysteries concerning Dugan's carnival production. Several Dugan carnival patterns that had been regularly featured in the wholesale catalogs abruptly vanished from them early in 1912, never to re-appear. These include Ski-Star, Wishbone & Spades, Petal & Fan, Stippled Petals, and the Fishnet Epergne, to name just a few. Several other assortments of non-iridescent Dugan designs also vanished from the wholesale catalogs at this same time. This fire could also explain why so many Dugan carnival patterns are found far less often than those made later by Diamond. After all, you can only produce so much glass in three years and with many of the molds now gone, some of Dugan's carnival patterns likely had very short production runs. Patterns like Wishbone & Spades and the Four Flowers Chop Plate made their first appearance in the wholesale catalogs only a few months earlier. They, too, vanished from the catalogs at this time.

The 1912 fire could also explain the limited variety of carnival shapes produced in many patterns that were made in a much greater variety of non-iridescent shapes prior to the carnival era. The S Repeat pattern might be a good example. Prior to the carnival era, this pattern was made in just about every shape imaginable, yet only a few carnival shapes are known. Perhaps the design was just entering iridescent production at the time of this fire, and the bulk of the molds was lost. Regardless, it does seem quite certain that some of Thomas Dugan's best efforts went up in smoke on that bitterly cold February morning. Surely, it must have been a devastating blow to him and may well have been a contributing factor in his decision to leave Indiana, Pennsylvania.

We will never know the exact circumstances surrounding Thomas Dugan's departure. Perhaps he simply wanted a fresh start elsewhere. Perhaps there were growing differences between his own ethics and those of the firm's board of directors. There is some evidence, however scant, to indicate that the latter may be the case. Both Thomas and Alfred Dugan left the plant at the same time. W. G. Minnemeyer, the firm's longtime salesman, likewise departed. While several trade journal reports from January of 1913 indicated that Thomas Dugan had "resigned" as plant manager, H. Wallace Thomas, who was to eventually become the new plant manager, wrote that Thomas Dugan had been "dismissed."

Regardless of the exact circumstances, by January of 1913 Thomas Dugan had left Indiana, Pennsylvania. The firm remained in operation as the Dugan Glass Company until July of that year, when the name was changed to the Diamond Glass Company.

Diamond's Carnival Glass Production, 1913 - 1931

Edward J. Rowland became the new plant manager in early February of 1913, and the name change to the Diamond Glass Company became official on July 1st of that year. Changes in name and management were not the only ones to occur. We now begin to see dramatic changes in the iridescent ware that was produced there as well.

Like his cousin Harry Northwood had been obliged to do 12 years earlier, Thomas Dugan apparently left the bulk of his surviving molds behind. Iridescent production of many of these designs was continued by Diamond for several years. Some remained in production right up until the plant closed in 1931.

The 1912 fire would certainly necessitate the need for the creation of new molds. Some, like Grapevine Lattice and Grape Delight, were created by Thomas Dugan in early 1912, and production of these designs continued. However, by 1913 we begin to see a whole new generation of patterns emerge from the Diamond Glass Company. A listing of a representative sample of some of these patterns is quite revealing.

Stork in the Rushes	Windflower	Peach & Pear
Double Stemmed Rose	Cosmos Variant	Coin Spot
Vintage Banded	Lattice & Daisy	Five Hearts
Rambler Rose	Golden Harvest	Golden Grape
Apple Blossom	Weeping Cherry	Malaga
Peacock at the Fountain	Wreath of Roses	Pony

All the above designs appeared for the first time, in the wholesale catalogs or in Diamond advertising, after the departure of Thomas Dugan, so there is no doubt that he had virtually nothing to do with their creation. And his absence shows. Like the designs listed earlier that were all Dugan creations, these Diamond Glass Company patterns show many similarities. But, they are similarities of a nature very different from the earlier Dugan designs. Most are much more simplistic in design and seem to lack the flowing, graceful appeal that was typical of Thomas Dugan's patterns. They seem, somehow, more awkward and more hastily conceived. In many cases, they lack the attention to pattern detail that was typical of Dugan's work, and the high degree of molding relief is also absent.

Perhaps I should point out that I am not attempting to label these designs as inferior products. Many of them do indeed have their own distinctive appeal with collectors. I am merely attempting to point out the distinct differences between the patterns created by Dugan and by Diamond. They are, in many ways, a world apart when it comes to a close comparison.

Likewise, the carnival glass colors that Diamond produced and the iridescent treatments applied to them are different than those made earlier by Thomas Dugan. Not that they are necessarily inferior in quality (though in some cases I personally feel that some of them are), they are just different.

Diamond produced a much wider variety of carnival glass colors than did the Dugans. This is only logical when you consider the fact that Thomas Dugan only produced carnival glass for a four-year period, while Diamond's iridescent lines remained in production, in varying degrees, for over 17 years. Some of the carnival colors developed by Dugan remained in production for many years after his departure. These were augmented by the development of several new iridescent colors that were developed between 1913 and the late 1920s.

Amethyst: Diamond produced huge quantities of this color, and it remained in production well after most of the firm's competitors ceased its production. We know this because some Diamond carnival designs that were not produced until the late 1920s, like Intaglio Daisy, are known in this color. Diamond's amethyst tends to be of a softer, lighter tone than that made by Dugan. Gone was the dense, deep purple color produced by Thomas Dugan, replaced by a somewhat lighter shade of amethyst more closely resembling that made by Fenton. While we do see some examples with a brilliant, rich iridescent blend, most tend to be of a softer, lighter and more satiny iridescence, and many are beautifully done.

Peach opalescent: Diamond definitely continued production of this color after Thomas Dugan's departure. For a time, it was of a quality that rivaled any produced by Dugan. However, by the mid to late teens, we begin to see a change. Many of the patterns made in this color after about 1915 tend to be found with a much weaker marigold iridescence and a much lighter degree of opalescence, which tended more and more to be confined mostly to the edges. The Question Marks bon-bon might be a good example to illustrate this. This piece was produced well into the late 1920s, and many of the peach opalescent examples found tend to have rather weak marigold color with very light opalescence.

White: This is another color carried over after Thomas Dugan's departure. Diamond's white carnival is usually of good frost and iridescent lustre, though some examples seem to have a very slight lavender tint in the base. Actually, this can sometimes result in a most pleasing effect, and some collectors actively seek out these examples. We find this color in a fairly extensive variety of Diamond's patterns but to nowhere near the degree of Dugan's production of the color. Its popularity with the buying public seems to have waned rather quickly. By the late teens, production of the color was shifted to the plainer shapes of what we call stretch glass today.

Marigold: Diamond's production of marigold carnival was far more extensive than was Dugan's. In fact, it was second only to that of the Imperial Glass Company. Nearly every carnival glass pattern that Diamond produced can be found in this color, and with few exceptions, most can be found quite easily. Examples of Diamond's marigold carnival continued to appear in the wholesale catalogs right up into 1931, so the color was still in production when the fire destroyed the plant that year.

Cobalt blue: The bulk of the cobalt blue carnival produced at Indiana, Pennsylvania, was made by Diamond, after Thomas Dugan's departure. The plant did begin to make the color while he was still there, in early 1912. It is interesting to note that this date closely coincides with an increase in cobalt blue carnival production by both Fenton and Northwood. Apparently the color became popular with the buying public at about this time.

Most of Diamond's water sets can be found in this color in reasonable quantity. These include Lattice & Daisy, Stork in the Rushes and Peacock at the Fountain. The full line patterns created by Dugan that remained in production after his departure, like Maple Leaf, are also found in cobalt blue. In fact, this was one of the key factors in determining that it was Diamond and not Dugan that produced the bulk of this color. In almost every case it is the Dugan patterns that were continued in production after he left that are found in cobalt blue! Cobalt blue examples of Dugan patterns not carried over into the Diamond years are actually very scarce.

Diamond's use of the color for novelty items seems to have been much more limited. While a fairly large number of Diamond's novelty patterns are known in cobalt blue, most are not that easily found. Patterns like Question Marks, Cosmos Variant, Windflower, and Double Stemmed Rose are good examples of this.

Green: Like the Dugan Glass Company before it, Diamond seems to have produced precious little green carnival. Only a mere handful of Diamond patterns, like Double Stemmed Rose for example, is found in green.

Ice green: Diamond's production of this color dates from the early 1920s and was primarily used for Stretch Glass. However, some patterned carnival items are known, like the Pony bowl, Windflower nappy, Adam's Rib water set, and the Coin Spot compote.

Celeste blue: Diamond actually made two different shades of this pastel blue. The lighter of the two, called cerulean blue, was introduced in 1916, while the darker, called Vesuvius blue, dates from 1924. They are so close in tone that it is often difficult to distinguish between them, so collectors have collectively labeled them "celeste blue." This is another of the colors developed primarily for use on plainer stretch glass designs, but some patterned carnival pieces are found. Designs like Double Stemmed Rose, Big Basketweave, Coin Spot, Vintage Grape, and a few others are known in this color.

Sapphire blue: Basically, this is the same base glass color shade that we commonly refer to as Celeste. The difference is in the iridescent treatment. While the celeste blue pieces have the onionskin stretch effect, the sapphire pieces have a satiny, multi-color iridescence more closely resembling the effect of other carnival iridescent treatments. Examples of this color were made by Diamond from around 1916, and are rarely found.

Red: The only items known in this color are candlesticks and console bowls from the Royal Lustre line. Often they are found with a brilliant, almost mirror-like silver iridescence; however items from this line are also found with a brilliant, near "electric" multi-color iridescence. This color dates from about 1924, and most examples have been mistakenly called Imperial Jewels in the past.

Pink: A handful of novelty items in iridescent pink from the Diamond Glass Company have surfaced over the years. These are part of a line called After Glow and date from the 1928 – 1931 period. All are rarely found today.

Diamond apparently experimented with a few other carnival colors on an extremely limited basis. A few designs like Double Stemmed Rose and Target have been found in olive green. These pieces likely date from about the same time that Northwood introduced their version of the color called "russet" about 1920. A few items, like the Target vase and the Floral & Grape water pitcher for example, occasionally surface in colors like aqua, vaseline, and lime green but are so rare that they are likely surviving "experiments." I also know of a precious few pieces in cobalt blue opalescent, and these, too, are likely experimental.

The Dugan trademark, a diamond with extended sides enclosing a capital letter "D," is very rarely found on any of their iridized ware. An occasional item in the Wreathed Cherry pattern turns up trademarked but rarely anything else.

The trademark is found more often on non-iridized opalescent and colored glass pieces in the Fan pattern line. A few items in the Filigree line have it, and it has also been documented on a few blue opalescent Jewelled Heart pieces. But, the vast majority of Thomas Dugan's glass is not trademarked in any manner.

The Diamond Glass Company (1913 – 1931) is not known to have used any form of a trademark.

This interesting title page from the 1907 Dugan factory catalog illustrates the Dugan "D-in-a-Diamond" trademark quite well. It is also interesting to note that the Dugan logo, in the lower right, is strikingly similar to the stylization of the famous Northwood "Script Signature."

DIAMOND "D" stands for Quality and Originality. We take great pride in being the factory from which such famous lines originated as "Klondyke," "Louis XV," "Pagoda," "Nestor," "Victor," "Venetian," "Japanese," and many others, while to-day we offer such successes as

Intaglio, Filigree, ◇D◇ Lines

We manufacture the Latest and Best

| Gold Decorated Opalescent Colored | Table Ware | Gold Decorated Opalescent Colored | Lemonade and Wine Sets |

Vases, Novelties, Night, Lamps, Toilet Bottles, etc.

If you want "Something Different and Artistic," come or write to

Dugan Glass Company INDIANA PA.

Dugan & Diamond Carnival Glass Colors

We have a rather unique situation when it comes to the carnival glass colors produced by these two firms, for there was a change of ownership and management in mid stream, so to speak. When the ownership of this plant changed at the veritable height of the iridescent glass era, the variety of colors made changed with it. Nowhere else in the field of carnival glass production does this circumstance exist.

During the carnival production years under the ownership of Thomas Dugan, iridescent glass was primarily produced in four colors: marigold, amethyst, white, and peach opalescent. We see these same colors appear over and over again in the vast majority of Dugan carnival patterns that date from the 1909 – 1913 period. Only rarely do we see carnival pieces from this period in other colors, such as cobalt blue or green.

When the plant became the Diamond Glass Company, under the watchful eyes of H. Wallace Thomas and Edward J. Rowland, we begin to see a greater variety of carnival glass color emerge. These include green, ice green, lime green, olive green, vaseline, celeste blue, more cobalt blue, and even true red. By this time, around 1913, Diamond's iridescent glass competitors were expanding their own varieties of carnival colors, so the introduction of expanded color lines was no doubt a decision born out of competition. Most of the Diamond carnival patterns that appear in the wholesale catalogs after 1913 are found in a greater variety of colors than those made earlier under Dugan management.

The following list describes the carnival glass colors known to have been produced by both Dugan and Diamond.

Marigold: Orange or clear glass with an orange iridescence.

Peach opalescent: Marigold carnival with a white opalescent edge and/or undersurfaces.

Amethyst: Purple. Some of Dugan/Diamond's amethyst is so dark and dense in tone that it almost appears red. Some collectors refer to this deep, reddish tone as oxblood, but it is not true red. This dense, near opaque oxblood color was actually a true black amethyst, which Dugan marketed under the name African Iridescent.

Lavender: A light, pastel shade of purple with pastel iridescence.

White: A frosty, translucent white with pastel iridescence.

Cobalt blue: A dark, rich royal blue.

Cobalt blue opalescent: Cobalt blue with opalescent edges and/or undersurfaces.

Ice blue: A frosty, light translucent blue with pastel iridescence.

Celeste blue: A slightly darker shade of pastel blue with the onionskin effect of stretch glass to the iridescence.

Sapphire blue: This is pretty much the same basic tone as celeste blue, but it has the more satin-like multicolor tones of true carnival glass, lacking the "onionskin" stretch effect. Note: Both celeste blue and sapphire blue are actually iridized examples of two very similar shades of blue introduced by Diamond between 1915 and 1921, which were marketed under the names Cerulean blue and Vesuvius blue.

Teal: A medium to dark blue/green color, tending more to a stronger blue tone.

Aqua: A lighter blue/green color with a slightly stronger green tone.

Green: A medium to dark shade of emerald.

Ice green: A light, frosty, translucent green with pastel iridescence. Many of Dugan/Diamond's pieces in this color tend to be slightly darker than those made by their competitors.

Lime green: A light, pastel green with a slight yellow tone.

Olive green: A medium olive color, similar to army olive drab.

Vaseline: Yellow. Will fluoresce under black/light.

Pink: A late iridescent color found primarily in candlesticks and a few novelty items, often with a stretch effect, but sometimes with a more satiny, carnival like lustre or a marigold iridescent overlay. It dates circa 1927 – 1929 and was marketed under the tradename After-Glow.

Red: Ruby. A true cherry red color. Many readers may be surprised to see red listed as one of the carnival colors made at Indiana, Pennsylvania. The Diamond Glass Company did make a true iridized ruby glass that qualifies as carnival. The Royal Lustre line, made in the 1920s, has an all-over heavy silver iridescence, lacking any stretch effect. This line was made in cobalt blue and true red and is illustrated in this book. Many of the pieces in this line have, in the past, been mistakenly attributed to Imperial and Fenton.

The Wholesale Catalogs

Among the most important tools in researching glass are the surviving issues of the wholesale catalogs from the carnival glass production era. From the late 1800s through the early 1940s, the majority of the merchandise offered by the retail stores in this country was purchased by them from several large wholesale outlets. Butler Brothers, Charles Broadway Rouss, G. Sommers & Company, and The Baltimore Bargain House were among the largest of these wholesale suppliers. Through them, glassware of every description was offered, in wholesale priced assortments, to the retail trade. Because these assortments were packed at the factories of their origin, these catalogs are priceless sources of documentation in attributing glassware patterns to their specific makers. They also offer some unique insight into the trade names under which the glass we call carnival was marketed, the time frames in which various carnival glass colors and patterns were in production, and the wholesale prices at which the glass was sold.

Throughout this book, you will find examples of these wholesale catalog assortments, pertaining to the specific patterns, shapes and colors being presented. I hope they will add to your understanding and enjoyment of carnival glass collecting.

The 1907 Dugan Factory Catalog

Also shown in this book are portions of the only known Dugan factory catalog. This catalog was found at the factory site 10 years after the 1931 fire. It predates the carnival glass era by just one year, but many of the patterns and shapes carried over into carnival glass productions are featured in it and have been included in this book, where relevant.

Along with this catalog, several original Dugan/Diamond factory mold drawings were also found at the plant site. Some of these are also included in this book.

These have all been reproduced with the gracious consent of their owner, Steve Jennings.

Notes on Value and Condition

In the early days of our carnival glass collecting, we bought what appealed to us. Prices were low and investment potential was really only a minor factor in our purchase selection. We bought strictly for color and beauty with little regard for what the piece was worth. There were no nationally promoted carnival glass specialty auctions as outlets for selling our glass, so investment potential was of little concern. Times and collecting attitudes have certainly changed and, in many ways, it's a shame that they have. However, with the price levels of today, brought on by the dramatic increase in the number of active collectors, change was inevitable. Now price and investment potential have become key factors in our decisions to buy.

Yet, ironically, the same standards we used many years ago, color and beauty, have the greatest impact on price and investment potential today! Carnival glass is unique in that respect. To quote the motto of the San Diego Carnival Glass Club, "Iridescence is the Essence." How very, very true! If you are buying as a collector, remember that motto whenever you purchase your glass. If you are a dealer, remember it when you price your glass for resale. The quality of the iridescent finish is what carnival glass is all about. Without it, it's just another piece of colored pattern glass. Even if the piece is in physically perfect condition and is an extremely rare pattern or shape, if it is of only average or lower iridescent quality, the desirability factor and the investment potential simply aren't there!

The quality of the molding also plays a role in determining value. It may vary considerably from example to example. Pieces with sharp, crisp pattern detail will always command a premium price. Those that are poorly molded or misshapen will not, regardless of scarcity.

Condition is also a key factor in both buying and selling. Beautifully iridized, perfect examples bring premium prices and offer the best investment potential. But is it okay to buy a damaged example? Of course it is, as long as it is kept in the proper perspective. We all have a damaged piece or two in our collections. We often use them as "fill ins," until we can purchase a perfect example. So, what's a damaged piece of carnival glass worth? (If I had a nickel for every time I've been asked that question. I could retire tomorrow, a very wealthy man!) The truth is that this is a virtually impossible question to answer, with a specific dollar amount. There are far too many variables, and I think the reader should consider them all.

What is the specific piece in question? Damaged examples of common, easily found patterns and shapes have little or no monetary value. However, less than perfect examples of extremely rare patterns, shapes and colors do retain some value and investment potential, particularly if they are beautifully iridized.

What is the degree of damage? It's pretty much common sense. The greater the degree of damage, the less the value. Generally, I would much rather have a piece that is chipped rather than one that is cracked. Cracks do "travel" and expand, with time; chips don't. A small flake or surface chip in a hidden area on the underside of a piece will not affect its value as much as a more prominent one in a more noticeable place.

So, what's it worth? It's worth whatever someone is willing to pay for it and that is a matter of personal choice. It's purely a judgment call on the part of the buyer and that varies from person to person. A person who collects purely out of love for the glass will likely be far more willing to buy a damaged piece than will a person who collects strictly as an investment. A collector with limited financial resources who cannot afford to pay several thousand dollars for a perfect example may be willing to pay a couple hundred dollars for a damaged piece while the collector for whom money is not a problem may be unlikely to do so. I have a standing personal philosophy regarding damaged pieces; perhaps it is the best way to answer the question of the value of damaged pieces.

"Whatever you paid for the piece, knowing that it was damaged, was what it was worth to you for your collection. Therefore, that is its value! Consider any future monetary gain derived from it a 'windfall,' and let it go at that. In the meantime, you've filled a gap in your collection and enjoyed the piece for its beauty."

Reproductions of old, collectible glassware are nothing new to the field of antiques. Whether you realize it or not, they have been around, in varying degrees, since the 1940s! Since the mid to late 1960s, the field of reproductions has grown in leaps and bounds, and we are now reaching a point where it is rapidly becoming a serious problem. Virtually anything of collectible value has become victim to re-issues and reproductions. There are now reproductions of Nippon china, R.S. Prussia china, Royal Bayreuth china, Flow Blue, Majolica, Roseville pottery, Depression glass, opalescent glass, custard glass, colored pattern glass, art glass, and of course, carnival glass. The list could go on and on. You name it! If it's a popular collectible, sooner or later, reproductions will appear.

I have no problem with reproductions as long as they are clearly marked to distinguish them from the originals. Sadly, this is not always the case. In fact, unmarked reproductions, or those with very misleading marks, are starting to show up on the market in alarming numbers! I have witnessed many instances of people paying good money for brand new glass, china, and pottery, at auctions and antique malls, no doubt believing they had made a "great find." Don't let it happen to you! Educate yourself. Learn how to distinguish old from new. Seek out the retail stores and shops that sell new glass and keep yourself up to date with what is being made. Pay attention to antique mall booths featuring new glass. Handle and examine it. Get to know the look and feel of new glass and you will soon be able to tell the difference for yourself. You will soon discover that most new carnival glass is much thicker and heavier than the old. The iridescence lacks the subtle blending of color tone of the old and has a much more garish and gaudy look. If you are unsure or if the dealer is unwilling to guarantee its authenticity by allowing a return privilege, play it safe. Don't buy it.

Dugan & Diamond Glass After 1931

After the 1931 fire that ended production at the Diamond Glass Company, a number of the surviving Dugan and Diamond molds were acquired by other glasshouses. The Fenton Art Glass Company purchased some of the Dugan and Diamond molds shortly after the fire. Eight years later, in May of 1939, the L.G. Wright Glass company of New Martinsville, West Virginia, purchased many of the remaining molds for the sum of $600. (That may seem like a bargain price, but in 1939 that was a pretty fair piece of change, about the price of a good automobile!) As a result, there have been numerous reproductions of many Dugan and Diamond carnival patterns. Foremost among these are those marketed by the L.G. Wright Glass Company. This firm has been in business for 60 years. I suppose that they could rightfully be called a "marketing concern," as the bulk of their glassware is made for them by other manufacturers from molds owned by Wright. Among the plants that have produced glassware for L.G. Wright are Fenton, Imperial, Westmoreland, Fostoria, Mosser, Summit, Viking, and Gibson, to name but a few.

Starting in 1972, Wright began marketing carnival glass reproductions, many of which were made in old Dugan and Diamond molds. Between 1972 and 1974, many of these pieces were marked with a very misleading trademark, consisting of a slightly altered version of the old Northwood "N in a circle" mark. A new trademark, consisting of an underlined capital letter "W," enclosed by a circle, was adopted in 1974 and continues in use today. Both of these trademarks are shown here. Learn to recognize them.

**L.G. Wright trademark
1969 – 1974**

**L.G. Wright trademark
1974 – present**

While a considerable number of Wright's carnival reproductions bear one of these two marks, I have seen many, many examples that are not trademarked in any manner. It should also be noted that Wright leased molds to other glasshouses, including Gibson and Mosser, and these two firms have made carnival glass from old Dugan and Diamond molds as well. The Gibson pieces that I have seen were all signed "Gibson," and many are also dated. The Mosser reproductions are often signed with a capital letter "M," but here too, I have seen countless examples that were not trademarked!

Most of the Wright, Gibson, and Mosser reproductions are of an exceptionally thick, heavy glass. The iridescence is very heavy but has an unusually bright, glassy and gaudy look to it, often with a near mirror-like finish. L.G. Wright, Gibson, and Mosser continue to market carnival glass today.

St. Clair also produced some carnival reproductions of old Dugan/Diamond patterns starting in the late 1960s. Most of these are either toothpick holders or tumblers. Some are signed "St. Clair" or "Joe St. Clair," but here again, many are not marked in any manner. Some of these are of exceptional quality and people are constantly fooled by them. The base glass colors and iridescent quality really do rival that of the old glass!

Recently, the Fenton Art Glass Company has begun reproduction of at least one old Dugan carnival pattern, the Christmas compote. They have also manufactured some Dugan reproductions for Singleton Bailey, including the Farmyard bowl and plate. These are all being made in colors not originally produced by Dugan and Diamond, and all are trademarked with the Fenton logo.

Still, one wonders about the future and where it will all end. Cannot the glasshouses of today create anything new or innovative? Can they not create new patterns and designs rather than relying on reissues of the old? Must everything be made in imitation of what once was? What has happened to the creativity and originality upon which the American glassmaking industry was built?

The following is a listing of the carnival glass reproductions of Dugan and Diamond carnival glass patterns. These are the ones that I can document at present. There are likely some that I have missed; there will likely be others in the future.

Beaded Shell: L.G. Wright, mug in ice blue and in non-iridized custard glass. Also a variety of pieces in non-iridized light blue glass and clear to white opalescent.

Cherry with Jewelled Heart Exterior: L.G. Wright, deep, round 7 – 8" bowls in electric blue and purple. They are not trademarked! A purple tumbler with the cherry interior and Jewelled Heart exterior was also made.

Christmas Compote: Made by Fenton from original Dugan mold, in ice blue, red, and iridized topaz (vaseline) opalescent. The red and iridized topaz opalescent compotes were made for Dave Richardson of *Antique Publications.* They are marked with the Fenton logo and the initials "AP."

Dahlia: L.G. Wright and Mosser, water set in amethyst, white, pink, and ice blue. Also made in non-iridized blue and green opalescent. No old opalescent items were made. The new tumblers have the dahlia flowers on three sides, while the old has it on all four. The old tumblers have a 33-rayed star on the underside of the base; the new ones do not.

Farmyard: Made in a new mold in an 8 – 9" bowl and plates in amethyst, red, and white. Many are marked with the letters "MIMI." Also made in a variety of iridescent colors for Singleton Bailey. They are clearly trademarked (Fenton) and should present no problem.

Floral & Grape: L.G. Wright, water set in purple carnival, tumblers also made in non-iridized custard.

God & Home: L.G. Wright, water set in purple, red, ice green, and cobalt blue carnival. Yes, a limited edition of 1,000 water sets was made in cobalt blue in 1982. The blue sets are reportedly all trademarked. (The old sets are known in cobalt blue only.) A limited edition was also made in non-iridized blue slag.

Golden Harvest: L.G. Wright & Gibson, wine set in purple, electric blue, and iridized custard. Some are signed "Gibson" and dated.

Grape Delight: L.G. Wright & Mosser, rose bowl and nut bowl in purple, cobalt blue, ice green, and ice blue. Some are marked with either of the two Wright trademarks and some are marked with the Mosser "M." However, some are not marked! (No old ice blue or ice green examples are known.)

Grapevine Lattice: L.G. Wright, water set, small bowls and small plates in purple carnival, tumblers, small bowls and plates in non-iridized custard. Most are trademarked.

Harvest Flower: L.G. Wright & Westmoreland, water set in a very gaudy red carnival.

Heavy Iris: L.G. Wright & Gibson, water set in purple. The new water pitcher has a plain, un-patterned area of about 1½ – 2" between the end of the patterned area and the ruffled top. On the old pitcher, the pattern extends all the way to the beginning of the ruffled top. The new tumblers are slightly fatter, but are otherwise extremely well done. Most of these sets are not trademarked! A handled whimsey basket, shaped from the tumbler mold, was also made in electric blue and red. They have a very gaudy look to them and are signed "Gibson" and dated.

Inverted Fan & Feather (Feather Scroll): St. Clair, the toothpick holder in marigold, amethyst, and cobalt blue. These are fabulous reproductions with a color tone and iridescent quality that rivals old carnival. Many people are fooled by them. (No old carnival toothpick holders are known.) Tumblers were also made in ice blue and cobalt blue. The cobalt blue tumblers were made in 1969 for O. Joe Olsen and the Original Carnival Glass Collectors Society. Most are so marked on the base and are beautifully done. However, some were apparently run after the order for O. Joe Olsen was complete, and they are not marked on the base. Watch out for these! There are also new tumblers in ice blue, and these too are beautifully done. No old ice blue tumblers are known.

Maple Leaf: L.G. Wright & Mosser, water set in purple, cobalt blue, and ice green. Table set in purple and cobalt blue. Some pieces are found with the Mosser "M" trademark. Some are unmarked.

Nautilus (Argonaut Shell): L.G. Wright & Mosser, table set and berry set in purple and cobalt blue. (No old carnival sets are known.) Also made in non-iridized chocolate glass, custard, cobalt blue, and ruby glass. Toothpick holder also made in cobalt blue carnival. (No old carnival toothpicks are known.)

Pony: L.G. Wright, bowl and plate in marigold and purple. Be especially careful on the marigold ones. They are very well done.

Rambler Rose: L.G. Wright, water set in purple carnival. Tumbler also made in non-iridized custard (often decorated).

S-Repeat: St. Clair (and later others), tumbler in marigold and toothpick holder in a variety of both iridescent and non-iridescent colors. (No old carnival toothpicks are known.)

Stork in the Rushes: L.G. Wright, water set in marigold (beaded version). The marigold water sets are very well done. The new tumblers have a slight barrel shape to them, slightly wider in the middle than at the top and base. Master berry bowl in purple; creamer, spooner, and covered sugar in marigold. (The new covered sugar has a different cover than the old). Also made in a non-iridized light blue opaque glass.

Vintage Banded: L.G. Wright, water set in purple carnival.

Wreathed Cherry: St. Clair & L.G. Wright, the toothpick holders (St. Clair) in cobalt blue fool many people. They have the color, look, and feel of old glass, and they are not trademarked. (All the old Wreathed Cherry toothpick holders are in amethyst only.) The water set and table set were made by L.G. Wright in non-iridized blue and vaseline opalescent, so future iridized pieces are a distinct possibility. (No old opalescent pieces are known in this pattern.)

It should also be noted that L.G. Wright has marketed many reproductions of Dugan and Diamond patterns in a wide variety of non-iridized shapes and colors, so future iridescent production of many of these items is always possible. The patterns include Wreathed Cherry, Maple Leaf, Beaded Panels, Corn Vase, Jewelled Heart, S Repeat and Question Marks. There are likely others, as we have no idea just how many of the Dugan and Diamond molds Wright owns.

Additional information on reproductions may be found in the pattern texts of this book.

Dugan & Diamond Carnival Patterns, 1909 – 1931

Presented here, in alphabetical order, are the carnival glass patterns, shapes, and colors made by both the Dugan Glass Company and the Diamond Glass Company between 1909 and 1931. A great deal of input from collectors all over the country went into the preparation of this text and every effort was made to ensure its accuracy. However, no one can know it all, and some colors and shape variations of some patterns have no doubt been unintentionally overlooked. There are also a few carnival glass patterns that some have credited to these two firms for which we have no conclusive evidence to substantiate such an attribution. These designs have not been included. Should such evidence surface one day, it would be far less confusing to the reader to include them in a future update than to include them here and have to retract them.

Beside the name of each pattern is the name of the firm that originated the carnival glass version of the design. They are presented as follows:

Dugan: This indicates that the pattern was a Dugan creation and all known production occurred under Dugan management.

Dugan ✧: This indicates that the design was of Dugan origin with production continued by Diamond.

Diamond: This indicates that the pattern was a Diamond Glass Company creation and all known carnival production occurred under Diamond management.

These attributions are based on the data currently available and are not written in stone. Existing records for both Dugan and Diamond are fragmentary, and it has been a painstaking, often frustrating task to sort out just who made what. So, these attributions are based on a great deal of detective work that involved putting together the bits and pieces gleaned from trade journals, wholesale catalogs, and many other sources.

The color listed as amethyst refers to the colors known as both purple and amethyst. Both were intended to be the same color at the time of manufacture.

Oxblood is listed as a separate color. This was Dugan's version of what we sometimes call black amethyst today, and it was marketed as a separate color line that Dugan called African Iridescent. Items listed in this color are those that I can confirm at the time of this writing. Others likely exist.

As we approach the millenium, we also approach a time when we must begin to re-think our definition of the term "rarity," as it pertains to carnival glass. In less than a decade, carnival glass will reach its one hundredth birthday, and the hobby of collecting and preserving it is now nearly 40 years old, as well. During the last five to seven years, more new collectors have joined the fold than at any other time in the history of the hobby. With this dramatic increase in collectors has come a tremendous impact on the availability of the glass. Quality examples of the glass are rapidly disappearing from the antique malls, shops, and antique shows. Because of this, the term "rarity" becomes more and more relative with each passing day. Patterns, shapes, and colors that were considered common and easily found just a few years ago no longer are.

The values of many of the traditional rarities are now approaching levels that are out of the financial reach of a growing number of collectors. This may seem discouraging, but it need not be. Consider the following: many of these rarities were not considered as such just 10 or 12 years ago. Likewise, there is a large number of carnival glass patterns, shapes, and colors that are still quite available at reasonable prices. But, will they be so, 10 or 12 years from now? I doubt it. Many of them will no doubt be the next generation of future rarities, just like their rare predecessors of today!

So, before you pass up that common, but beautifully iridized and reasonably priced peach opalescent six petals bowl, or amethyst cosmos variant bowl, stop and give the term "rarity" a little perspective. Think not only of what is, but what will likely be in the future.

With these thoughts in mind, you must put in perspective the terms used to describe the availability of the various patterns, shapes, and colors noted in the following pattern texts. A little thought will not only one day pay off but will also greatly add to your present enjoyment of the hobby.

Dugan's Decorated Peach Opalescent

During the 1910 – 1911 period, the Dugan Glass Company produced a wide variety of peach opalescent carnival shapes and patterns that were factory decorated with various enamel floral motifs. Several Butler Brothers wholesale catalogs feature assortments of these pieces. Some of the molded patterns that may be found with these enameled decorations include Caroline, Stippled Petals, Stippled Flower, Footed Cherries, Single Flower Framed, and Dogwood Sprays, to name a few.

On occasion, an absolutely plain, unpatterned piece of peach opalescent turns up with this painted decoration. I have included an illustration of one of them here that shows this decoration to best advantage.

Throughout the pattern texts of this book, you will find listings of the pieces known to have this type of decoration in the Shapes & Colors Known boxes. Of course others are always possible, but these are the ones that I can currently confirm. I have never personally seen or heard of any enamel decorated Dugan pieces in colors other than peach opalescent, but their existence is always possible.

Adam's Rib

This is the first of several iridescent lines produced by Diamond that truly bridge the gap between carnival glass and stretch glass. It is a fairly late line, introduced in 1925, and originally marketed as Diamonds #900. It can be found with the typical onionskin iridescent effect of stretch glass, a brilliant carnival-like lustre, or a soft, satiny iridescence. In non-iridized colors of blue, green, amber, crystal, and pink, it can be found in a tremendous variety of shapes. These include bowls, sandwich servers, pitchers, cups, saucers, creamers, sugars, plates, candlesticks, bonbons, compotes, and just about every other imaginable shape. Not all of these are yet known in iridized form, but I suspect many of them do exist.

The most familiar iridescent shape is the lemonade pitcher, even though it is rarely found. It has a separately applied handle and has been documented only in ice green and celeste blue to date.

Other known iridescent shapes include fan vases, mugs, stemmed compotes, collar based bowls, a large pedestal footed console, and two styles of candlesticks. The fan vase has been documented in marigold and celeste blue and the compote in celeste blue and ice green. The pressed candlesticks with their flared out base were part of the three-piece console set and have been documented in marigold, ice green, and celeste blue. The other candlestick shape is mold blown and hollow. These have been documented only in marigold and Celeste blue, to date. The handled mug was actually intended to accompany the lemonade pitcher. Strangely, it has been documented only in ice green, to date. There must surely be some celeste blue examples out there somewhere. Without any doubt, among the rarest of the iridized Adam's Rib pieces are that of a single known large, pedestal footed console bowl in milk glass with a marigold iridescent overlay. Some collectors refer to this shape as a large open compote, but it is pictured in Diamond Glass Company advertising as part of the three-piece console set. This leads to a very interesting possibility. Could the matching candlesticks exist in marigold on milk glass? None have yet been reported, but they could well exist. This large console bowl is also known in celeste blue. I also know of a large 10 – 11" flared bowl in iridized milk glass. This bowl does not have a marigold overlay, but a more delicate, pastel iridescent, and is actually an example of an iridescent treatment that Diamond advertised as their Moresque Line. I have yet to see any other examples of this, but they must surely exist.

The rare Adam's Rib lemonade pitcher in celeste blue and the handled lemonade mug in ice green.

While the non-iridescent pieces of Adam's Rib are seen quite frequently at shows and in shops, the iridized items are quite hard to find.

Shapes & Colors Known	
Lemonade pitcher	ice green, celeste blue
Mug	ice green
Covered candy jar	ice green
Open sugar, 2-handled	ice green
Vase, 9¾"	celeste blue
Compote	ice green, celeste blue
Candlesticks, blown hollow	marigold
Candlesticks, flared base	marigold, ice green, celeste blue
Fan vase	marigold, ice green, celeste blue
Large console, pedestal footed	celeste blue, marigold on milk glass
Bowl, 10 – 11"	pastel iridized milk glass

Amaryllis

We all make mistakes; if we didn't, there would be no need for erasers. I made a good one when I included this pattern in my Northwood book. During its preparation, several collectors reported examples of this design that were definitely signed with the N in a circle trademark. I have since examined several of these very examples, and of course, they are not! I learned a valuable lesson because I had violated one of the primary rules of glass research; hearsay or word of mouth is not confirmation.

Amaryllis is definitely a Dugan product. Examples of this pattern are found in white and cobalt blue, so the design was likely in production around 1912 when Dugan began producing those colors.

Only four shapes, all fashioned from the same mold, are known. Three of these are small compotes, usually standing from two to three inches in height. They may be ruffled, triangular, or a deep, round shape. Ruffled examples seem to be the most plentiful, especially in marigold and amethyst. White examples are much harder to find and a few rare cobalt blue compotes are known. Triangular compotes are seen far less often and have been reported in marigold, amethyst, and white. The deep, round examples are very rare and to date have surfaced only in marigold.

The little, stemmed whimsey plate is quite rare in any color; it is known in marigold, amethyst, and white. In my opinion, all are just about equal in rarity, but the amethyst examples usually bring the highest prices.

The exterior surface carries a design called Poppy Wreath. This is a carry-over from earlier non-iridescent production and Poppy Wreath appears in the 1907 Dugan factory catalog.

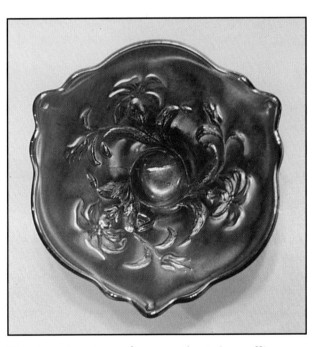

This interior view of an amethyst Amaryllis compote shows both the pattern detail and the slight triangular shape quite well.

Shapes & Colors Known

Compote, ruffled	marigold, amethyst, white, cobalt blue
Compote, triangular	marigold, amethyst, white
Compote, deep round	marigold
Whimsey plate	marigold, amethyst, white

Apple Blossom

This is one of the designs that dates from late in the carnival production era. In fact, it appears in the wholesale catalogs during the last few years of Diamond's production, from 1928 to 1931. The iridescence on many examples is often very light and weak, which is typical of many of Diamond's late efforts. However, some beautifully iridized examples do exist.

Small, 6" – 7" bowls, which may be ruffled or a round, deep shape are plentiful in marigold. Amethyst is a little tougher to find but still quite available. White bowls are actually quite scare, as are the cobalt blue bowls, but both do exist. I know of two or three examples in green, always a rare color from this firm. Peach opalescent bowls are rumored to exist, but I have never personally seen one.

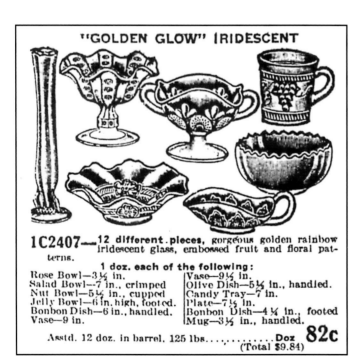

Amethyst Apple Blossom bowls like this one are not easily found.

Most carnival references list a 7" – 8" plate in this pattern. I wish someone would place one in my hands. In over 28 years of carnival collecting, I have never seen one, nor have I spoken with anyone who ever has! Perhaps they do exist, but until I can personally confirm that, I will not list them. There are too many pieces being listed based only on hearsay and speculation; I will not do that. If someone out there has a true, flat plate in this design, please let me hear from you.

A small, collar-based rose bowl shaped from the bowl mold does indeed exist. They are rather scarce and to date, have been reported only in marigold.

"GOLDEN GLOW" IRIDESCENT

1C2407—12 different pieces, gorgeous golden rainbow iridescent glass, embossed fruit and floral patterns.

1 doz. each of the following:

Rose Bowl—3½ in.   Vase—9½ in.
Salad Bowl—7 in., crimped   Olive Dish—5½ in., handled.
Nut Bowl—5¼ in., cupped   Candy Tray—7 in.
Jelly Bowl—6 in. high, footed.   Plate—7½ in.
Bonbon Dish—6 in., handled.   Bonbon Dish—4¼ in., footed
Vase—9 in.   Mug—3½ in., handled.

Asstd. 12 doz. in barrel, 125 lbs...........Doz **82c**
(Total $9.84)

The Apple Blossom pattern is featured in this Diamond Glass Company assortment from the April 1929 Butler Brothers catalog.

Rarer still is this round Apple Blossom bowl in cobalt blue.

Shapes & Colors Known

Bowl, 6" – 7" marigold, amethyst, white, green, cobalt blue
Rose bowl   marigold

Apple Blossom Twigs

Found exclusively on plates and bowls of various shapes, Apple Blossom Twigs is one of the most popular of all Dugan carnival glass patterns. The design is simple yet graceful and seems to jump right out at you. The initial production likely dates from the 1911 – 1912 period, with some limited production continued by Diamond until about 1914 when it disappeared from the whole-sale catalogs.

The 8 – 9" bowls are found in a variety of shapes. Most carry the big basketweave exterior pattern and have a fluted edge with 48 points. They are known in a ruffled shape, ice cream bowl shape, or with a three-in-one-ruffle. This latter shape is the least often seen of the three. Some of the ruffled bowls are very low in profile. Some collectors call these ruffled plates and some call them low ruffled bowls. I tend to agree with the latter, but you call them what you like.

Peach opalescent is far and away the most often found color, followed by amethyst. White is next in line, with the beautiful, pastel lavender examples and the equally scarce cobalt blue just about tied for fourth place. The big surprise here is the rarity of the marigold bowls. Comparatively few are found. Two examples have been reported in smoke, an extremely rare color for either Dugan or Diamond!

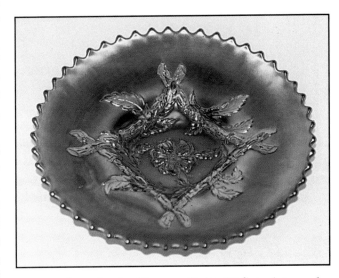

Much rarer are the bowls with a plain exterior and a smooth edge. These have been reported only in amethyst and peach opalescent, to date. At least one in each color has been reported in a banana bowl shape, with two sides pulled up.

Likewise, there are two versions of the 9" flat plate. Examples with the fluted edge and the Big Basketweave exterior pattern are the most often found. Surprisingly, it is the cobalt blue examples that seem to surface the most often. Far more of them have changed hands at the carnival glass auctions than any of the other known colors. Amethyst, white, and peach opalescent plates are on near equal footing for third place, with the white ones just slightly more available. Here again it is the marigold plates that seem to be found least often.

An amethyst Apple Blossom Twigs 9" flat plate and a peach opalescent bowl with the three-in-one ruffle. Both of these examples carry the Big Basketweave exterior pattern.

The late Don Moore once reported the existence of an ice blue (possibly celeste blue) 9" plate. I have virtually no reason to doubt this. His credibility is above reproach! What I would like to know is simply this: where is it? Does anyone out there have this ultra-rare, one-of-a-kind plate?

Plates with a smooth edge and a plain exterior are also known, but they are far more rare than the version described above. They have been reported in peach opalescent and amethyst, with the amethyst examples the more rare of the two.

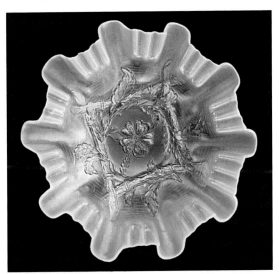

Bowl, 8" – 9", fluted edge	marigold, amethyst, peach opalescent, white, cobalt blue, lavender, smoke
Bowl, 8" – 9", plain edge	amethyst, peach opalescent
Banana bowl, plain edge	amethyst, peach opalescent
Plate, 9", fluted edge	marigold, amethyst, peach opalescent, white, cobalt blue, ice blue, (celeste)?
Plate, 9", plain edge	amethyst, peach opalescent

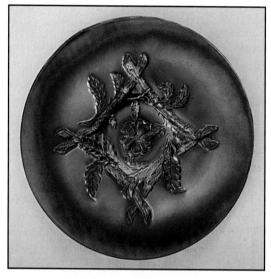
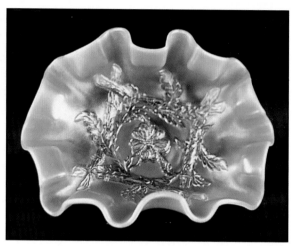

This smooth edged, plain exterior Apple Blossom Twigs 9" plate in amethyst is also a very scarce and desirable piece. Rarer still is this beautiful peach opalescent Apple Blossom Twigs banana bowl shape. Note the 10 broad, flat ruffles. This is a characteristic quite typical of many Dugan pieces.

Band

This simple design is quite familiar to most carnival collectors. The little hat-shaped vases, usually found with two sides pinched in and pulled up, are quite abundant in marigold and even in amethyst. They are often found with metal holders, making for an attractive little basket.

They can also be found with a separately applied, clear glass handle. These are sometimes called violet baskets and are actually quite scarce. The handles are very delicate and there were likely a lot of casualties over the years. Marigold is the only color reported on these, but I would not be surprised if amethyst examples also exist.

Hat-shaped vase	marigold, amethyst
Basket	marigold

Band hat shapes in amethyst and marigold. This same shape is sometimes found fitted into a handled, metal holder.

Diamond

Beaded Basket

It seems as though nearly every novelty piece made by Dugan can be found in peach opalescent. The Beaded Basket has never been found in that color. Add to that the fact that it did not appear in any of the known wholesale catalogs until 1915 and it becomes clear that we are likely dealing with a Diamond Glass Company pattern here.

Even today with all the years of collecting, the marigold Beaded Basket is quite abundant on the market, another good indication of a Diamond origin. Several other colors are known and most will present a challenge. Amethyst examples are known but are found far less often. Rarer still are the cobalt blue and white baskets. A few are known in lime green with a marigold iridescent overlay. I also know of two or three examples in aqua, and one in pink with a marigold iridescent overlay. This pink basket and the lime green basket are no doubt iridized examples of Diamond's After Glow line, which dates from 1928 – 1929. These last three colors are yet another indication of Diamond Glass Company production. Nearly all the carnival patterns made at Indiana, Pennsylvania, that are found in those two colors are Diamond ones.

Shapes & Colors Known
Two-handled basket	marigold, amethyst, cobalt blue, white, lime green w/ marigold overlay, aqua, pink w/marigold overlay

White is a rare color for Diamond's Beaded Basket.

Beaded Panels

This design, found only on compotes with a most unusual stem, was initially produced in non-iridized opalescent colors as early as 1900. So there can be no doubt that Dugan's carnival version was produced from one of the molds that Harry Northwood left behind.

The top portion of the compote may be found with a variety of shapings. I have seen examples that were round and broadly ruffled or triangular and ruffled. Both shapes may also be found with a tightly crimped edge. I have seen a non-iridized blue opalescent example that was fashioned into a Jack-in-the-Pulpit shape, so a similar carnival version is possible, though un-reported. The unique stem is comprised of four curved, beaded columns with the area between them open.

Peach opalescent is by far the most often seen color. They are very attractive pieces and remain a popular item with collectors. Marigold examples are actually much harder to find, but they do exist. The

Beaded Panels tri-shaped, crimped edge compote in peach opalescent.

amethyst compotes are very scarce and it will take a good deal of searching to come up with one. Over the years, I have seen only a few. The only other confirmed color is cobalt blue and these are very rare, with only three or four reported.

Caution: This compote has been reproduced in non-iridized opalescent colors of blue and vaseline, so iridized examples are always a possibility though I have not personally heard of any. The reproduction compote has a solid fill of glass between the four curved, beaded columns that make up the stem.

"ETRUSCAN" DECORATED GLASSWARE ASST—Iridescent.

Every item in this assortment will bring a dime or more.

C2408—Golden iridescent, rustic, fruit and mosaic embossed. 1 doz. each of 12 items.

7¼ in. vase.   4 in. handled mug.   6½ in. card tray.
8 in. plate.   4x3¼ footed bowl.   6¾ in. crimped marmalade.
Tumbler.   Footed sugar.   6½x5 mayonnaise boat.
6¾ in. crimped dish.   "   creamer.   Fancy bonbon.
                      12 doz. in bbl., about 128 lbs.   Doz.   **48c**

The Beaded Shell creamer and spooner, from the four-piece table set, were often offered separately as a two-piece breakfast set, as shown by this assortment from the July 1914 Butler Brothers catalog.

Beaded Shell

The original factory pattern name for this design is New York. It was first introduced in non-iridized colored glass in 1903 and remained in production for many years. The carnival glass version of the pattern likely went into production early in the carnival era, circa 1910, and examples continued to appear in wholesale catalogs through 1916.

A full line was made in carnival, including the berry set, table set, water set, and mug. However, the variety of colors known is extremely limited. The berry set and table set have been documented only in marigold and amethyst. The water set is known in these same colors and the tumbler has also been documented in cobalt blue. The cobalt blue tumblers are quite scarce. As of this writing, I have not been able to conclusively confirm a cobalt blue water pitcher, but there must be one out there somewhere. It would have to be classed as extremely rare! A few very rare lavender tumblers are also known. The handled mug is found in a greater variety of colors, including marigold, amethyst, cobalt blue, lavender, and a true, frosty white. The cobalt blue and lavender mugs are quite scarce, while the white examples are very rare.

The only other shape reported is a flared, ruffled whimsey, shaped from the mug mold. Only a white example has been confirmed.

In non-iridized colored and opalescent glass, a wider variety of shapes is known, including a cruet, salt and pepper shakers, and a toothpick holder. None of these have ever been found in carnival, but you never know! They could well exist.

Dugan ✦

The marigold Beaded Shell mug is much harder to find than its amethyst counterpart. White ones are really very rare.

The Beaded Shell water pitcher and tumbler are not easily found, even in marigold.

Beauty Bud

Diamond

This simple, pedestal footed bud vase was a permanent fixture in the wholesale catalogs from the late teens right up through 1931. If we were ever to select the most commonly found carnival glass vase, I have no doubt that the Beauty Bud would win the contest, hands down! You would likely be hard pressed to find an antique mall that does not contain a few examples. Most are found in the 7" – 9" height range, and marigold is the only reported color.

Shapes & Colors Known
Bud vase   marigold

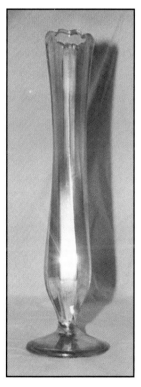

Bells & Beads

This attractive yet often overlooked pattern is found in a variety of shapes and, based on the known colors, likely dates from the 1909 – 1911 period. Some of these shapes are found in oxblood (black amethyst), so the design was in production in March of 1910 when Dugan introduced that color. It is not the easiest pattern to find.

Ruffled and crimped edge bowls, generally in the 7" size range, are the most frequently found shapes; peach opalescent is the most available color, followed by amethyst, marigold, and oxblood, in that order. A single green bowl takes the top honors in rarity. The same mold was used to fashion a variety of other shapes, all of which are much harder to find. These include a card tray with two sides turned up; a triangular shaped 7" bowl; a 7" round, flat plate; and a rare triangular counterpart. All of these have been reported only in amethyst and peach opalescent, with the latter slightly more available.

A rare, stemmed compote has been reported in marigold and amethyst, but strangely, no peach opalescent examples have been documented. A handled nappy, sometimes ruffled and sometimes spade-shaped, is the only other reported piece. The spade-shaped version is often called a gravy boat. These are known in

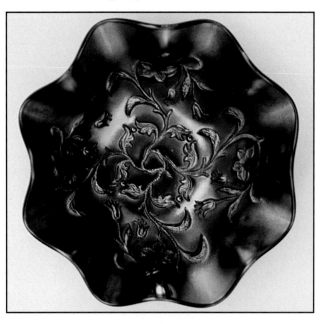

The tri-shaped peach opalescent Bells & Beads bowl is not often found, but it certainly takes a back seat to this stunning purple ruffled bowl. Just look at the beautiful blend of iridescent colors on this little jewel!

peach opalescent, amethyst, marigold, and oxblood, in about the same rarity order as the ruffled bowls.

No white examples of this pattern have ever been reported. Dugan's white carnival line had only been in production for a few weeks when the February 1912 fire destroyed a large number of molds. I suspect that Bells & Beads may have been one of them.

Shapes & Colors Known

Bowl, 7", ruffled or crimped	marigold, amethyst, oxblood, peach opalescent, green
Bowl, 7", triangular	amethyst, peach opalescent
Card tray	amethyst, peach opalescent
Plate, 7" – 8", either shape	amethyst, peach opalescent
Compote	marigold, amethyst
Nappy, handled	marigold, amethyst, peach opalescent, oxblood

Big Basketweave

Both the Dugan and Diamond Glass companies got a lot of mileage out of this pattern. As a primary design, it was used on vases and on two sizes of handled baskets. As a secondary pattern, it was used on the exterior surface of several different items, as well as the base to the Persian Gardens two-piece fruit bowl.

The vases are among the most popular of the known shapes, and for good reason. Not only are they attractive, but they are known in one of the most extensive varieties of colors of any of the patterns from these two firms. Many of these colors were not developed until well into the Diamond years, so from this we know that the pattern was produced for many years.

The vases fall into two basic size categories. The first and perhaps the most eagerly sought is the squat vase. These stand from 5" – 6" tall, and have been reported in marigold, amethyst, peach opalescent, oxblood (black amethyst), and white. They are not easy to find in any color. I must admit to having seen more white ones than any of the others, with marigold next in line. The amethyst and oxblood examples are quite rare, but I would have to give peach opalescent the top ranking here.

The standard size vases, which vary in height from 8" to as much as 14", are seen more often, but are still not easily found in most colors; amethyst and white seem to turn up the most. Marigold examples turn up far less often, as do the oxblood vases. The cobalt blue vases are quite scarce, like most novelty items in that color, from both these firms. Rare indeed are the beautiful, pastel lavender vases. Running very high both in scarcity and popularity are the beautiful celeste blue, ice blue, and sapphire blue examples, but the top honors must go to the peach opalescent vases. Very few are known.

Big Basketweave swung vases in marigold and white, with a scarce squat vase in amethyst.

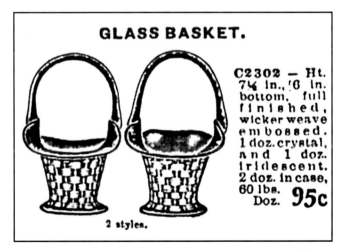

GLASS BASKET.

C2302 — Ht. 7½ in., 6 in. bottom, full finished, wicker weave embossed. 1 doz. crystal, and 1 doz. iridescent. 2 doz. in case, 60 lbs. Doz. **95c**

2 styles.

The Big Basketweave large handled basket is offered in this spring 1915 Butler Brothers ad, in both marigold carnival and non-iridized crystal.

One of the most desirable colors in the Big Basketweave swung vases is this beautiful sapphire blue example.

The **Big Basketweave Variant** pattern as it appears on the exterior surface of several Dugan/Diamond bowls and plates.

Two sizes of handled baskets are also known. The large one has a separately applied, clear handle. They are not that easily found, but a fair number of marigold examples exist. It is the amethyst baskets that are truly rare, with relatively few known. The small basket has a molded handle and is known only in marigold. They turn up in pretty fair numbers.

Big Basketweave may also be found as an exterior design on bowls and plates in the Apple Blossom Twigs, Round-up, and Fanciful patterns, as well as the base pattern on the Persian Gardens two-piece fruit bowl.

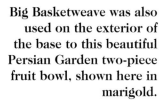

Big Basketweave was also used on the exterior of the base to this beautiful Persian Garden two-piece fruit bowl, shown here in marigold.

Shapes & Colors Known	
Vase, squat 5" – 6"	marigold, amethyst, peach opalescent, white, oxblood
Vase, 8" – 14"	marigold, amethyst, white, lavender, cobalt blue, celeste blue, sapphire blue, peach opalescent, oxblood, ice blue
Basket, large	marigold, amethyst
Basket, small	marigold

Blossoms & Band

I'm not 100% convinced that this car vase was made at Indiana, Pennsylvania: only 90% convinced. If it did originate there, then it was no doubt made by Diamond, likely during the late teens through the 1920s when car vases were in vogue. The stylized flowers around the top portion show similarities to other floral patterns produced by Diamond. The Diamond Glass Company was a major producer of car vases. They had a contract to provide glass parts with the Benzer Company, a large supplier of automotive accessories, and the Blossoms & Band car vase may be one of those made for Benzer. So, I have included it here as a probable Diamond product.

These car vases are found with either a ruffled or cupped-in top, and marigold is the usual color. I also know of at least one example in light green with a marigold iridescent overlay.

Shapes & Colors Known	
Car Vase	marigold, light green/ marigold overlay

A pair of marigold Blossoms & Band car vases.

Border Plants

Thomas Dugan apparently had a fondness for dome-footed shapes. The Dugan Glass Company produced more of them than any other carnival glass manufacturer, and I suspect there was a practical reason for this. Nearly all of Dugan's dome-footed shapes were used for the production of peach opalescent carnival, and Thomas Dugan was very proud of this color. You could not pick a better shape on which to show it off!

Border Plants is the first of many patterns shown in this book used primarily on dome-footed shapes. Like the vast majority of Dugan patterns used for peach opalescent production, it likely dates from the 1910 – 1911 period. It is a classic Dugan dome-footed design in which the pattern radiates outward from the central point. We see this design characteristic over and over on Dugan's dome-footed carnival shapes.

Handgrip plates are always popular items with today's collectors and are not easily found. Examples like this beautiful amethyst Border Plants one ranks right up there with the best of them.

Dome-footed 8" – 9" bowls seem to be the most available shape, but even these are not easily found. They may be a round, deep shape, or have a ruffled edge. Peach opalescent is the usual color found, but scarce amethyst and very rare oxblood examples also exist. I have also heard of a precious few marigold examples, Like so many Dugan novelty patterns, very few marigold examples are found. A very scarce handgrip bowl, with one edge curled up, is also known. These are reported in peach opalescent and amethyst; neither one is often found.

The dome-footed handgrip plate is rarer still and has been reported only in peach opalescent and amethyst. Amethyst is by far the rarer of the two.

The only other reported shape is that of a dome-footed rosebowl fashioned from the same mold. Peach opalescent and amethyst are the only reported colors and only a couple of examples of each are known.

No Border Plants pieces have ever been reported in white, and I suspect that none ever will be. Dugan's white carnival line entered production around December of 1911, and the catastrophic 1912 fire occurred just a few weeks later. I would be willing to bet that the Border Plants mold was among those destroyed. It would also account for the relative scarcity of this pattern.

Shapes & Colors Known

Bowl, 8" – 9", dome-footed	marigold, amethyst, peach opalescent, oxblood
Bowl, 8", handgrip	amethyst, peach opalescent
Plate, 8" – 9", handgrip	amethyst, peach opalescent
Rose bowl	amethyst, peach opalescent

Diamond

Brooklyn Bridge

This may well be one of the last carnival production designs made at the Diamond Glass Company. Reportedly, a large quantity of these bowls was found in a storage room, just after the 1931 fire that destroyed a large portion of the plant. These were allegedly given to local townspeople after the fire clean-up.

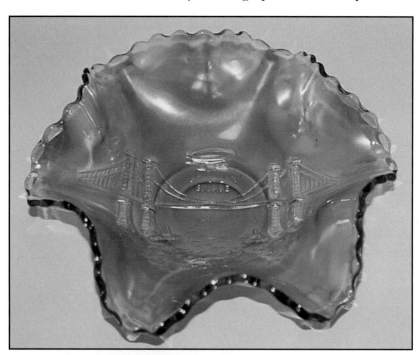

This six-ruffled Brooklyn Bridge bowl is actually a pastel pink with a marigold iridescent overlay.

The ruffled bowl is the only shape known. Some have six ruffles, some have eight, and some have ten. Most are lettered with the words "Brooklyn Bridge," but rare examples that lack this lettering also exist. Marigold is the usual color, and the iridescence has a brilliant, transparent radium quality. While not considered terribly rare, these bowls are quite scarce and it will take some searching to come up with one.

The motorized zeppelin floating over the bridge adds a nice touch to the design, and therein lies the major clue as to the time frame for the production of these bowls. Some have speculated that these bowls were made very early in the carnival production era, circa 1907 – 1908, for the 25th anniversary of the Brooklyn Bridge. However if you know your history, then you realize this is not possible.

Motorized airship travel for the masses was virtually unknown in 1907 – 1908. That was only five years after the Wright Brothers first flew! But by 1930 – 1931, it was all the rage with regularly scheduled flights between the United States and Europe. It is far more likely that these bowls were produced at that time in preparation for the 50th anniversary of the Brooklyn Bridge in 1932. It would certainly explain the quantity of them found in storage after the 1931 fire.

In addition, a few examples in pink with a marigold iridescent overlay are also known. These are undoubtedly part of Diamond's After Glow line. After Glow was a line of pastel pink and green glass that was introduced around 1928. It is found in several well-known Diamond carnival patterns, in both non-iridized and iridized forms. So, the iridized pink Brooklyn Bridge bowls must date from after that time. This would tend to confirm that the Brooklyn Bridge bowls were in production shortly before or at the time of the 1931 fire.

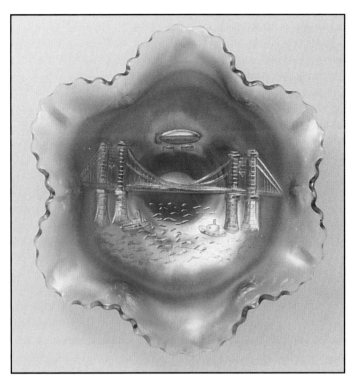

This very rare example is one of only two known to lack the lettering Brooklyn Bridge.

Shapes & Colors Known	
Bowl	marigold, pink w/marigold overlay

Butterfly & Tulip

This handsome pattern is one of the most eagerly sought of all of the Dugan carnival designs. The mold work is of the highest quality and the iridescence is unusually superb. These large 10" – 13" footed bowls are an impressive sight and always command attention and high prices whenever they are sold. Depending on color and shape, they range from very scarce to extremely rare.

The most desirable of the shapes is the large square bowls that are usually fashioned with eight broad ruffles. The amethyst examples seem to generate the highest interest, but in reality, the marigold ones are of near equal rarity. The more rounded, deeper version is somewhat more easily found, especially in marigold, but still very scarce. This shape also exists in amethyst, but is seen less often than its marigold counterpart. Even this round, deep version is often somewhat square in appearance due to the

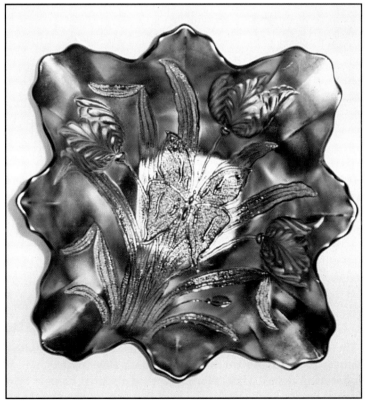

Is it any wonder that Butterfly & Tulip bowls are so highly treasured? Just look at the fabulous color and pattern detail on this beautiful square ruffled amethyst example!

manner in which the edge is shaped. No other carnival colors have been reported to date.

The exterior surface carries the Inverted Fan & Feather pattern, another of the carry-over designs from the pre-iridescent era; some collectors call it Feather Scroll. Prior to the introduction of carnival glass, this exterior design was made in a wide variety of shapes and colors, including non-iridized opalescent, colored glass, custard, and opaque pink.

The general scarcity of these bowls and the extremely limited variety of colors suggest a relatively short production run. Perhaps the Butterfly & Tulip interior mold plate was a casualty of the 1912 fire.

Most of the known marigold Butterfly & Tulip bowls, like this beautiful example, are found with a brilliant, radium type of iridescence.

Shapes & Colors Known	
Bowl, large square	marigold, amethyst
Bowl, large round	marigold, amethyst

Caroline

Caroline is one of Dugan's early carnival creations, dating from 1910 when examples of it appeared in the Butler Brothers wholesale catalogs. The pattern was used almost exclusively for production in peach opalescent, primarily as an exterior pattern, combined with the Smooth Rays interior design. Several shapes are known, all of which were fashioned from the same mold.

The most often seen shapes are 8" – 9" bowls, usually deep in shape, with a tightly crimped edge. Shallow, ruffled bowls also exist but seem to turn up less often. Peach opalescent is the usual color, but a few scarce marigold examples are known. A scarce banana bowl shape is also known but only in peach opalescent. On rare occasions, some of the bowls are found with an enameled, floral decorated interior surface. These decorated peach opalescent bowls were regularly offered in the 1910 wholesale catalogs. A handgrip plate, fashioned from the same mold, is also known. Here again, peach opalescent and enamel decorated peach opalescent are the only colors reported to date.

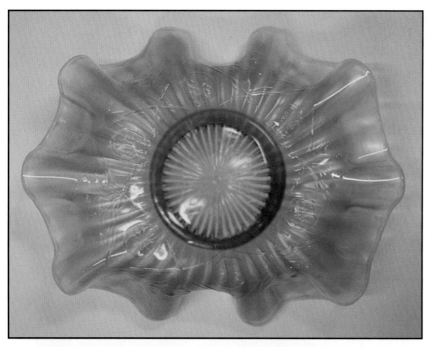

The Caroline pattern is one of the most difficult to photograph. It is faintly molded and the interior Smooth Rays pattern shows through, obscuring detail. This exterior view of a scarce banana bowl shape in peach opalescent is about the best that can be produced.

The handled basket is the most highly treasured item here. It has a separately applied, clear glass handle and is not a whimsy, but a regular production item. However, make no mistake about it, these are still very rarely found. Until recently, peach opalescent was the only reported color for these. Now, a single example in iridized lavender opalescent has been confirmed, an extremely unusual color for Dugan!

The peach opalescent Caroline handled basket, a very rare and popular item.

Shapes & Colors Known	
Bowl, 8" – 9"	marigold, peach opalescent, decorated peach opalescent
Banana bowl	peach opalescent
Handled basket	peach opalescent, lavender opalescent
Handgrip plate	peach opalescent, decorated peach opalescent

Cherry, Dugan's

There are two distinct versions of this popular design. One is always collar-based while the other is always footed. In order to gain a clear picture of the shapes and colors known and the production time frame for each version (which is important), we will look at each one separately.

Collar-Based Version

The collar-based version of Dugan's Cherry is found on bowls of varying size and shape, and on small, crimp-edged plates. Virtually all known examples carry the Jewelled Heart exterior design. Jewelled Heart was one of the carry-over patterns from the pre-carnival era, so from this we can say with fair certainty that the collar-based Dugan's Cherry pattern was likely in production during the 1909 – 1913 period.

Large, ruffled, 8" – 10" bowls, along with a smaller 5" – 6" counterpart, are the most frequently seen items. Combined, they make up a most attractive berry set. Peach opalescent is the most available color, yet

This beautiful Dugan's Cherry 9½" low ice cream-shaped bowl in amethyst is a very scarce item.

The peach opalescent berry set shown here is one of the hardest to find of all carnival glass! Very few are known.

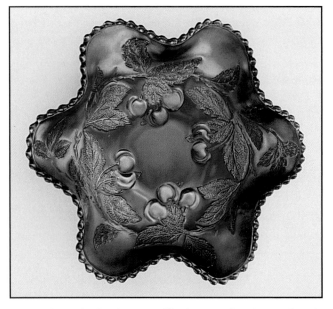

Even though the large ruffled Dugan's Cherry bowls are the most available of the known shapes, amethyst examples with iridescence of this quality are very seldom found and highly treasured.

they are not really easily found. This is particularly true of the large bowls. The large amethyst bowls are very scarce, with the small ones more easily found. The same can be said of the oxblood examples. A mere handful of both large and small bowls is also known in white and these must surely take top honors in rarity and desirability. Marigold examples also exist and are likely on par with the white, as far as actual numbers known. However, the white examples would still win the desirability contest. (Comparatively little marigold carnival was made during the Dugan years of operation. Diamond was far more prolific when it comes to marigold.)

Both the large and small bowls may also be found in a round, deep, more classic berry bowl shape. These have been reported in peach opalescent and amethyst and are really quite rare in either color.

The large bowl turns up on rare occasion in a true round low ice cream shape. These are the rarest of all the bowl shapes in this pattern and are known in amethyst and peach opalescent. I have never seen one of the small bowls in this shape, but there are likely a few out there.

The only other confirmed shape is that of a small, 6" – 7" plate, usually found with a tightly crimped edge. They are known in amethyst, oxblood, and peach opalescent and are rarely found. A white one would be a real treasure, but none has been reported to date.

It is interesting to note that virtually all the Dugan bowl and plate patterns that carried the Jewelled Heart exterior design (including this one) disappeared from the wholesale catalogs after the 1913 change of management, when the plant became the Diamond Glass Company.

Caution: The collar-based Cherry bowl, with the Jewelled Heart exterior has been reproduced by L.G. Wright in purple and electric blue carnival. These bowls are roughly 7" – 8" in diameter and are of a round, deep, non-ruffled shape. They are not trademarked!

Shapes & Colors Known: Collar-based version/Jewelled Heart exterior	
Bowl, 8" – 10", ruffled	marigold, amethyst, peach opalescent, white, oxblood
Bowl, 5" – 6", ruffled	marigold, amethyst, peach opalescent, white, oxblood
Bowl, 8" – 9", round deep	amethyst, peach opalescent
Bowl, 5", round deep	amethyst, peach opalescent
Bowl, 8" – 9", low ice cream	amethyst, peach opalescent
Plate, 6" – 7"	amethyst, peach opalescent, oxblood

The footed version of this design had a much longer and in some ways more mysterious production run. There is no doubt that the footed version was also a Dugan creation. It appears in the fall 1910 Butler Brothers catalog and again in the special Christmas 1910 edition. However, it then vanished from them completely and did not re-appear until 1917, four full years after the Diamond take-over. It then appeared continually through 1923, often sold in company with the Double Stemmed Rose pattern bowls. Strange!

There are actually two versions of this bowl. One has the Cherry pattern on both the interior and exterior while the other has the design only on the exterior with a plain, unpatterned interior. In fact, it is the version with the plain interior that was featured in the 1910 wholesale catalogs. They were offered in peach opalescent with enamel decorated floral interiors. The version with the pattern on both interior and exterior surfaces did not appear in the catalogs until 1917. Still, based on the known colors, production of both versions likely spanned both the Dugan and Diamond years.

While all examples are footed, a wide variety of shapes and edgings can be found. I have seen them with a smooth, broadly ruffled edge; a tightly crimped edge; an edge with either eight or 10 square, flat ruffles; a tightly crimped, near vertical ribbon candy edge; and a three-in-one crimped edge. Examples in both round and triangular shapes are known.

Bowls with a plain interior are known in marigold, amethyst, peach opalescent, and peach opalescent with painted floral decoration on the interior. Of these, the latter would be considered the most desirable. The other colors are all still quite available.

Bowls with the pattern on both surfaces are

The footed version of Dugan's Cherry shown here in a rare banana bowl shape in amethyst.

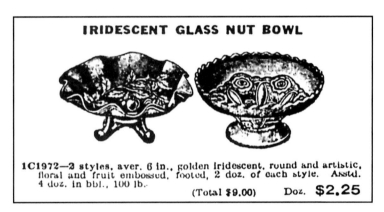

IRIDESCENT GLASS NUT BOWL

1C1972—2 styles, aver. 6 in., golden iridescent, round and artistic, floral and fruit embossed, footed, 2 doz. of each style. Asstd. 4 doz. in bbl., 100 lb.

(Total $9.00)   Doz. $2.25

The footed version of Dugan's Cherry appeared in the wholesale catalogs for many years. Often it was sold in company with the Double Stemmed Rose pattern, as in this ad from the July 1922 Butler Brothers issue.

known in a wider variety of colors. These include marigold, amethyst, peach opalescent, white, oxblood, and cobalt blue. Of these, marigold is abundant, peach opalescent a close second, with amethyst and oxblood harder to find. Both the white and cobalt blue are rarely seen, with the cobalt blue the scarcer of the two. I also know of a single example in deep, rich vaseline with a marigold iridescent overlay. Green has also been reported, but remains unconfirmed at this writing.

Shapes & Colors Known: Footed version/Plain interior

Bowl, 8" – 9½"   marigold, amethyst, peach opalescent, peach opalescent w/painted floral decoration

Footed version/Patterned interior

Bowl, 8" – 9½"   marigold, amethyst, peach opalescent, white, cobalt blue, oxblood, vaseline w/marigold overlay, (green?)

Christmas Compote

Make no mistake about it — this is one of the rarest and most desirable pieces in the entire spectrum of Dugan/Diamond carnival glass! They bring raves whenever they are shown and very serious prices when they change hands. These massive pieces of glass are truly impressive examples of the mold maker's art.

They have been documented only in marigold and amethyst and either color is extremely rare. The quality of the iridescence, especially on the amethyst examples, is often quite stunning. The design characteristics are so strikingly similar to the Holly & Berry pattern shown elsewhere in this book, that I have often wondered if the 6" – 7" Holly & Berry bowls might have actually been intended to accompany these compotes. This is merely a speculative theory on my part, and there is no concrete evidence to support it at present; but they would certainly have made an impressive set.

The Christmas Compote rarely surfaces outside the carnival glass auction circuit, and lucky indeed is the person that happens to find one.

In the spring of 1997, the original Dugan mold for the Christmas Compote was discovered in private holdings in West Virginia. It reportedly weighs a whopping 400 pounds and has the D-in-a-diamond trademark molded on the exterior surface! Little time was wasted getting a reproduction on the market; the Fenton Art Glass Company has produced a limited number of them for *Antique Publications* of Marietta, Ohio, in ice blue, red, and topaz (vaseline) opalescent carnival. They are marked with the Fenton logo and the initials AP, so they should present no problems for collectors of old carnival. Aside from that, they are also very expensive reproductions, retailing from $200 to $250 each, so I would not expect to see them turning up in your local antique mall.

One of the true masterpieces of carnival glass: the amethyst Christmas Compote.

<table>
<tr><td colspan="2">Shapes & Colors Known</td></tr>
<tr><td>Large compote</td><td>marigold, amethyst</td></tr>
</table>

Circle Scroll

Just prior to the carnival era, Circle Scroll underwent an extensive production in non-iridized opalescent colors. A full line consisting of berry set, table set, water set, salt and pepper shakers, condiment tray, jelly compote, and cruet were made. So it seems likely that the subsequent carnival glass production of the design occurred fairly early, probably circa 1909 – 1910.

The berry set, table set, water set, and jelly compote are all known in carnival. In addition, a ruffled hat and a swung vase, both fashioned from the tumbler mold, are also known in carnival. No carnival examples of the cruet, salt and pepper shakers, or the condiment tray has ever surfaced. Still, its always possible that they could exist, so be on the lookout for them.

The extremely rare jelly compote has been reported only in amethyst to date, with only one confirmed example known. Virtually all the other carnival shapes may be found in amethyst or marigold, with the amethyst examples receiving the most attention from collectors. However, this is not the easiest of carnival patterns to find, with most shapes really quite scarce, even in marigold. It is also very hard to find examples in absolutely perfect condition. The sharply raised vines within the circle were highly prone to chips and nicks. Finding an example without them is tough!

A Circle Scroll master berry bowl in marigold, and an amethyst spooner. Circle Scroll pieces in perfect condition are difficult to find.

The table set and water set are popular items and always bring very respectable prices, especially in amethyst. The berry sets often receive little attention, but in reality are equally difficult to find. The ruffled hat is still quite available, but the Jack-in-the-Pulpit version will take some patient searching. The swung vases, which will usually be found in the 7" – 9" range, are particularly popular items and not easily found. The amethyst ones are especially desirable and always bring top dollar.

No Circle Scroll pieces have ever surfaced in any colors other than marigold or amethyst. Still, just about anything is possible in the field of carnival glass. One thing I have learned over the years is, when it comes to carnival glass, never say never!

Shapes & Colors Known	
Berry set, Table set, Water set	marigold, amethyst
Jelly compote	amethyst
Hat shape, ruffled or JIP	marigold, amethyst
Swung vase	marigold, amethyst

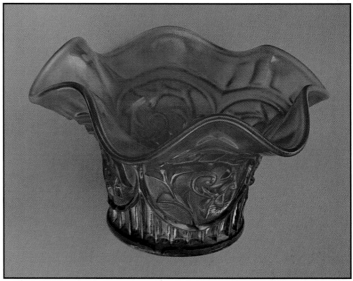

A Circle Scroll swung vase in amethyst and a ruffled hat shape in marigold. Both were fashioned from the tumbler mold. The vases can sometimes be difficult to identify because of the pattern distortion caused by the swinging out process.

Coin Spot

Spanning both the Dugan and Diamond production years, Coin Spot had a lengthy production and was made in a wide variety of carnival colors. Examples continued to appear in the wholesale catalogs as part of Diamond's Golden Glow assortment right up until 1931, so it seems likely that the pattern was still in production at the time of the fatal fire that year.

Most collectors are familiar with the Coin Spot compote since they are still quite available in marigold and peach opalescent. Amethyst examples are much harder to find but do turn up on occasion. All of the other known colors would have to be classed as rare to extremely rare. These include cobalt blue, celeste blue, and ice green. Of these, ice green is the rarest. Green has also been reported, but is unconfirmed at this writing.

The only other shape reported is that of a goblet that was fashioned from the same mold. Only one example, in ice green, has been confirmed.

The peach opalescent Coin Spot compote is one of the more easily found colors in this pattern.

Shapes & Colors Known	
Compote	marigold, amethyst, peach opalescent, cobalt blue, celeste blue, ice green, (green?)
Goblet	ice green

The Diamond Glassware Company's Golden Glow assortment of marigold carnival novelties was a regular feature in the wholesale catalogs for many years. The Coin Spot compote was a permanent fixture in these assortments, like this one from the July 1928 Butler Brothers issue.

Examples of the Coin Spot compote in amethyst are few and far between.

Compass

Thomas Dugan produced very few geometric or near cut type designs in carnival. In fact, Compass is the only one, and it was used strictly as an exterior design for the Ski-Star and Heavy Grape pieces. It was likely because of this that Dugan's Heavy Grape bowls were once thought to be Millersburg products. That firm used numerous geometric designs as the exterior motif on their larger bowls.

The design appears on the exterior of several sizes of Ski-Star bowls and on both sizes of Heavy Grape bowls. I have neither seen nor heard of an iridized example of Compass without an accompanying interior pattern, but such examples do exist in non-iridized opalescent colors.

Shapes & Colors Known
Exterior design only

The Compass pattern as it appears on the exterior of Dugan's Ski-Star and Heavy Grape bowls.

51

Constellation

Constellation is found only on the interior surface of rather small, delicate looking, ruffled compotes. The exterior carries the S Repeat pattern, but somehow along the way, it received the name Sea Foam from carnival collectors. The carnival version of this compote was made by using the existing mold for the S Repeat jelly compote, an item that was produced in non-iridized form just prior to the carnival era.

Six carnival colors are known and white seems to be the most available. Marigold seems to be much harder to find and the amethyst examples even more so. Peach opalescent examples are seldom found and eagerly sought, a strange situation when you consider the volume of that color that was made by Dugan. A few examples in a very pastel shade of lavender are known. The only other color known is a most unusual one. I know of one example that is a true, frosty white with a marigold stem. Exactly how this unique color treatment was achieved is uncertain. It is likely either a surviving experimental piece or an iridescent treatment whimsey of sorts. I have heard rumors of a blue example but have been unable to confirm it as of this writing.

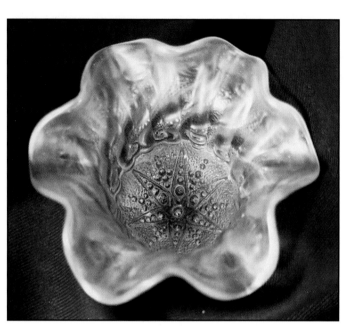

Interior view of a Constellation compote in white.

This exterior view shows the S Repeat pattern variation that some collectors call Sea Foam.

Shapes & Colors Known	
Compote	marigold, amethyst, white, peach opalescent, white w/marigold stem, lavender

The non-iridized opalescent glass version of this unusual vase first appeared in the October 1905 Butler Brothers wholesale catalog. The design was a natural for iridescent production. So, the carnival version likely dates from the 1909 – 1910 period and was one of the molds rushed into iridescent production. Why so few were apparently made, or why only one perfect example has survived, remains a mystery.

Dugan's Corn Vase differs considerably from the version made by Northwood. It stands taller, about 8¾", and the husks form double open handles. These handles could perhaps offer a clue con-

cerning the rarity of this vase. It must have been a rather difficult piece to make, with a considerable degree of breakage when removed from the mold. Even the earlier opalescent glass version appeared in the wholesale catalogs for only a short time, so there may indeed have been molding problems with it.

Marigold is the only color reported, to date, and only one perfect example is known to exist, making Dugan's Corn Vase a rarity of the highest possible order! For years I have heard rumors of a second, damaged example, but this remains unconfirmed.

Caution: This vase has been reproduced in non-iridized opalescent colors so new carnival examples are always a possibility. On the reproduction, the handles are solid with glass rather than open. This would tend to confirm my theory of molding difficulties on the old ones. Molding the handles solid instead of open would indeed eliminate such problems.

The ultra-rare marigold Dugan's Corn Vase is shown here with an amethyst Northwood's Corn Vase. The double open handles formed by the husks likely created molding problems and a lot of breakage during the manufacturing process. This is the only known example in perfect condition!

Shapes & Colors Known
Husk-handled vase   marigold

Cosmos Variant

For many years this pattern was considered a Fenton product. In fact, most carnival references still list it as such. However, we now have conclusive proof that it is a Diamond Glass Company design. It appears in company with the Double Stem Rose pattern in the mid-winter 1927 Butler Brothers catalog. This is one of Diamond's later carnival creations. Its first appearance in the wholesale catalogs did not occur until 1922.

Cosmos Variant bowl in marigold. Once thought to be a Fenton pattern, its appearance in company with other known Diamond Glass Company items in Butler Brothers wholesale catalogs confirm that it was indeed made in Indiana, Pennsylvania

Rather large 9" – 10" ruffled bowls, shallow ice cream-shaped bowls, and a flat plate, large enough to qualify as a true chop plate, are the only known shapes. All three shapes rest on a collar base and were fashioned from the same mold.

To say that the marigold-ruffled bowls are abundant would be a considerable understatement. They are surely one of the most easily found carnival glass bowls. They are somewhat harder to find in amethyst, but still do turn up in reasonable numbers. Examples in cobalt blue are actually rather scarce; it will take some patient searching to come up with one. I also know of one example in true vaseline with a marigold iridescent overlay. These are the only confirmed colors for this bowl! Rumors persist regarding the existence of them in green, white, marigold on milk glass, and red. To the best of my knowledge, none of these has ever been confirmed. I would not be too surprised if white and green examples might well exist, but I have serious doubts about the other two.

The ice cream-shaped bowls are known in marigold, amethyst, and cobalt blue. All are much harder to find that the ruffled version, with the cobalt blue examples the scarcer of the three.

The plates are not easily found in any color, but the marigold examples do turn up from time to time. Amethyst is very scarce and I can only confirm one example in cobalt blue, though others likely exist. No other colors have been reported in the plate shape.

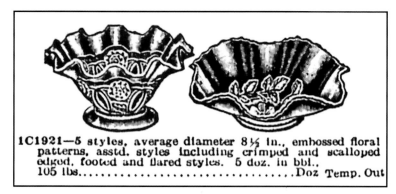

1C1921—5 styles, average diameter 8½ in., embossed floral patterns, asstd. styles including crimped and scalloped edged, footed and flared styles. 5 doz. in bbl., 105 lbs..................................Doz Temp. Out

The Cosmos Variant bowl with the Double Stemmed Rose bowl, from the mid-winter 1927 Butler Brothers catalog.

Shapes & Colors Known

Bowl, ruffle, 9" – 10"	marigold, amethyst, cobalt blue, vaseline
Bowl, ice cream shape	marigold, amethyst, cobalt blue
Chop plate, 10" – 11"	marigold, amethyst, cobalt blue

This pattern dates from the 1912 period and was used exclusively for carnival production. It came about as a result of a mold re-tooling of Dugan's Fan pattern. A full line, including the berry set, table set, and water set, was made. It is a very popular pattern with collectors.

All items are known in three colors, and none of them is easily found. While the white pieces are among the most popular and usually bring the highest prices, they are in reality probably the most often seen of the three colors. They are often decorated with red and gold trim and are on rare occasion found with fired-on blue and gold trim. Amethyst examples are a little harder to find but are well worth the search. They usually exhibit exceptionally nice iridescence. The marigold pieces are much more difficult to find than amethyst or white examples. I personally believe that there are far fewer marigold pieces of Dahlia than is generally thought. Very few have changed hands at the carnival auctions.

Caution: The Dahlia water set was reproduced by the L.G. Wright Glass Co., starting in 1977 in ice blue, white, and purple carnival, and in both iridized and non-iridized blue opalescent. There are more recent reproductions of the water set by the Mosser Glass Company in red, pink opalescent, sapphire blue, and black amethyst. Some of these colors are iridized and some are not. The new tumblers have only three Dahlia flowers on them instead of the original four. The old tumblers have a 33 rayed star on the underside of the base, while the new ones are plain. With the exception of the white and amethyst pieces, none of these other colors was ever made in the originals.

The Dahlia master berry bowl with four small berry bowls in amethyst. This pattern was created by retooling the molds to the Fan pattern.

Shapes & Colors Known

Berry set, Table set, Water set   marigold, amethyst, white

Daisy Dear

This simple pattern was likely one of those rushed into iridescent production at the start of the carnival era. It shows many similarities to Single Flower, which dates from the 1909 – 1910 period. Still, examples are known in white, so some production of the design carried over through 1912 when Dugan introduced his white carnival lines. It is also very similar to another Dugan pattern called Triplets. The main difference between them is that Daisy Dear has four stemmed flowers on the exterior surface, while Triplets has only three.

Daisy Dear is found on the exterior surface of bowls, which may be from 7" to 8" in diameter. It has been reported in marigold, amethyst, peach opalescent, and white with the marigold and amethyst examples the most often found. Peach opalescent and white examples are actually quite scarce, but like most exterior only patterns, they receive little attention from collectors.

Rarities can be found in even the most common patterns and Daisy Dear is a good case in point. I know of two Jack-in-the-Pulpit-shaped whimsey bowls, both of which are in marigold.

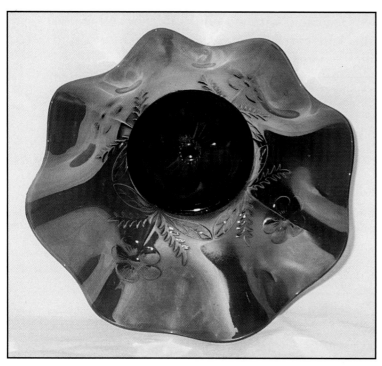

The Daisy Dear ruffled bowl in amethyst.

Even the most common patterns can turn up in rare shapes, as evidenced by this Daisy Dear Jack-in-the-Pulpit whimsey in marigold.

Shapes & Colors Known	
Bowl, 7" – 8"	marigold, amethyst, peach opalescent, white
Jack-in-the-Pulpit whimsey bowl	marigold

Daisy & Plume

Both Northwood and Dugan made versions of this popular pattern. It has long been assumed that Dugan simply copied the Northwood design. However, recent evidence indicates that quite the opposite is likely true. The Dugan version appears in non-iridized opalescent colors in the April 1906 Butler Brothers wholesale catalog and is featured prominently in the 1907 Dugan factory catalog. The Northwood version does not appear in the 1906 Northwood factory catalog or in any of the wholesale catalogs until late 1909. In this case, it appears that Dugan may have originated the pattern and Harry Northwood was the copycat!

There are ways to distinguish between the two versions. Most Northwood pieces are trade-marked with the N-in-a-circle, and the Dugan version is unmarked. The Dugan version has 80 beads surrounding each flower, while the Northwood examples have from 74 to 76 beads. It has also been recorded that the Dugan version has three equally spaced, round holes in each of the three feet, and that these were lacking on the Northwood version. However, this is not written in stone; I have owned peach opalescent Dugan examples that did not have three holes. In fact, at least one of the examples shown in the 1906 Dugan factory catalog does not appear to have them either. Also, the Northwood version is most often found in the rose bowl shape. All the Dugan ver-

sions I have ever seen were in the ruf-fled candy dish shape; I have never seen a Dugan carnival example in the rose bowl shape.

Dugan's Daisy & Plume is found primarily on the exterior surface of three footed, ruffled candy dishes. The variety of known colors is very limited, and all are not that easily found. I suspect that the pattern had a relatively short iridescent production. Examples are known in marigold, amethyst, lime green with marigold overlay, and peach opalescent. Amethyst is probably the least often seen, but the peach opalescent commands most of the attention. I only know of one example in lime green. The interior surface is plain on most examples.

The only exception to the plain interior is a ruffled bowl that carries the Dugan's Cherry interior pattern. Only a couple of examples have been reported and both are in amethyst.

Dugan's Daisy & Plume footed candy dish in peach opalescent. Note that this example does not have the three holes through the feet, as some have insisted that all Dugan examples of this pattern do.

Shapes & Colors Known

Candy dish, footed	marigold, amethyst, peach opalescent, lime green w/marigold overlay
Bowl, 8 – 9", footed, Cherry interior	amethyst

Daisy Web

This design shows a good deal of similarity to Heavy Web and I suspect they are both variations of the same design. Daisy Web is found only on the interior surface of small ruffled or crimped hat shapes and small handled baskets, fashioned from the same mold. The baskets have a separately applied, clear handle.

An amethyst Daisy Web crimped hat shape with two sides turned up.

The hat shapes may be ruffled or crimped, and a few very rare examples are Jack-in-the-Pulpit-shaped. They have been reported in three colors to date, marigold, amethyst, and peach opalescent. They are very seldom found in any of the three, but there are probably a few more marigold ones than there are of the other two. The amethyst examples can be positively stunning, often exhibiting a brilliant, "electric blue" iridescent. These examples bring very healthy prices. There are probably fewer peach opalescent examples around, but they usually take a back seat to the amethyst ones when it comes to price.

The handled baskets are very rare in any color, but they have been reported in marigold and amethyst. I have not seen or heard of a peach opalescent example, but they likely exist.

The Daisy Web Jack-in-the-Pulpit hat, a favorite with collectors.

Shapes & Colors Known	
Hat shape	marigold, amethyst, peach opalescent
Hat shape, Jack-in-the-Pulpit	amethyst
Basket	marigold, amethyst

Dogwood Sprays

The known colors and general mold characteristics all seem to indicate that this design dates from the Dugan era, circa 1909 – 1913. Dogwood Sprays is found only on the interior of dome footed bowls and a dome-footed compote that was shaped from the same mold. The scalloped domed foot is of the same configuration as that found on the Stippled Petals bowls, and that pattern appeared in the wholesale catalogs in 1910. Both patterns also carry the Long Leaf exterior design.

The dome-footed bowls are generally found in the 8" – 9" size range and are usually broadly ruffled. I have seen examples with six, eight, or ten ruffles. Occasionally, an example will be found with the three-in-one edge treatment, or even an unusual edging consisting of 10 flat, squared ruffles. A few examples have been reported with two sides turned up to form a banana bowl shape. Amethyst is probably the most often found color, followed closely by peach opalescent. Oxblood examples are also known but harder to find. Marigold is seen less often. A few very rare cobalt blue examples are also known, but the top honors go to the iridized blue opalescent bowl. Only one example has been confirmed. The dome-footed "compote" was fashioned from the same mold. These have been pulled up to depth of as much as 5" – 6", with a top diameter of only 6" – 7". These are harder to find than the normal bowl shape and have been reported only in amethyst, oxblood, and peach opalescent. Of the three colors, amethyst is likely the most often seen, but it's really a pretty close call. All are becoming scarce and are most attractive.

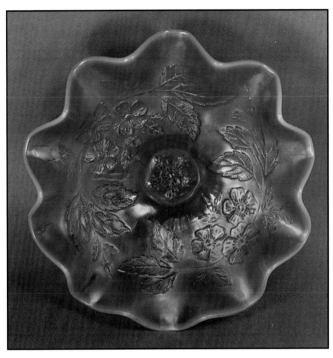

The Dogwood Sprays dome-footed bowl in peach opalescent.

Shapes & Colors Known

Bowl, dome-footed	marigold, amethyst, peach opalescent, cobalt blue, blue opalescent, oxblood
Compote, dome-footed	amethyst, peach opalescent, oxblood.

Double Stemmed Rose

One of many dome-footed patterns produced by this firm, Double Stemmed Rose had one of the longest production runs of any of the Dugan/Diamond carnival designs. It first appeared in the wholesale catalogs in 1916 and continued to appear through 1927. Even though this is a comparatively late appearance, I am convinced that the design is a Dugan one, likely dating initially from the 1911 – 1912 period. There are simply far too many peach opalescent and white examples known for it not to date from that time. Its production longevity, coupled with the unusually wide variety of carnival colors in which it can be found, indicates that this was an extremely popular pattern with the buying public.

The dome-footed bowl is the most frequently found shape in this pattern. Generally, they are from 8 to 9" in diameter and may be found with three different edge shapings. Round, deep examples seem to be the most often seen, followed closely by the ruffled bowls. The ruffled version can be found with 10, eight, or six ruffles. The third style of edge shaping is three-in-one, which seems to be found far less often.

Marigold, amethyst, and white seem to be the most abundant colors in the bowl shape. Peach opalescent is a bit harder to find, but persistence will usually turn one up. The cobalt blue examples are also rather tough to find. All of the other reported colors range from rare to extremely rare. These include lavender, aqua, celeste blue, green, ice green, olive green, and cobalt blue opalescent, so there's a lot to collect here. I personally know of only two examples in green, one in ice green, one in olive green, and another in cobalt blue opalescent, so these are without doubt the rarest colors. The cobalt blue opalescent example would likely win the desirability and popularity contest.

A round, ice cream-shaped Double Stemmed Rose dome-footed bowl in cobalt blue, not the easiest color found.

The dome-footed plate is the only other confirmed shape in this design. The fluted edge is sometimes turned up slightly, but the piece is still regarded as a plate. It is the white examples that seem to turn up most. Amethyst plates are harder to find, and surprisingly, the marigold plates are rarer still! Peach opalescent is the only other confirmed color and these too are very scarce. None of the other colors has yet surfaced in the plate shape, but I wouldn't be surprised if at least some of them existed.

With such a wide variety of colors known, this long taken for granted and overlooked pattern is gaining rapidly in both collector popularity and value. And, rightly so, for there is a lot of very pretty glass to hunt for in this design.

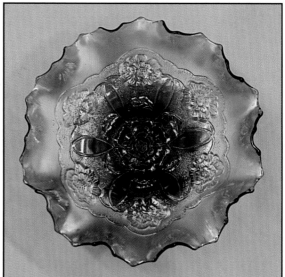

The ruffled olive green example is extremely rare. In fact, this is the only example in that color I have seen.

If you look closely, you can see the opalescent edges on this one-of-a-kind cobalt blue opalescent Double Stemmed Rose ruffled bowl.

Shapes & Colors Known	
Bowl, dome-footed	marigold, amethyst, white, peach opal, blue, green, lavender, aqua, celeste blue, olive green, ice green, cobalt blue opalescent
Plate, dome-footed	marigold, amethyst, white, peach opal

A rare Double Stemmed Rose ruffled bowl in celeste blue.

Elks Nappy

Between 1910 and 1914 both Fenton and Millersburg made a variety of commemorative pieces for the Fraternal Order of Elks. They were made for specific conventions in Detroit, Atlantic City, and Parkersburg, to name a few. Apparently, Thomas Dugan also received at least one order from the Elks for a convention commemorative, and the rare little Elks Nappy was the result.

The base mold for the Leaf Rays Nappy was used for this piece, with the elk's head substituted in place of the usual interior mold plate. The problem is that we don't know for which Elks' convention this piece was made. Unlike the pieces made by Fenton and Millersburg which were lettered with the location and date of the conventions, the Dugan Elks Nappy has no lettering or date. This ultra-rare nappy is known only in amethyst and only four examples have been confirmed to date. Three of these are spade-shaped and the other more rounded with a ruffled edge.

There are several possibilities that could explain the mystery surrounding the Elks Nappy. A few years ago a Fenton's Elks bell surfaced with the name Portland molded on it. This one-of-a-kind piece is the only known Elks commemorative to bear the name of that city. It has been theorized that this bell was made for an Elks Convention that, for reasons unknown, never took place. With only four examples of the Dugan Elks Nappy known, it is possible that these could be surviving "test pieces" for the very same event!

Of course, there are many other possibilities. They may well be samples that were made on approval, in anticipation of a possible order from the Elks, and the

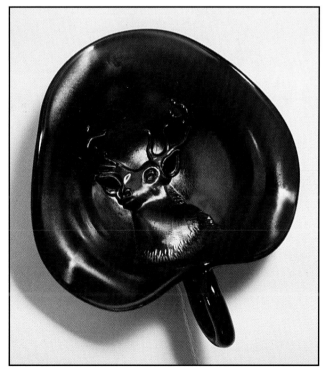

One of the three known spade-shaped Elks Nappys. The only other known example is ruffled. All are in amethyst.

61

design was rejected by them in favor of those made by Millersburg and Fenton. They could have been intended as generic Elks souvenirs, to be given away wherever and whenever desired. (Personally, I tend to favor that theory). And, there is also the possibility that this little nappy had nothing to do with the Fraternal Order of Elks at all! It may have been created and test molded as an Elks pattern and then rejected as part of the normal design/production process. We will probably never know for certain.

Regardless of that, fortunate indeed is the collector who finds one of these rare little treasures.

Dugan

Fan

Once thought to be a Northwood creation, we now know that Harry Northwood had nothing whatsoever to do with the production of this pattern. It was originally marketed as Dugan's Diamond D line, and it appears prominently in the 1907 Dugan factory catalog, offered in non-iridized decorated emerald green, cobalt blue, ivory (custard), blue, green, and flint (white) opalescent. In these colors, a full line was made, including berry sets, table sets, water sets, and a variety of novelty items, most of which were fashioned from the creamer and spooner molds. Many of these non-iridescent pieces are found signed with the Dugan D-in-a-diamond trademark.

The carnival version of this pattern is found only on two shapes, both of which were fashioned from the creamer and spooner molds. For some unknown reason, most collectors have labeled these two items as a gravy boat and sauce dish. Yet when placed side by side, it should quickly become obvious that they were intended to be used as an open breakfast creamer and sugar. Besides, this old glass is not heat tempered to accept hot liquids, like modern glass. I certainly would not want to put hot gravy in them! Would you?

Both shapes have been documented in only two carnival colors, peach opalescent and amethyst. Of these, peach opalescent is found far more often than the much scarcer amethyst.

8   DUGAN GLASS CO., INDIANA, PA.

"DIAMOND D" GOLD DECORATED
TABLE WARE ASSORTMENT

TEA SET

WATER SET   BERRY SET

THIS assortment is composed of four 4-piece Tea Sets, four 7-piece Berry Sets, four 7-piece Water Sets, all decorated heavily with Fired Gold Edges and base. The colors are the newest effects in fancy glassware, viz :—Rich Ivory, Royal Blue and Emerald Green.

⅓ doz. Tea Sets (2 Ivory, 1 Green, 1Blue) , @ $9.00.....	$3 00
⅓ " Water Sets (2 Ivory, 1 Green, 1 Blue), @ $13.00 ..	4 33
⅓ " 10-in Berry Set (2 Ivory, 1 Green, 1 Blue),@ $13.00	4 34
Cost of 12 Different Sets..............................	$11 67
Package...................................	35
Weight 100 lbs.	———$12 02

"DIAMOND D" OPALESCENT
TABLEWARE ASSORTMENT

This pattern is the same as the above except that it is made in the finest opalescent glass.

⅓ doz. Tea Sets (2 Flint Opalescent, 1 Green Opalescent, 1 Blue Opalescent), @ $4.00................	$ 1 33
⅓ doz. Water Sets (2 Flint Opalescent, 1 Green Opalescent, 1 Blue Opalescent), @ $5.50...........	1 84
⅓ doz. Berry Sets (2 Flint Opalescent, 1 Green Opalescent, 1 Blue Opalescent), @ $4 30..........	1 43
	$4 60
Package...........................	35
Weight 100 lbs.	———$4 95

An assortment of Dugan's Fan from the 1907 Dugan factory catalog. This is a non-iridized assortment, but it has been included here because it shows the two pieces from which the two known carnival shapes were fashioned: the creamer and spooner. All of these molds were re-tooled, circa 1911 – 1912, to create the Dahlia pattern.

None of the other shapes has ever surfaced in carnival glass, and I suspect they never will. We now know that sometime around 1911 or 1912 the fan molds were re-tooled and the result was the Dahlia pattern, shown elsewhere in this book. Still, it's always possible that an iridized fan water set, table set, or berry set could turn up. Thomas Dugan could have run a few before the mold re-tooling took place. You never know!

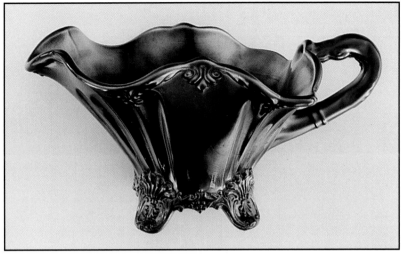

Dugan's Fan breakfast creamer in amethyst and the open breakfast sugar in peach opalescent. Some collectors persist in calling these pieces gravy boats and sauce bowls, but a 1912 wholesale catalog confirms that they were marketed as breakfast sets.

Shapes & Colors Known	
Breakfast creamer & open sugar	peach opalescent, amethyst

Fanciful

Based on the known colors, design characteristics, and iridescent quality, there seems little doubt that Fanciful is a Dugan creation, likely dating from the 1911 – 1912 period. We have no evidence to suggest that production of the pattern was carried over by Diamond. Fanciful is one of the more popular Dugan patterns and is found in a fairly extensive variety of colors.

Bowls in the 8" – 9" size range are found in a variety of shapes including broadly ruffled, low ruffled, with a three-in-one edge, or in an ice cream shape. Of these, the three-in-one edge shaping is found least often. White is by far the most available color, followed closely by peach opalescent and amethyst, in that order. Marigold is seen less often and cobalt blue bowls are quite scarce. I have seen a few oxblood examples, but the pastel lavender bowls win the top spot, with only three or four reported. Not all colors are known in each bowl shape. The ice cream-shaped bowl has not yet been reported in lavender and the three-in-one edged bowl is not reported in lavender or oxblood.

The 9" flat plates are the only other reported shape. Here again, white is the most available color. Surprisingly, the cobalt blue plates are the next most available color, a most unusual situation when you consider the scarcity of the bowls in that color and the general scarcity of most Dugan patterns in cobalt blue. Amethyst is next in line with the marigold plates in a rather tough to find fourth place. Another surprise is the rarity ranking of the peach opalescent plates. The bowls are far more numerous. A few oxblood examples are known, but the top honors go to the green plate. While more may exist, I personally know of only one example! For some unknown reason, both Dugan and Diamond just didn't do much with green carnival.

All known Fanciful shapes carry the Big Basketweave exterior design.

Three Fanciful shapes in three colors: a plate in cobalt blue with electric blue iridescence, a low ruffled bowl in amethyst, and a peach opalescent example with the three-in-one edge treatment.

Shapes & Colors Known	
Bowl, 8" – 9", ruffled	marigold, amethyst, white, cobalt blue, peach opalescent, oxblood, lavender
Bowl, ice cream	marigold, amethyst, peach opalescent, white, oxblood
Bowl, 3-in-1 edge	marigold, amethyst, peach opalescent, white, cobalt blue
Plate, 9"	marigold, amethyst, peach opalescent, white, cobalt blue, oxblood, green

Without any doubt, Farmyard is the most eagerly sought, most highly treasured, and most highly valued of any of the carnival designs to come out of Indiana, Pennsylvania. The mold work, quality of iridescence, and the very design itself combine to make a real winner. The pieces always generate a good deal of excitement and admiration wherever they are shown, and very serious prices whenever they change hands.

There are actually several shapes known, all of which were fashioned from the same mold. These large 10" – 12" bowls are found with six broad ruffles or, on occasion, eight. The eight-ruffled versions have a somewhat squareish appearance. Rarer still are the examples found with the more tightly crimped three-in-one type of edging. Climbing up another notch on the rarity ladder we have the true square Farmyard bowls with four sides turned up. Only eight or nine examples are known in this shape; all of these shapes are found primarily in amethyst. A single peach opalescent example with six ruffles has also been confirmed. Only three green examples are known. One of these is an eight-ruffled shape and the other two have the three-in-one edge.

One round, flat plate is known in amethyst. The edge on this example does turn up slightly but not enough to disqualify it as a true plate.

All of the known Farmyard shapes carry the Jewelled Heart exterior pattern.

This design dates from the Dugan years (1909 – 1913), so it was quite a surprise when the green examples turned up a few years back. Very little green carnival seems to have come from this plant under Thomas Dugan's management. Even more surprising is the fact that no marigold examples have ever surfaced, and I've always been amazed that a white one hasn't turned up. Virtually all the other Dugan patterns that carry the Jewelled Heart exterior design, as the Farmyard pattern does, are found in those two colors. But, who knows? Just about anything is possible in carni-

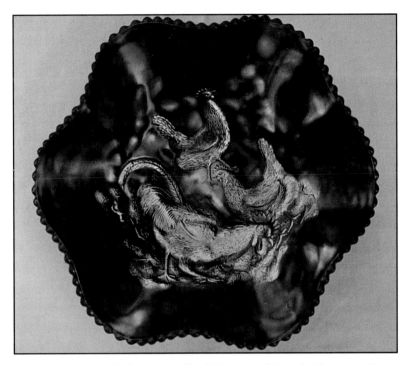

Two examples of the six-ruffled Farmyard bowl. The amethyst one is probably the most available of the various shape and color combinations. The peach opalescent bowl is the only known example in that color.

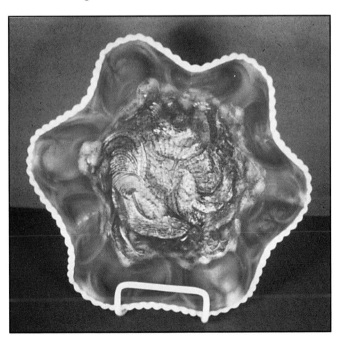

Shapes & Colors Known

Bowl, 6", ruffled	amethyst, peach opalescent
Bowl, 8" ruffled	amethyst, green
Bowl, square, 4 sides turned up	amethyst
Plate	amethyst

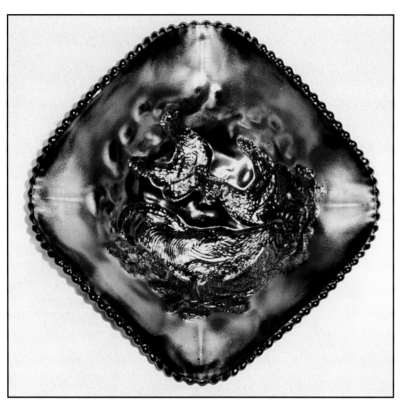

One of the rarest of the Farmyard shapes is this true square bowl in amethyst.

val glass and maybe one day a marigold or white one will be found.

The Farmyard bowl has been reproduced; however these new pieces were not made in the original mold. The new bowls measure only about 9" in diameter and are dome-footed. They were made in red, white, and amethyst and the examples I have seen all had a very garish and gaudy iridescence. Some are signed with the letters "MIMI" molded on the base. These were made by L.G. Wright. More recently, larger bowls and plates were made by Fenton for Singleton Bailey in a variety of iridescent colors. Here again, these should present no problems since all of them are clearly trademarked to distinguish them from the old.

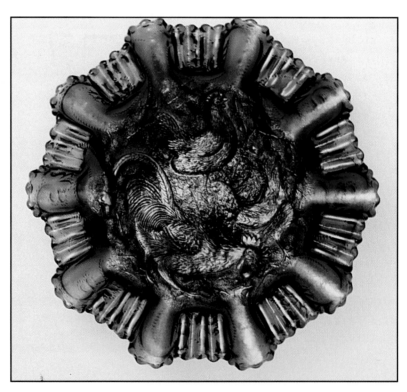

One of only two known three-in-one edge green Farmyard bowls.

Some collectors call this pattern Inverted Fan & Father. The design first entered production in non-iridized form in 1900 when the plant was operating as the Northwood Works of the National Glass Company. At that time, it was produced in custard glass, opalescent glass, and an unusual opaque pink that collectors have erroneously dubbed "Pink Slag." It is really not true slag glass as it was actually made from a single heat-sensitive batch of glass that changed color when warmed in. The pattern was also made in gold decorated emerald green and blue opalescent as late as 1909. A few pieces have also surfaced in a most unusual opaque gray color, which was no doubt experimental. In non-iridized form, a full line was produced including berry sets, table sets, water sets, salt and pepper shakers, toothpick holders, cruets, jelly compotes, a massive footed punch set, and a wide variety of novelty shapes fashioned from many of the above molds.

In carnival glass, the pattern is found as an exterior design on the Butterfly & Tulip and Grape Arbor footed bowls, and I also know of one example of the covered sugar, in marigold. It is missing the cover. I have personally examined this piece and I have virtually no doubt of its age and authenticity. Its existence suggests that at least one or a few table sets must surely have been made.

The only other documented carnival shape is a very controversial one: marigold carnival tumblers exist and some have questioned their age. I do not and I'll tell you my reasons. In 1973, I purchased six of these from a central Maine antique shop. I have known the dealer I purchased them from for over 25 years and her honesty is above reproach. I distinctly remember her telling me that she had had them in her stock for several years. This would pre-date any L.G. Wright carnival reproductions. Wright did not begin making carnival glass until 1972. The iridescent quality of these tumblers was quite typical of Dugan's marigold. They varied in iridescence and depth of color considerably, which is a characteristic not typical of new glass! They showed wear and age, with a couple of them having base chips. One of them was also quite misshapen, another characteristic that is typical of old glass and not new. I have no doubt that they were old and neither did the people to whom I sold them.

No matching water pitchers have ever surfaced, but I feel certain that there's probably one out there somewhere.

Caution: There are some carnival reproductions of this pattern. There are new tumblers in ice blue and cobalt blue. They were made by St. Clair, circa 1969. The cobalt blue ones were made for O. Joe Olsen and the Original Carnival Glass Collector's Society. They are so marked on the base and there were about 250 of these made. St. Clair also made some toothpick holders in marigold, amethyst, cobalt blue, and ice blue carnival. These are beautifully done with iridescence very close to that of old carnival glass. However, no old carnival Feather Scroll toothpick holders are known.

This marigold Feather Scroll sugar, missing the cover, is the only known example. Its existence would tend to confirm that the full, four-piece table set was indeed made in carnival glass. This example shows age wear on the feet and very uneven coloring on the interior. I am convinced that it is old!

Shapes & Colors Known

Covered sugar	marigold
Tumbler	marigold
Exterior pattern on Butterfly & Tulip and Grape Arbor bowls	

67

Filigree Vase

Dugan's Filigree line appeared for the first time in the 1907 Dugan factory catalog. The line consisted of a number of stylized patterns and shapes in iridized ruby, cobalt blue, emerald green, and ivory (custard). The slightly raised patterns were highlighted in silver and later, gold trim. They were no doubt intended to compete with the Northwood Verre D'or line, which had been introduced in 1906. Northwood and Dugan may have been cousins, but they were also fierce competitors.

Only one carnival glass example of this line is known to exist. It is a large, mold-blown vase in an unusual color that seems to be of a bronze/amethyst shade. While the blend of iridescent colors is of very high quality, it is somewhat uneven and spotty. While most of these mold-blown items in the Filigree line had finished and smoothed bases, this particular vase shows a rough pontil scar. The Filigree line made its last appearance in the wholesale catalogs in 1909, just about the time Dugan began production of his new iridescent glass. So it was no doubt experimental, and it may hold the distinction of being one of the first test pieces for Thomas Dugan's newly formulated iridizing process. This one-of-a-kind piece was reportedly found in the Indiana, Pennsylvania, area. No other iridized pieces of the Filigree line have ever been found.

The only known iridized Filigree Vase, quite possibly the test piece for Dugan's newly formulated iridizing process.

Shapes & Colors Known
Vase   bronze/amethyst

Fisherman's Mug

This mug first appeared in 1911 and production was continued at least through 1914, spanning both the Dugan and Diamond eras. The design shows many close similarities to the Waterlily & Cattails pattern, which is now known to have been made by Northwood, Fenton, and Dugan. Of course, the main difference here is the addition of the fish. The pattern is found only on the front of the mug, while the back is plain.

Amethyst is by far the most available color. In fact, one could call amethyst pieces plentiful. Still, they are popular items with collectors and usually don't hang around long in shops and antique malls. A fair number of these amethyst mugs are found with souvenir lettering stenciled on the unpatterned back. Marigold Fisherman's Mugs are far more difficult to find, often commanding two to three times the price of their amethyst counterparts. A handful of rare cobalt blue examples has also been reported. Peach opalescent is the big rarity here. Comparatively few are known and they bring very serious prices on the rare occasions when they are sold.

Fisherman's Mugs in amethyst and marigold

Shapes & Colors Known
Mug   marigold, amethyst, cobalt blue, peach opalescent

The Fishnet Epergne is one of the earliest carnival items to emerge from the Indiana, Pennsylvania, factory. It was produced during the Dugan years and made its first appearance in the wholesale catalogs in 1910. The pattern for which it is named is confined to the surface of the lily. The separate bases, which may be ruffled or have a three-in-one edge, are unpatterned and rest on a raised dome foot.

There are only two colors known: peach opalescent and amethyst. Neither one of them could be called abundant, but a fair number of peach opalescent examples do surface. It is the amethyst examples that are really quite rare and underrated. The few I have seen had a rich, satiny, multi-color iridescence and were really quite striking.

Like all epergnes, these are highly prone to damage and should be checked very carefully before you spend your money. Putting together an example from separately purchased parts can also be frustrating. Often there are slight variations in the diameter of the fitting hole in the base. As a result, separately purchased lilies do not always fit well. Of the two parts, the lilies seem to be somewhat easier to find, and there is a shortage of matching bases.

Two examples of the Fishnet Epergne in peach opalescent and amethyst. Both are rarely found with the amethyst examples especially hard to come by.

Shapes & Colors Known
Epergne   amethyst, peach opalescent

The Fishnet Epergne was a regular fixture in the wholesale catalogs during the 1910 – 1912 period. This ad for the peach opalescent version is from the fall 1910 issue of Butler Brothers.

69

Fishscale & Beads

Fishscale & Beads had a long production run, spanning both the Dugan and Diamond years. Often it is combined with Flower & Beads as an exterior pattern, a design carried over from earlier opalescent production.

Small, 5" – 7" ruffled bowls are the most commonly found shapes and are quite abundant in

A rare color for the Fishscale & Beads low ruffled bowl, a real beauty in cobalt blue.

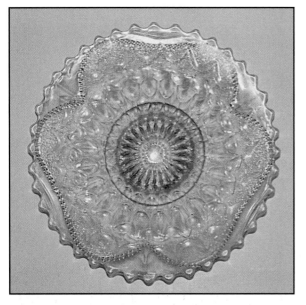

The Beads part of the Fishscale & Beads pattern is actually part of the Flowers & Beads exterior design. It shows through on this 7" flat plate in white.

marigold. They are somewhat harder to find in amethyst, white, and peach opalescent, but are still reasonably available with a little searching. The oxblood examples are very scarce and a couple of very rare cobalt blue examples are known. On rare occasions, these bowls are found with enamel souvenir lettering, usually the name of a town or popular tourist attraction. Some examples, usually in peach opalescent, have been found in a metal holder, which makes for a cute little miniature bride's basket.

The same mold was also used to fashion a card tray, with two sides turned up. Peach opalescent is the most frequently found color, but examples are also known in marigold, white, and amethyst. Triangular-shaped bowls, with three sides turned up, have also been reported in marigold, amethyst, and peach opalescent. These are seen far less often than the card tray shape.

The flat plates usually measure about 7" in diameter and are much harder to find than the bowls. Most have a fluted edge, but a few rare smooth-edged examples are known. Marigold is the most available of the known colors. White examples are harder to find but still turn up from time to time. Amethyst examples are very scarce and always command a pretty fair price when offered for sale. The iridescence on them is often dazzling. Peach opalescent seems to be the rarest color here. Very few have surfaced in recent years. Like the bowls, these plates have been found with enamel souvenir lettering, and these always command premium prices.

Being a resident of Maine, I can't resist a personal note here. Over the years, I have owned three pieces of this pattern that had enamel souvenir lettering: two bowls and a plate. All three were in peach opalescent with the same lettering on them, "Souvenir of Harmony, Maine." I don't know if any of you have ever been to Harmony, Maine, but it's a real big place. Sneeze and blink while you're driving through and you've missed it! Yet, someone once sold these pieces there.

Shapes & Colors Known

Bowl, 5" – 7"	marigold, amethyst, white, peach opalescent, cobalt blue, oxblood
Card tray	marigold, amethyst, white, peach opalescent
Bowl, triangular	marigold, amethyst, peach opalescent
Bride's bowl w/holder	peach opalescent
Plate, 7"	marigold, amethyst, white, peach opalescent

Not much is known about this scarce and often over-looked Dugan carnival pattern. It does not appear in any of the known Dugan advertising or in any currently known issues of the whole-sale catalogs. However, based on the known colors and design characteristics, there seems little doubt that it is a Dugan creation. The general scarcity of Five Hearts tends to indicate a rather brief production.

Dome-footed 8" – 9" bowls (a favorite shape for Dugan), a rare dome-footed rose bowl, and a whimsey bowl are the only known shapes. The bowls may be a round, deep shape with a scalloped edge, or they may be tightly crimped or ruffled. Peach opalescent is the usual color, but scarce marigold examples and even rarer amethyst examples do exist. There is also a single known marigold bowl that is perfectly round, 4½" deep with a widely flared rim. It has been called a whimsey bowl by collectors. The rose bowls, fashioned from the same mold, have been reported only in peach opalescent and marigold to date, with only three or four confirmed examples known.

A Five Hearts bowl in marigold.

This unusually deep, flared Five Hearts bowl in marigold has been called a whimsey shape. One could also classify it as a dome-footed compote.

Shapes & Colors Known

Bowl, 8" – 9", dome-footed	marigold, amethyst, peach opalescent
Rose bowl, dome-footed	peach opalescent, marigold
Whimsey deep, flared bowl	marigold

Floral & Grape

It came as a big surprise to everyone when shards of this pattern turned up in the Helman diggings. The design had long been credited to Fenton and indeed, that firm did produce a version of Floral & Grape. There are differences between the two and it was always assumed that one of the two versions was merely a variant and the likely result of a re-tooling of a worn-out mold. The Helman shards changed all that and we now know that the Floral & Grape water set is a Dugan creation. It is the Floral & Grape Variant water set that is a Fenton product.

The Floral & Grape water set first appeared in the April 1912 Butler Brothers catalog, in company with the Dugan Grapevine Lattice water set. It continued to appear through 1919, spanning the Diamond production years as well. It was often sold in company with other Diamond water sets, such as Lattice & Daisy.

There are some simple ways to distinguish Dugan's Floral & Grape from the Fenton Floral & Grape Variant water sets. On the Dugan version, the wide band of slanted ribs that encircles the pitcher is bordered by horizontal, cable-like bands. The Fenton version lacks these horizontal bands. The Dugan pitchers have more flowers, leaves, and grapes covering a larger portion of the pitcher.

While the marigold floral & Grape water set is still very available, the marigold Jack-in-the-Pulpit hat, fashioned from the tumbler mold, is very seldom seen.

The Fenton version is far more sparse, showing a good deal of un-patterned area. The Dugan pitcher has a second band of slanted ribs that encircles the neck; the Fenton pitcher lacks this.

The Dugan/Diamond Floral & Grape water sets are quite easily found in marigold. The tumblers are especially abundant; just about every antique mall or flea market will have a few. Often the iridescence is only fair at best, but some beautifully iridized examples do turn up. Amethyst sets are harder to find, but I would by no means class them as rare. It may take a little searching, but they're still out there. I would, however, classify the cobalt blue pitchers as scarce. The tumblers turn up from time to time, but the pitchers are tough. The white examples are scarce, with the tumblers also surprisingly hard to find. A few rare pitchers in lime green with a marigold iridescent overlay are also known. I have yet to see a matching tumbler, but they likely do exist.

The only other shape known is that of a ruffled hat shape, fashioned from the tumbler mold. These are actually quite scarce and have been reported only in marigold and amethyst to date, but other colors likely exist. A few rare examples in a Jack-in-the-Pulpit shape are also known, but only marigold to date.

Shapes & Colors Known:

Water pitcher	marigold, amethyst, cobalt blue, white, lime green w/marigold overlay
Tumbler	marigold, amethyst, cobalt blue, white
Ruffled hat	marigold, amethyst
JIP hat	marigold

Floral & Wheat

This unusual stemmed, two-handled bonbon made its debut just about the time that Thomas Dugan left Indiana, Pennsylvania, in 1913. It appeared in the wholesale catalogs until 1916, but likely remained in production until the 1920s. Its namesake pattern is found on the exterior surface. Most of the known examples carry the Puzzle pattern on the interior, but a few are known with a plain interior. The top portion is usually round, but an occasional variation turns up. Some are ruffled and some are formed into a card tray shape, with two sides pulled out.

Peach opalescent is really the most often encountered color. Often the opalescence is scant and confined to the fluted edge only, but some examples with heavy opalescence do turn up from time to time. Marigold is found slightly less often, but is still available. I must admit to seeing a pretty fair number of white examples over the years. Often it is these white examples that are fashioned into the ruffled and card tray shapes. Amethyst Floral & Wheat bonbons are really quite scarce but are overshadowed by the few known cobalt blue examples. While I cannot confirm an iridized celeste blue example, I wouldn't be too surprised to learn of one. I have seen them in non-iridized celeste blue, so it's entirely possible that an iridized one could exist.

Flowers and wheat sheaves adorn the exterior of this amethyst Floral & Wheat stemmed bonbon. The interior surface features the Puzzle pattern.

Shapes & Colors Known

Stemmed bonbon	marigold, amethyst, peach opalescent, white, cobalt blue

Flowers & Beads

Flowers & Beads is one of the early Dugan carnival patterns that was carried over from non-iridized opalescent production. The opalescent version appeared in 1907, so the carnival version likely dates from the 1909 – 1910 period. It was used as a primary pattern on the exterior surface of small, 7" – 8" flat plates, with a plain interior. These are usually hexagonal in shape and are not that easily found in any color.

Amethyst examples are the most frequently seen, but even these are rather

The Flowers & Beads pattern on the exterior of this six-sided 7" flat plate in amethyst.

73

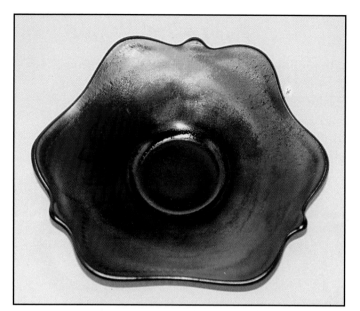

scarce. Peach opalescent is seen far less often and the oxblood examples are rarer still. Like so many Dugan carnival novelties, marigold examples do exist but are rarely found.

Round and ruffled 6" – 7" bowls are also found in all of the above listed colors. These are really no more easily found than the plates.

This design was also used in combination with the Fishscale & Beads interior design, which can be found in 5" – 6" ruffled bowls and on 7" – 8" round, flat plates, with a fluted edge. (See Fishscale & Beads for information on these).

The iridescence on the plain interior of the Flowers & Beads plate is often quite stunning.

Shapes & Colors Known (plain interior)	
Bowl, 6" – 7"	marigold, amethyst, peach opalescent, oxblood
Plate, 7" – 8", hexagonal	marigold, amethyst, peach opalescent, oxblood

Flowers & Frames

Found only on the interior surface of dome-footed bowls, Flowers & Frames is a relatively scarce Dugan carnival pattern. Some examples are found in Dugan's African Iridescent (oxblood), so the design must have been in production around March of 1910, when that line was introduced.

A beautiful triangular-shaped Flowers & Frames bowl in oxblood.

The dome-footed bowls are generally found in the 8" – 9" size range, in a variety of shapes and edgings. Examples have been reported in a round, ruffled shape, triangular shape, and even in an unusually deep version that some collectors call a dome-footed compote. This latter shape was apparently a favorite of Thomas Dugan, for we find it in several of his dome-footed carnival designs. Edge shapings known include broadly ruffled, three-in-one, flat, square ruffles, and tightly crimped.

Only three colors can be confirmed as of this writing. None is that easily found, but amethyst seems to be the most available, followed closely by peach opalescent. The oxblood (black amethyst) examples are very rare. Some reference sources list marigold and green as well. I have never seen any example of either color, so for now, both remain unconfirmed.

Shapes & Colors Known	
Bowl, 8" – 9", ruffled	amethyst, peach opalescent, oxblood
Bow, 8" – 9", triangular	amethyst, peach opalescent, oxblood
Compote shape	amethyst, peach opalescent, oxblood

74

Flowers & Spades

This design never seems to receive much fanfare or publicity, but make no mistake about it, this is a very rare Dugan carnival pattern! Since 1982, only about a half dozen examples have changed hands at the carnival glass auctions. In 28 years of collecting, I have owned only one example! The design shows many similarities in concept to the Wishbone & Spades and Four Flowers patterns, both of which were in production in the 1911 – 1912 period. So, Flowers & Spades likely dates from the same time frame. Because of its rarity, the design likely had a very short production run. It is possible that the molds may have been a casualty of the 1912 fire.

Flowers & Spades is found only on the interior surface of large, 10" bowls and their smaller counterparts, 5" – 6". The exterior surface is unpatterned. (I have received a report of one example with the Big Basketweave exterior design, but this is unconfirmed.) Most examples are broadly ruffled, and have been confirmed in peach opalescent and amethyst. A few very rare ice cream-shaped bowls are also known in amethyst. I suspect peach opalescent ones also exist but remain unconfirmed to date.

Many reference sources list this pattern in marigold and green. I have never seen an example in either color, nor have I spoken with anyone who ever has. It's entirely possible that they could exist, but until such time as one is placed in front of me or a good, clear photo of one is shown to me, I will pass on listing them.

Flowers & Spades 10" ruffled bowl in peach opalescent.

Shapes & Colors Known

Bowl, 10", ruffled	amethyst, peach opalescent
Bowl, 5" – 6", ruffled	amethyst, peach opalescent
Bowl, 10", ice cream	amethyst

Fluted Scrolls

Only one carnival shape is found in this design and it is a true rarity of very high order. Fluted Scrolls was originally called Klondike when it was introduced by Harry Northwood in 1898. At that time, the design was made in a full line of non-iridized colors of blue, canary yellow, and clear to white opalescent. The shapes included a berry set, water set, table set, cruets, and salt and pepper shakers. None of these shapes has ever surfaced in carnival.

The only carnival item known is a footed rose bowl that was quite obviously shaped from the spooner mold. It is also quite obvious that this must have been made in one of the molds that Harry Northwood left behind when he moved on to Wheeling, West Virginia, in 1901. Yet another obvious fact is that this is one of the rarest of all Dugan carnival items. I know of only two examples, one in marigold and one in amethyst. There must surely be others out there somewhere. It is also quite possible that other carnival shapes could one day surface, but none has as yet. Then again, Fluted Scrolls may have been among the molds lost in the 1912 fire.

The extremely rare Fluted Scrolls rose bowl in amethyst. This version, with the molded floral band around the center, is called Jackson by some collectors.

Dugan

Folding Fan

This design bears a striking resemblance to that found on the lily of the Fishnet Epergne. Here it is known only on the interior surface of short-stemmed compotes, found in a variety of shapings. I have seen them with a ruffled top, a round, deep-shaped top, a tightly crimped edge, and a "banana" dish-shaped top (two sides turned up), also with a tightly crimped edge. I would have to say that I have seen more of the crimped edge shapes than any of the others.

Only three colors have been documented to date. As far as actual numbers are concerned, I have seen more of the peach opalescent examples than any other. There seem to be far fewer marigold examples and I would classify the amethyst ones as really quite rare. I have never seen or heard of a white one, but I wouldn't be surprised if there's one out there somewhere. Most Dugan carnival designs that are found in marigold, amethyst, and peach opalescent eventually turn up in white.

Interior of a Folding Fan compote with a crimped edge in peach opalescent.

Formal

Dugan

Formal is one of the earlier Dugan carnival designs, likely from the first few years of the carnival era. It was one of the carry-over patterns made earlier in opalescent glass.

Only two carnival shapes are known, both fashioned from the same mold. Both are rarely found. The pedestal-footed vase is usually found in a Jack-in-the-Pulpit shape in marigold or amethyst. The other shape is commonly called a hatpin holder. The top is slightly cupped inward. In all likelihood, this shape was actually intended to be used as a bud vase. Here again, marigold and amethyst are the only colors reported, with amethyst slightly edging out marigold in rarity.

These are very popular pieces and always command very respectable prices when they change hands. The quality of the iridescence is usually top notch.

Shapes & Colors Known
Vase	marigold, amethyst
Hatpin holder (bud vase)	marigold, amethyst

The rare Formal hatpin holder in amethyst. In actuality, it was more likely intended to be used as a bud vase.

Four Flowers

Dugan

One of the most popular Dugan carnival patterns, Four Flowers made its debut in the wholesale catalogs early in 1911. It was often marketed with another popular Dugan pattern, Wishbone & Spades. Just one year later, both designs abruptly vanished from the wholesale catalogs, and I suspect that the molds may have been among those lost to the February, 1912 fire. Such a short production run would certainly account for the relative scarcity of both designs. Some collectors call this design Pods & Posies.

Two sizes of plates and several bowl shape variations are the primary items found here. Most examples found will have a plain, unpatterned exterior, but there are a few exceptions. Some small plates are found with a Basketweave Variant exterior. Some bowls, the rose bowl, and at least one known example of the large chop plate have been documented with the Soda Gold (Tree of Life) exterior pattern.

Just look at the fabulous electric iridescence on this beautiful amethyst Four Flowers plate.

77

This peach opalescent Four Flowers 9" ruffled bowl is also a beauty.

The large 10" chop plates and the small 6½" plates were often marketed as a seven-piece cake set. Peach opalescent is by far the most often found color for both sizes of plates. Amethyst examples are seen far less often and should be classified as very rare. Like so many Dugan carnival designs, it is the marigold examples that are actually the rarest color. I know of only one chop plate and three small plates. A single example of the large chop plate in peach opalescent is known with the Soda Gold (Tree of Life) exterior.

Perhaps one of the rarest of the known shapes is the large 10" ice cream bowl. It was fashioned from the same mold used for the chop plate. I know of only one each in amethyst and peach opalescent. To the best of my knowledge, no matching small ice cream bowls have surfaced, but they could well exist.

Large 8½" – 10" bowls, along with a small 5" – 6" size, make a most attractive berry set. Examples may be found ruffled or in a round, deep shape. Surprisingly, the large bowls seem to surface most often in amethyst, yet the small ones are very rare in that color. Quite the opposite is true of the peach opalescent examples. The small bowls are found more often than are the large ones. Very scarce large marigold bowls exist. Strangely, these often have the Soda Gold (Tree of Life) exterior pattern. I have yet to see a matching small bowl in marigold, but they likely exist. The large bowl has also been documented in a few other colors, all of which must be classified as extremely rare. I know of two in amber, two in green, one in cobalt blue, and one in vaseline. I have not been able to document any small bowls in any of these colors as of this writing.

Three other shapes are known, all very rare and all fashioned from the molds for the chop plate or large bowl. The banana bowl, with two sides pulled up, is known in amethyst and peach opalescent. I know of six in amethyst and only one in peach opalescent. A few triangular-shaped bowls have been documented, but only in peach opalescent to date. The only other reported shape is that of a large rose bowl. It carries the Soda

The Four Flowers chop plate, along with six of the small plates, was offered in this ad from the mid-spring 1911 Butler Brothers issue as a seven-piece cake set for 45¢ a set! If you could piece one together at today's prices it would likely cost you from $2,000 to $4,000, depending on color.

Shapes & Colors Known

Chop plate, 10"	marigold, amethyst, peach opalescent
Small plate, 6½"	marigold, amethyst, peach opalescent
Ice cream bowl, 10"	amethyst, peach opalescent
Bowl, 8" – 9"	marigold, amethyst, peach opalescent, cobalt blue, amber, green, vaseline, teal
Bowl, 5" – 6"	amethyst, peach opalescent
Banana bowl	amethyst, peach opalescent
Triangular bowl	peach opalescent
Rose bowl	marigold, amethyst

Gold (Tree of Life) exterior pattern and has been documented only in marigold and amethyst. I know of only one of each.

This design was also produced by The Rhiimaki Glass Company of Finland. It is shown in one of their surviving factory catalogs. Their version was made in a 9½" ruffled bowl, with a plain, unpatterned exterior. Marigold is the only confirmed color, usually with a brilliant radium finish. It is not known whether they copied the Dugan design or possibly purchased the mold from Dugan. Personally, I feel that a copy is the more likely of the two possibilities.

A variation of this pattern, called Four Flowers Variant, also exists, but it, too, was not made by Dugan. It is believed to be of European origin, but the exact maker is not known. The Four Flowers Variant pattern has an extra flower between the tusk-shaped pods, and a thumbprint and panel design on the exterior surface. It also lacks a collar base, with a ground base instead. It is found on 9" plates and ruffled bowls in a wide variety of colors.

The Four Flowers Variant 9½" plate, believed to be of European manufacture.

Garden Path and Variant

Considerable mystery surrounds this elaborate pattern. Just exactly why two versions of the design were made with such minor differences remains unclear. Many theories about this have

been put forth, so I'll add my two cents' worth. The pattern is found in white carnival, so it must have been in production late 1911 to early 1912, when Dugan began producing his White Carnival line. This would place its manufacture at exactly the time of the catastrophic 1912 fire. Perhaps one mold was destroyed and another had to be created. Or, perhaps the mold was damaged and salvaged by adding a few modifications. We may never know for certain, but it's food for thought.

The differences between Garden Path and Garden Path Variant are confined to the outer edge of the pattern. The Garden Path Variant pattern has six small, winged heart-like devices, and six five-

How's this for a real knock out? This stunning amethyst Garden Path Variant chop plate is one of the rarest and most treasured of all Dugan carnival pieces.

79

This beautiful white Garden Path Variant 7" plate is one of the rarest color and size combinations in the plate shape.

A very rare and desirable peach opalescent Garden Path Variant 10" ice cream-shaped bowl.

petalled palm-like fronds bordering the outer edge of the pattern; Garden Path lacks these. Aside from that, the two patterns are identical.

None of the known shapes is easily found, but the bowls seem to be the most available. The larger bowls may vary from 8" to as much as 10" in diameter, and may be ruffled, a deep, round shape, or ice cream-shaped. The ice cream-shaped bowls are the rarest of the three. They are known in marigold, amethyst, peach opalescent, and white. White and peach opalescent are the most available of the four colors, with both amethyst and marigold seen far less often. The small bowls range from 5" to 7" in diameter and are known in the same three shape variations. Peach opalescent seems to be the most available color, followed by white, amethyst, and marigold, in that order. Soda Gold is the usual exterior design.

Large 11" chop plates, along with smaller 6" – 7" plates, were likely marketed as seven-piece cake sets. The chop plate is the most eagerly sought and highly treasured of all the shapes in this design. Even in amethyst, by far the most often found color, they always command high prices. Only two or three marigold examples are known and only one in peach opalescent. It seems strange that no white chop plates have surfaced, for that is by far the most often found color for the small plates. Peach opalescent is next in line, but even so, comparatively few are known. Examples also exist in marigold and amethyst. Both are very rare. Here again, Soda Gold (Tree of Life) is the usual exterior design, but some examples with a plain exterior are known.

The bowls are found in both Garden Path and the variant. All known plates are in the Garden Path Variant pattern. Mention should also be made of the report of a 8" ruffled bowl in green, but it remains unconfirmed.

A large rose bowl was fashioned from the same mold used for the large bowls. It is very rare, with only a few examples known, and has been reported only in marigold to date.

By far, the rarest known shape is the compote. Only a handful are known in marigold, amethyst, and white. All are extremely rare. In fact, I don't recall one ever selling at auction!

Shapes & Colors Known

Bowl, 8" – 9", ruffled	marigold, amethyst, peach opalescent, white, (green?)
Bowl, 8" – 9", round, deep	marigold, amethyst, peach opalescent, white
Bowl, 10", ice cream	marigold, amethyst, peach opalescent, white
Bowl, 6-7"	marigold, amethyst, peach opalescent, white, aqua w/marigold overlay
Chop plate, 11"	marigold, amethyst, peach opalescent
Plate, 6" – 7"	marigold, amethyst, peach opalescent, white
Rose bowl	marigold
Compote	marigold, amethyst, white

Georgia Belle

Georgia Belle is an exterior design usually found in combination with the Puzzle and Question Marks patterns on pedestal-footed compotes and plates. It is one of the very few intaglio designs to come from this firm and was likely one of the carry-over patterns from Dugan's Intaglio line, which was made just prior to the carnival glass era.

The design of impressed peaches and leaves would be a most attractive primary pattern, but I have never seen it as such. It is always found in combination with the Question Marks interior design, with the Puzzle pattern on the pedestal foot.

Shapes & Colors Known
Exterior pattern only – see Question Marks and Puzzle

The Georgia Belle pattern as it appears on the exterior surface of a Question Marks stemmed plate.

God & Home

Even though many carnival collectors were appalled by all the unmarked reproductions made by L. G. Wright, I suppose that this is one instance that we should thank him for. For many years, all efforts to track down the maker of this extremely rare water set, proved fruitless. We know that Wright purchased many of the Dugan/Diamond molds after 1931. So, when the Wright reproductions of this set appeared amidst the Dugan/Diamond boom of reproductions in the early 1980s, we finally had a clearer picture. It now seems pretty certain that the original version was made at Indiana, Pennsylvania.

Make no mistake about it, this is one of the rarest and most

The extremely rare cobalt blue God & Home water set. As rare as they are, their values have been stagnant for a good many years, primarily due to the reproductions by the L. G. Wright Glass Company.

desirable of all the water sets produced by this firm. They are seldom offered for sale and always bring top dollar. They are known only in cobalt blue, a most curious situation. This would tend to make me think these sets were produced on an extremely limited basis for some special event or for a specific customer. We are now reasonably certain Thomas Dugan did not produce any cobalt blue carnival until early in 1912 when the first cobalt blue items from this firm began to appear in wholesale catalogs. Dugan left the firm less than a year later. So, it is possible that the God & Home water set was made by Dugan. However, Diamond's production of the color was far more prolific, for a much longer period, so the odds actually favor Diamond as the maker.

It is also interesting to note that in the early years of carnival collecting, a large number of these sets consistently turned up in the same areas: the junction of the Ohio and Mississippi rivers southern Illinois, western Kentucky, and eastern Missouri. Perhaps they were made for a customer in that area and shipped there via boat down the Ohio River. There has also been some speculation that these sets may have been made as a commemorative, marking the end of WWI in 1918. This is entirely possible and would, in fact, serve to confirm Diamond as the maker.

Caution: The reproduction God & Home water sets by L. G. Wright are very nicely done. They were initially made in amethyst only, and later in red and ice green, so distinguishing them from the old sets was never a problem. Then, and this may come as a big shock to many collectors, in 1982 Wright produced a limited edition of 1,000 sets in cobalt blue carnival! They are reportedly all trademarked, but as we all know, marks can be removed. So, be advised!

Shapes & Colors Known	
Water set	cobalt blue

Golden Grape

Production dates for this simple design coincide with the Apple Blossom pattern. It does not appear in the wholesale catalogs until 1928 and continued to do so until 1931. The known shapes are also comparable and like many of the later Diamond carnival patterns, the iridescence is often rather weak.

It is found on the interior surface of 6" – 7" bowls, which may be ruffled or a round, deep shape. The exterior is plain. Marigold examples are plentiful and a handful of amethyst bowls is also known. Green has been reported but is, as yet, unconfirmed.

A collar-based rose bowl, fashioned from the same mold, is known in marigold, and these are rather scarce.

Shapes & Colors Known	
Bowl, 6" – 7"	marigold, amethyst, (green?)
Rose bowl	marigold

A Golden Grapes 7" ruffled bowl in marigold.

Golden Harvest

For many years the origin of this design remained a mystery. Some were convinced it was a product of the U.S. Glass Company, while others believed it was made by Fenton. Several shards of this pattern turned up in Helman diggings, so we now know for certain it was made in Indiana, Pennsylvania. This pattern dates from the Diamond Glass Company era, and made its debut in the wholesale catalogs in 1916.

Wine sets are the only known shapes and the variety of colors available is also very limited. The stopper to the decanter is unusual in that it is a solid piece of glass, while the stoppers for virtually all other carnival wine decanters are hollow. The stemmed wine glasses are far less elaborate than the pattern on the decanter. They actually appear to be a variation of the Vintage pattern, and in fact, many collectors call them that. But, they are the proper ones for this set.

Marigold and amethyst are the only reported colors. The marigold decanters are not terribly difficult to find and often the quality of the iridescence is only fair. While the amethyst wines turn up in fair numbers, the matching decanter is really quite scarce. Here again, the iridescent quality is often only fair, but some beautifully iridized examples do exist.

Caution: This set has been reproduced by L.G. Wright in amethyst. Apparently, the molds were also leased to Gibson, as there are reproduction decanters in electric blue and iridized custard that are signed "Gibson" and often dated.

Golden Harvest wine decanter and stemmed wine in amethyst.

"GOLDEN IRIDESCENT" WINE SET.

C1856—Allover grape and leaf embossed, 12 in. 1 qt. decanter, SIX 2 oz. ftd. wines. 2 sets in case, 20 lbs.
(Total, 90c)   Set, **48c**

The Golden Harvest wine set in marigold from the June 1916 Butler Brothers issue.

Shapes & Colors Known	
Wine decanter & stemmed wines	marigold, amethyst

Grape Arbor

This pattern caused a great deal of controversy back in the early 1980s. The handsome Grape Arbor water sets bear the Northwood N-in-a-circle trademark, so there was never any doubt they were products of that firm. So, it was only natural to assume that the large, footed Grape Arbor bowls were also Harry Northwood's creation. However, when some large chunks of these bowls

Dugan/Diamond's Grape Arbor large footed fruit bowl in marigold. All known examples carry the Feather Scroll exterior pattern. These bowls were made by adding the Grape Arbor design to the interior of the Feather Scroll master berry bowl, a mold revived from pre-carnival opalescent production.

Another view of the Grape Arbor fruit bowl, this one in amethyst.

turned up at the Dugan/Diamond dump site, it caused quite a stir. These large, footed bowls never saw the inside of the Northwood factory! They are indeed Dugan products and likely date from the 1910 – 1912 period. This would be in the same time frame as the Butterfly & Tulip bowls. Both patterns carry the Inverted Fan & Feather design on the exterior, and this is one of the carry-over patterns from the pre-iridescent era.

This actually leads us to a most interesting situation. Once these bowls were established as Dugan products, it was quickly assumed that Dugan had copied Northwood's design. Or did he? We know that the Northwood Grape Arbor water set was in production in 1912. This was when Northwood introduced his pastel carnival colors of white, ice blue, and ice green; surviving trade journals confirm this. The Northwood water set is found in all three of those colors. If Dugan's Grape Arbor bowl was in production during the 1910 – 1912 period, it may actually pre-date Northwood's version of the design! So, just who copied whom here? We may never know for certain, but it's certainly food for thought.

These large, deep, footed bowls are quite handsome Dugan products. Marigold examples turn up in reasonably fair numbers, but it takes a little searching. The amethyst bowls are far more difficult to find but are well worth the effort. Most exhibit beautiful iridescence. Rarer still are the cobalt blue examples, with comparatively few known. First prize in the rarity department goes to the peach opalescent Grape Arbor bowl. Only one example is known, and it hasn't changed hands for eight years!

Shapes & Colors Known
Bowl, large footed   marigold, amethyst, cobalt blue, peach opalescent

84

Grape Delight

This design first appeared in the wholesale catalogs in 1912 and continued to do so through 1916, spanning both the Dugan and Diamond production years. A close examination of the pattern reveals many strong similarities to the Vintage Perfume and Powder Jar shown elsewhere in this book, and I suspect that Grape Delight was really part of the same line. However, the lack of the rows of beads and the unique feet set it apart enough so that collectors have always called it by this name.

Only two shapes are known, a footed rose bowl and a nut bowl, fashioned from the same mold. Both rest on six unusual, squared, stubby feet, which are highly prone to damage, making perfect examples difficult to find. However, if you don't mind a nick or two on the feet, you shouldn't have too much trouble finding examples in several of the known colors.

The rose bowls, with their cupped-in tops, are found in two variations. One has a smooth, crimped edge, while the other has a scalloped top. The scalloped top variation is the harder of the two to find. White seems to be the most available color, with marigold and amethyst running a close second and third. Cobalt blue is harder to find, yet I would not classify them as rare. Some patient searching will turn one up. The rare colors here are a beautiful pastel lavender and a rarer still horehound, which was this firm's version of amber.

The nut bowl, with its straight-up sides, is known in virtually all the same colors but seems to be a little harder to find. It is seen most often in marigold, amethyst, and cobalt blue. I have seen far fewer white nut bowls than I have rose bowls. Here again, lavender and horehound are rare.

Caution: These pieces have been reproduced by L.G. Wright and Mosser in cobalt blue, purple, ice green, and ice blue. The new cobalt examples are more lightly iridized and more transparent looking than the old. No old ice blue or ice green examples are known. Some are signed with the Mosser "M" trademark, but many more are not marked, so watch out!

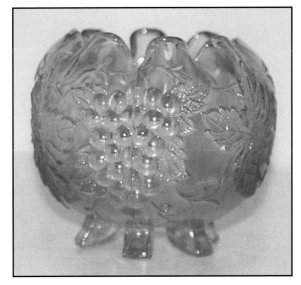

The marigold Grape Delight rosebowl and a Grape Delight nut bowl in amethyst. Both pieces were fashioned from the same mold.

The Grape Delight rose bowl and nut bowl, from the April 1912 Butler Brothers catalog. Note the word "OUT" where the price should be. They were apparently sold out!

IRIDESCENT ROSE AND NUT BOWL ASST.

C1826 — Prominent relief embossed grapevine dark metallic iridescent finish, rustic feet. Comprises 1 doz. each:
5 in. crimp rose bowl.
5½x4¼ deep nut bowl or jardiniere.
2 doz. case. 43 lbs.

Doz.   Out!

Shapes & Colors Known

Footed rose bowl & nut bowl   marigold, amethyst, cobalt blue, white, lavender, horehound

Grapevine Lattice

Grapevine Lattice is one of the designs that spanned both the Dugan and Diamond years at Indiana, Pennsylvania. It first appeared in the spring 1912 Butler Brothers catalog and continued to appear sporadically through the early 1920s. The water set was often sold in company with the Floral & Grape water set.

Amethyst Grapevine Lattice tankard water sets like this one are very scarce and eagerly sought.

The small, 6" – 7" ruffled bowls must surely be one of the most common of all carnival novelties, at least when it comes to the white and marigold examples. It often seems as though every antique mall has a few. They are not so easily found in amethyst, however. The small, 7" plates are another story; they do turn up in white, on occasion, but are rather scarce in marigold and rarely found in amethyst. They are also known in peach opalescent and these are quite rare.

The tall, tankard water set is often overlooked in marigold, probably because many examples tend to be rather light in color. However, they are really not all that plentiful and beautifully iridized examples do exist. The amethyst pitchers and tumblers are the next most available, but are really very scarce. The iridescent quality on these is usually top notch. The cobalt blue sets are very rare with comparatively few perfect pitchers known, and the same situation applies to the white water sets. The water pitchers are rather delicate, being mold-blown with an applied handle, so many of them have likely become casualties of time. It should be noted that a couple of rare tumblers in an odd shade of smoky blue have been reported, but no matching pitcher has surfaced. These were likely just the result of an off-color or misfired batch of cobalt blue.

This marigold Grapevine Lattice 7" plate has unusually frosty iridescence.

The only other known shape is a ruffled hat, fashioned from the tumbler mold. They are known in marigold and amethyst but are not easily found. At least one amethyst example is known in a Jack-in-the-Pulpit shape. I have not heard of a cobalt blue or white ruffled hat, but they could well exist.

Caution: The water set, small bowls, and plates have been reproduced by L.G. Wright in purple carnival. The tumblers, small bowls, and plates were also reproduced in non-iridized custard glass.

Shapes & Colors Known

Bowl, 6" – 7"	marigold, amethyst, white
Plate, 7"	marigold, amethyst, white, peach opalescent
Hat, ruffled	marigold, amethyst
Hat, Jack-in-the-Pulpit	amethyst
Tankard water pitcher	marigold, amethyst, cobalt blue, white
Tumbler	marigold, amethyst, cobalt blue, white, smoke blue

C1936. "Vineyard"–2 shapes, lattice and grape embossed, pearl, amethyst and royal blends. ½ gal. blown jugs, stuck handles, pressed tumblers. 2 sets each. 6 sets in bbl.. —lbs.   Sets, **67c**

The Grapevine Lattice tankard water set was sold in company with Dugan's Floral & Grape water set in the April 1912 Butler Brothers wholesale catalog

Harvest Flower

Precious little is known about the production of this pattern. For many years, all efforts to track down a conclusive connection to either Dugan or Diamond proved fruitless. It does not appear in any known wholesale catalogs or in any of the currently known advertising from either firm. In the early 1980s, L.G. Wright issued a reproduction of the water set, and at last we had a firm connection. Wright made this reproduction in original molds purchased in Indiana, Pennsylvania. As to which of the firms originated the design, my own opinion, based on mold characteristics and the known colors, favors the Diamond Glass Company.

Harvest Flower is found only on extremely rare water sets. The tankard pitcher is mold-blown with a separately applied handle. Both pitcher and tumbler are known in marigold; make no mistake, both are extremely rare with relatively few examples known. A handful of amethyst tumblers also exists, but no matching pitcher has yet surfaced. There must surely be one out there somewhere. A single tumbler in pastel green with a marigold iridescent overlay is also known to exist, but here again, no matching pitcher has been reported.

Caution: This water set was reproduced in a very gaudy red carnival glass. Reportedly, these sets were made by Westmoreland for L.G. Wright in the late 1970s or early 1980s.

The rare Harvest Flower Tumbler in marigold. Note how it is narrower in the middle than at the top and base. The water pitcher shows this effect in even more pronounced fashion, appearing almost hourglass-shaped.

Shapes & Colors Known

Water pitcher	marigold
Tumbler	marigold, amethyst, light green w/marigold overlay

Heavy Grape, Dugan's

Believe it or not, this design was once thought to be a Millersburg product! It was not until the shards from the Helman diggings were carefully examined that we learned this was indeed a Dugan creation. It was the geometric design called Compass found on the exterior surface of these handsome bowls that was the key. Several fragments of Ski-Star bowls turned up in these shards, and these carry the same Compass exterior pattern.

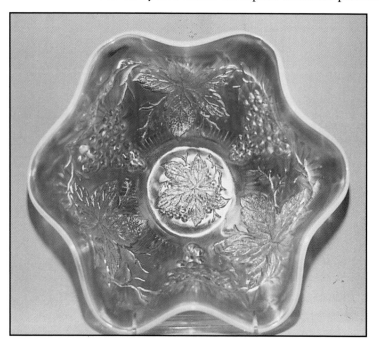

Even though the amethyst Dugan's Heavy Grape bowls receive all the raves, it is the peach opalescent examples, like this one, that are the rarest color.

The name Dugan's Heavy Grape should always be used when referring to this pattern, in order to avoid confusion with Imperial's design of the same name.

The design is found only on the interior surface of large 10" – 11" bowls, and a smaller 5" – 6" counterpart. Most of the known examples are broadly ruffled and make a most impressive berry set. The large bowls are very desirable items and very difficult to find. Surprisingly, the small bowls are even tougher to find, with comparatively fewer examples known. Amethyst is the most often encountered color, but even so, they are very scarce. The iridescence is often spectacular, especially on the examples found with a brilliant, all-over electric blue lustre. Marigold examples are really much harder still to find, even though they seldom bring the raves the amethyst ones do. The only other color reported is peach opalescent, and this is really the least often found.

I know of two large bowls, measuring 10½", in the low ice cream bowl shape. Both are in amethyst and one of them is an absolute knockout, exhibiting a stunning electric blue iridescence. I know of no small bowls in this shape, but they could well exist.

The amethyst Heavy Grape bowls rightfully deserve all the raves they get, as evidenced by this beauty.

Shapes & Colors Known

Bowl, 10" – 11", ruffled	marigold, amethyst, peach opalescent
Bow, 5" – 6", ruffled	marigold, amethyst, peach opalescent
Bowl, 10" – 11", ice cream shape	amethyst

Heavy Iris

The Heavy Iris tankard water set is, in my opinion, one of the most beautiful and impressive in the entire spectrum of carnival glass. That any of these delicate, mold-blown pitchers survived the years at all is really amazing. They have a separately applied handle and virtually all known examples, save for one, have a ruffled top. They are very difficult to find in any color. Marigold is the most often seen color, but even they are quite scarce. The positively stunning amethyst pitchers are a sight to behold and are highly treasured. Rarer still are the oxblood (black amethyst) pitchers. The white pitchers are very rare and always command serious attention and prices whenever they are offered for sale. A single peach opalescent tankard is known. It appears to have a very slight opalescence on the edge of the ruffled top and there is some controversy over whether or not it truly is peach opalescent, but most collectors accept it as such. A single white example with a straight, unruffled top also exists.

Tumblers are known in marigold, amethyst, oxblood, and white, with the rarity in that order. They are also found in a beautiful lavender shade. No peach opalescent tumblers have yet been confirmed.

A single known Jack-in-the-Pulpit hat, fashioned from the tumbler mold, is also known. White is the only reported color, but I wouldn't be surprised if an amethyst or marigold example surfaced.

Caution: This water set has been reproduced by The L.G. Wright Glass Company from the original molds. The new pitchers are quite easy to distinguish from the old. The new pitcher has a plain, unpatterned area, about 2", between the top end of the patterned area and the ruffled top. On the old pitcher, the ruffled top begins immediately at the top of the patterned area. The new tumblers present more of a challenge. Generally, they are of good quality, but they are not quite as sharply molded in pattern detail. As with most new carnival, the iridescence is rather gaudy. These new sets were made in amethyst during the 1980s. They are not trademarked in any way.

There is also a new whimsey handled basket in red and electric blue carnival. These were made by Gibson in 1987 and are so marked on the base.

The magnificent amethyst Heavy Iris tankard water set.

This drawing of a Heavy Iris tumbler, somewhat flattened out to show detail, was one of the Dugan pattern drawings done by the author in the late 1970s for William Heacock.

Shapes & Colors Known	
Tankard pitcher	marigold, amethyst, white, peach opalescent, oxblood
Tankard pitcher, straight top	white
Tumbler	marigold, amethyst, white, lavender, oxblood
Hat shape, JIP	white

89

Heavy Web

Fragments of this design were unearthed at the plant site, so we know this extremely rare pattern was made at Indiana, Pennsylvania. It is very similar in concept to the Daisy Web hat shape and likely dates from the same period, around 1910. Very few examples are known, so the production run must have been a very short one. Perhaps Heavy Web was a casualty of the 1912 fire.

Large 10" bowls and chop plates are the only shapes reported. Often the bowls have two sides pulled up, in the manner of a banana bowl, but round examples and even a couple of square ones are known. Most examples have eight broad ruffles and an exterior pattern of grapes and leaves that collectors call Grape Clusters. A few have been found with an exterior pattern that appears to be some form of Morning Glory flowers. Only one example of the chop plate is known, and it has the Grape Clusters exterior pattern.

Peach opalescent is the only reported color. Often, the opalescence tends to have a slight blue tone to it. Make no mistake, this is a very rare pattern and examples always command a great deal of attention whenever shown or offered for sale.

The rare Heavy Web Bowl in peach opalescent.

Shapes & Colors Known	
Bowl, all shapes	peach opalescent
Chop plate	peach opalescent

Heron Mug

Of all the various carnival mug designs produced by Dugan, this seems to be the one most difficult to find. This is likely due to a very short production run. It first appeared in the wholesale catalogs in the spring of 1912 and disappeared from them just a year and a half later in August of 1913. It is interesting to note that this disappearance coincides with the time that Thomas Dugan left Indiana, Pennsylvania, and the plant becoming known as the Diamond Glass Company. Apparently the new management did not continue the production of this mug, which accounts for its scarcity today.

Only two carnival colors are known. Amethyst is the most available, yet even this is difficult to find. Marigold Heron Mugs are very rare and always command a good deal of attention, and very respectable prices, on the rare occasions when they turn up.

Examples of the Heron Mug are difficult to find in either of the known colors, but the amethyst ones, like this, seem to be seen most often. The marigold mugs are very rare.

Shapes & Colors Known	
Mug	marigold, amethyst

This design dates from the Dugan years, ca. 1909 – 1913. It is so strikingly similar to the pattern found on the Christmas compote that I have often
wondered if the rather small 6" – 7½" Holly & Berry ruffled bowls were actually intended to accompany it. It
would certainly make a most impressive holiday serving
set, but we have no proof of this. It's merely speculative
food for thought.

The small 6" – 7½" ruffled bowls are the most often
seen shape, with the amethyst examples the most frequently seen color. The iridescence on these is often spectacular. Peach opalescent is the next most available color,
and these are also popular and attractive pieces. Most that I
have seen had good, rich color and heavy opal. Marigold
examples also exist but are actually seen far less often.
(When you think about it, this is true of many Dugan novelty pieces. It was the later production under Diamond
management that turned out more marigold!)

The only other known shape is that of a large, single-
handled nappy. Most are spade-shaped, typical of Dugan
nappies, but I have seen a few ruffled examples. I must
admit to seeing a near-equal number of peach
opalescent and amethyst examples over the years,
but the amethyst is likely the most popular of the
two. Here again, marigold examples exist but are
seen less often. A few very rare cobalt blue nappies
are also known. Some collectors refer to the spade-
shaped nappy as a gravy boat. However, this glass is
not heat tempered, like modern glass. I certainly
wouldn't want to put hot gravy in one of them!

For years, both shapes have been rumored to
exist in green. In nearly 29 years of collecting, I
have never had one placed in front of me, nor have I
ever spoken with anyone who had a green example.
If they are out there, they remain unconfirmed.

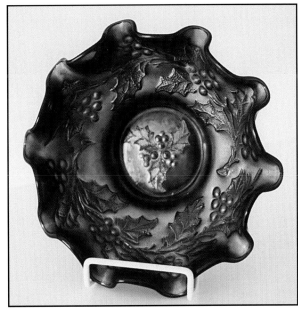

**Two styles of Dugan's Holly & Berry 8" ruffled
bowls. Both are in amethyst.**

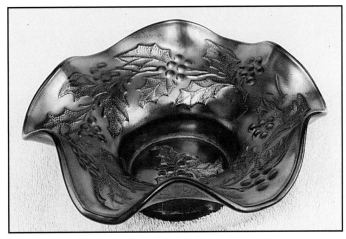

**A ruffled Holly &
Berry handled
nappy in amethyst.
Spade-shaped
examples also exist.**

Shapes & Colors Known	
Bowl, 6" – 7½"	marigold, amethyst, peach opalescent
Nappy	marigold, amethyst, peach opalescent, cobalt blue

Holly & Poinsettia

Ever have a "gut feeling" about something and your instincts just keep telling you to "go with it?" Such is the case with the Holly & Poinsettia pattern. We have virtually no concrete evidence to place it firmly in the Dugan family, yet based on pattern characteristics and shape, I'm firmly convinced that Dugan it is! In both design and shape, it is strikingly reminiscent of the Christmas compote.

The only known example of the Holly & Poinsettia pattern.

Only one example of this pattern is known to exist at this time, and it could best be described as a dome-footed compote. The color is a good, rich marigold with a radium-type iridescence. The pattern is on the interior surface and the exterior is plain, allowing the design to show through quite well. The dome-footed base is a favorite Dugan device. No other shapes or colors are known, but I would not be too surprised if a more shallow, ruffled, dome-footed bowl shape were to one day be found. Keep your eyes open for this one!

Shapes & Colors Known	
Compote, dome-footed	marigold

Honeycomb

There are actually two versions of this design, and they differ considerably. However, most collectors classify them under the same pattern name, as both versions came from Dugan about the same time, ca. 1909 – 1911.

The Honeycomb rose bowl is a carry-over from the pre-carnival Venetian and Japanese art glass lines. The pattern is on the exterior surface and the design is molded in fairly high relief. To date, these rose bowls have been documented in only two colors, peach opalescent and marigold. The peach opalescent examples are the most available, but they are by no means plentiful. Collectors eagerly snatch them up, and they do not remain in a shop or antique mall for very long. The marigold examples, like so many Dugan novelties in that color, are actually quite rare. There are far fewer known than many people realize.

The peach opalescent Honeycomb rosebowl is a very popular item with collectors and is not easily found.

A variation of the Honeycomb pattern is also found on the interior surface of small 5" – 7" bowls and 7" plates. The design is far less distinct than on the Honeycomb rose bowl. In fact, it is often confused with the very similar pattern called Fishscale & Beads, which is shown elsewhere in this book. There is an easy way to tell the difference. On the Honeycomb pieces, the center area is plain and unpatterned. The pattern on Fishscale & Beads covers the entire inner surface.

The bowls are usually found with a tightly crimped or ribbon-candy edge. The plates are also most often found with a tightly crimped edge. The known colors for both shapes include marigold, peach opalescent, amethyst, and oxblood. Of these, the latter is by far the rarest. I have seen examples with a plain exterior or with the Flowers & Beads exterior design.

A peach opalescent Honeycomb 6" bowl with a ribbon-candy edge and a 7½" crimped edge plate in oxblood.

Shapes & Colors Known	
Rose bowl	marigold, peach opalescent
Bowl, 5" – 7"	marigold, amethyst, peach opalescent, oxblood
Plate, 7"	marigold, amethyst, peach opalescent, oxblood

Hyacinth

To the best of my knowledge, the carnival version of this mold-blown vase has never before been shown in any carnival glass reference book. The name is one that I have heard several collectors use when referring to it, so I'll use it here.

There seems little doubt that this vase is a Dugan product and dates very early in the carnival production era, likely around 1909. An identical shape appears in several Butler Brothers assortments of Dugan's Venetian art glass, so the carnival version is no doubt one of the pieces rushed into iridescent production at the start of the carnival era. Add to that the fact that peach opalescent, one of the first carnival colors developed by Thomas Dugan, is the only reported color, and there seems little doubt of a Dugan origin.

I know only of a handful of these vases and all are in peach opalescent. The opalescence is fairly light on most of them, confined to just the top edge with some traces at the base as well. Perhaps these are some of Thomas Dugan's experiments with his new "Pearl Iris" (peach opalescent) iridizing formula.

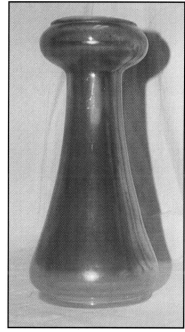

The Hyacinth vase is possibly one of Thomas Dugan's earliest carnival glass experiments.

Shapes & Colors Known	
Vase	peach opalescent

Intaglio Daisy

For many years, this design was believed to be an English product and was credited to Sowerby. We now know that this attribution was not correct and that this pattern never saw the white cliffs of Dover! It appears prominently in company with other Diamond Glass Company patterns in a 1929 G. Sommers & Company catalog assortment. Because the wholesale assortments were packed at the factory of origin, there is now no question that it is a Diamond Glass Company product.

Intaglio Daisy is an unusual design, combining both styles of molding: high relief and impressed or intaglio. Four shapes, all fashioned from the same mold, have been reported to date. Two of these are bowl shapes. One is very deep and nearly straight sided, while the other is slightly more shallow with the sides and edge flared outward. The other two shapes are both rose bowls. One of these is rather shallow with angular sides and a turned-in rim. It is the most often encountered of the two. The other is rounded, deeper, and of a more classic rose bowl shape. It is far rarer than the other rose bowl shape.

All four shapes are found in marigold. The example of the angular-shaped bowl, shown here in amethyst, is the first of any of these reported in that color. Diamond also produced this pattern in the non-iridized, pastel green and pink colors that were part of their After Glow line. An iridized example, in either of these colors, would be a great find. None has been reported but could well exist.

This Intaglio Daisy round, ball-shaped rose bowl is a very scarce shape.

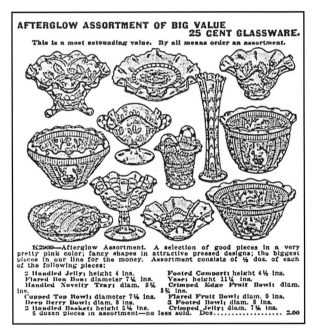

This assortment of Diamond's After Glow line, from a 1929 G. Sommers & Company wholesale catalog showing three styles of Intaglio Daisy bowls in company with other confirmed Diamond Glass company patterns, offers the proof that this design was definitely made at Indiana, Pennsylvania.

To the best of my knowledge, this angular sided Intaglio Daisy bowl is the only known example of the pattern in amethyst.

Shapes & Colors Known	
Bowl, two styles	marigold, amethyst
Rose bowl, two styles	marigold

The original factory pattern name for this design is Victor, and it made its debut in non-iridescent form in January of 1905. Between 1905 and 1909, the pattern underwent extensive production in blue, green, and flint opalescent, and a gold decorated color called Apple Green. A wide variety of non-iridescent shapes was made, including a berry set, table set, water set, cruet, syrup jug, sugar shaker, toothpick holder, condiment tray, and assorted novelties. Many items in this line appear in the 1907 Dugan factory catalog. A few blue opalescent Jewelled Heart pieces have been found with the Dugan D-in-a-diamond trademark.

The carnival production of this design was far more limited, but it began quite early on. Peach opalescent Jewelled Heart pieces appear in the fall 1910 Butler Brothers wholesale catalog, further confirming this as one of the first carnival colors produced by Thomas Dugan.

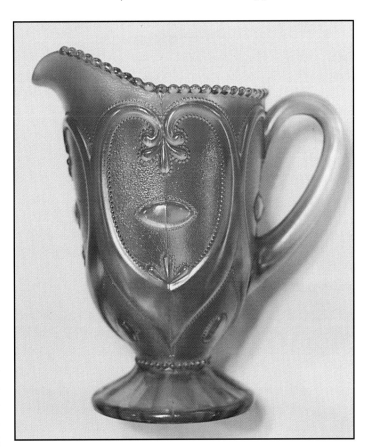

The rare Jewelled Heart water pitcher in marigold. It is one of the more difficult Dugan water pitchers to find.

As a primary carnival pattern, Jewelled Heart is found only on water sets. The handsome pitchers are of the pedestal-footed type, a style seldom found in carnival. Both pitcher and tumbler are found in marigold, but only rarely. It is one of the more difficult Dugan water sets to find, and those fortunate enough to own one treasure them highly. I know of at least one example of the tumbler in white, but no matching pitcher has yet surfaced. No other colors have been reported.

Jewelled Heart underwent extensive use as an exterior motif for bowls and plates that featured a variety of other designs as primary, interior patterns. These include the Farmyard bowl, Dugan's Cherry, Petal & Fan, and Smooth Rays. I do not recall seeing a carnival Jewelled Heart bowl or plate without some form of interior pattern.

Because Smooth Rays is such a simple, plain design, most carnival collectors refer to the bowls and plates in that pattern as Jewelled Heart pieces. Large, ruffled, 10" berry bowls, along with their small 5" – 6" counterparts, are the most often seen items. Peach opalescent is the most frequently found color, followed closely by amethyst, but even these are getting hard to find. White examples also exist, and these are very rarely found. Marigold is almost non-existent, but I have seen a few examples.

A very rare whimsey basket fashioned from the mold of the small, ruffled berry bowl is also known. It has a separately applied, clear glass handle and has been documented only in peach opalescent to date.

The only other known shape is that of a small, 6" – 7" plate, usually with a tightly crimped edge. This was fashioned from the small berry bowl mold, and it too carries the

Shapes & Colors Known	
Water pitcher	marigold
Tumbler	marigold, white
Ruffled berry set w/	
Smooth Rays interior	marigold, amethyst, white, peach opalescent
Plate, 6" – 7" w/	
Smooth Rays interior	amethyst, peach opalescent
Whimsey basket, small	peach opalescent

Smooth Rays interior design. They have been reported only in amethyst and peach opalescent to date. Either one is very scarce.

With such a wide variety of pre-carnival, non-iridescent shapes known, it seems strange that no other Jewelled Heart carnival pieces have surfaced, but such is the case. Still, you never know. Keep looking!

Caution: The Jewelled Heart bowl, with the Cherry interior pattern has been reproduced by L.G. Wright. They are round, deep bowls, about 7" – 8" in diameter and were made in purple and electric blue carnival. They are not trademarked, so be careful!

The Jewelled Heart pattern as it appears on the exterior surface of many different Dugan bowls and plates. This is one of the Dugan pattern drawings done by the author in the late 1970s for William Heacock.

Keyhole

This exterior pattern underwent extensive production in non-iridized opalescent colors during the 1905 – 1908 period. In carnival glass, it can be found on the exterior surface of dome-footed bowls and plates with the Raindrops interior pattern.

The Keyhole pattern shown on the exterior of this amethyst Raindrops dome-footed banana bowl.

Shapes & Colors Known
Exterior pattern — see Raindrops

Lattice & Daisy

Found primarily on tankard water sets and a rare berry set, Lattice & Daisy dates from the Diamond years and was in production during the 1915 – 1919 period. Until shards of this pattern turned up in the Helman diggings, it was thought to be a Fenton product.

The tankard pitchers are mold-blown with a separately applied handle. The tumblers are pressed. Like so many of Diamond's water sets, the marigold examples, which are the most often seen, tend to be rather light in color. The rare cobalt blue sets are another story, often exhibiting a rich multi-color iridescence. Amethyst is rarer still, with only a couple pitchers and a relative handful of tumblers known. I must admit that I have yet to see a white Lattice & Daisy pitcher, but at least one tumbler is known, so the pitcher likely exists too.

The berry set is one of the rarest items here. It was not even known to exist until a few years ago. At least one master bowl exists in marigold, as do a handful of small bowls. I know of one small bowl in white, but so far no master bowl has surfaced.

The only other shape known is that of a single known whimsey vase in amethyst, fashioned from the tumbler mold.

A rare Lattice & Daisy water pitcher in cobalt blue, and an equally rare tumbler in amethyst.

"FLORAL AND GRAPE EMBOSSED" LEMONADE SET.

C1868—Golden iridescent, 2 styles, 11 in. plain top tankard and 9 in. crimped top squat blown jugs, stuck handles, floral and grape embossed, 6 tumblers to match. 3 sets each, 6 sets in bbl., 53 lbs. Set, 62c

The Lattice & Daisy tankard water set appeared in company with the Floral & Grape water set in the mid-spring 1915 Butler Brothers catalog.

Shapes & Colors Known	
Master berry bowl	marigold
Small berry bowl	marigold, white
Tankard pitcher	marigold, amethyst, cobalt blue (white?)
Tumbler	marigold, amethyst, cobalt blue, white
Whimsey vase	amethyst

Lattice & Points and Vining Twigs

I may be called to task on this, but I'm convinced that Lattice & Points and Vining Twigs are slight variations of the same design, and, even more importantly, all known shapes in these two patterns were fashioned from the tumbler mold to the Grapevine Lattice water set! The lack of detail on the criss-crossed vines is either the result of shaping or possibly because of the use of a worn mold. Aside from the lack of detail on the vines, you will find the designs to be the same when comparing these two patterns to a Grapevine Lattice tumbler. Granted, some examples of the Vining Twigs and Lattice & Points patterns are found with a daisy impressed in the base, which the Grapevine Lattice tumbler lacks. However, this could be easily done by simply using a different base plate during the molding process.

This is not the easiest pattern to find and examples in any shape are rather scarce. Ruffled hat shapes are known in marigold, amethyst, white, and peach opalescent, with the latter the hardest color to find. A more widely ruffled 6" – 7" bowl is known in marigold, amethyst, and white. Swung vases, usually measuring about 7" – 9" in height, are found in a slightly wider variety of colors including marigold, white, amethyst, peach opalescent, lavender, and cobalt blue. The cobalt blue vases are by far the rarest. I know of only two, but the peach opalescent vases are not that far behind them. All of

these shapes may also be found in an extremely light pastel marigold that almost borders on a clambroth color. A single known example of a flat plate in white also exists. No other colors have yet surfaced in this shape, but they could well exist.

A tiny shot glass, known only in marigold, has also been given the name Vining Twigs. I have not personally seen it, so I will reserve crediting it to Dugan or Diamond until such time as I do. My reasons for this are simple. If all known Lattice & Points and Vining Twigs shapes were indeed fashioned from the Grapevine Lattice tumbler mold, and I am convinced that they were, then the tiny shot glass would be the only item in this pattern that required the making of a separate (and expensive) mold. It seems unlikely that either Dugan or Diamond would do so, just to make a few shot glasses.

Lattice & Points (Vining Twigs) ruffled hat shape and swung vase in amethyst, with a shorter swung vase in white. All of these pieces were fashioned from the same mold that was likely the Grapevine Lattice tumbler.

Shapes & Colors Known

Bowl, 6" – 7"	marigold, amethyst, white, pastel marigold
Hat shape	marigold, amethyst, white, peach opalescent, pastel marigold
Vase, 8" – 9"	marigold, amethyst, white, peach opalescent, lavender, cobalt blue, pastel marigold
Plate, 7" – 8"	white
Shot glass (Dugan?)	marigold

Lattice Hearts

This design is included here, with some reservations, as a possible Dugan or Diamond product. At present we have nothing concrete to firmly place it in the Dugan family, but based on shape, color, iridescent quality, and design characteristics, I strongly suspect that it was indeed made at Indiana, Pennsylvania. The edge shaping is highly reminiscent of that found on several Dugan/Diamond vases, such as the Squat Target vases. The amethyst examples exhibit a deep, rich, purple color virtually identical in tone to that produced by Dugan, and the iridescent quality appears the same as well. The pattern itself just seems to say "Dugan." Some sources list this as an English pattern. My only problem with that is that far too many amethyst examples have surfaced and we just don't find that much of this color in most English carnival patterns. The iridescent quality and tone just doesn't look English, at least to me.

Lattice Hearts is found on the exterior surface of round, deep bowls measuring from 6½" to 7½" in diameter, and on the exterior of 7" – 8" flat plates, often found with the very edge turned up sharply at a 90° angle. This would technically qualify them as Salvers, but most collectors simply refer to them as plates. The interior surface is plain. The bowls are often found with the iridescence on both surfaces, but the salver/plates are often iridized only on the interior. Amethyst is the only confirmed color to date, but I would not be surprised if there are a few marigold examples out there. This is not an easily found pattern and comparatively few examples are known.

Lattice Hearts deep, round bowl in amethyst.

Shapes & Colors Known
Bow, 6½" – 7½"   amethyst
Salver/plate, 7" – 8"   amethyst

Leaf Rays

If we were ever to hold a contest to determine which is the most common and available single-handled nappy in the entire spectrum of carnival glass, I have every confidence this design would win that title. The Leaf Rays nappy first appeared in the wholesale catalogs in 1912, and it continued to do so until 1931. With a 19-year production run, is it any wonder they are still so easily found?

The Leaf Rays nappy can be found in two shapes. The most easily found is the spade shape with a smooth edge. Examples in white and marigold are abundant, and even the amethyst and peach opalescent ones are not much harder to find. The only color I would label as scarce are the cobalt blue examples. Green has been rumored to exist, but I cannot confirm one as of this writing.

The other known nappy shape is more rounded with a tightly ruffled edge. These are actually a little harder to find, in any color. They are known in marigold, amethyst, and peach opalescent. I have not heard of any in white or cobalt blue, but I'm sure they likely exist.

This same base mold, without the Leaf Rays interior pattern, was used to make the ultra-rare Elks Nappy.

Spade-shaped Leaf Rays nappys in peach opalescent and white. The ruffled version seems to be harder to find.

Shapes & Colors Known	
Nappy, spade shape	marigold, amethyst, white, cobalt blue, peach opalescent
Nappy, ruffled	marigold, amethyst, peach opalescent

Lined Lattice

These unusual vases date from the Dugan era with production likely carried over through the Diamond years. Two versions of this vase are known with the difference centered on the unusual footed base. One version has nine rounded, spade-like feet, while the other has an equal number of sharply-squared feet. Because of this, examples in perfect condition are very difficult to find. The top edge of the vase also has nine "flame" points. The height may vary from the 5" – 6" squat vase, to the tall, swung 14" size. Most examples are found in the 8" – 11" size range. Of the two versions, the examples with the rounded, spade-like feet are the most available style. Vases with the sharply squared feet are more highly prone to base damage and much harder to find.

This is one of the few carnival vase patterns that is not easily found in any color. Even the marigold examples are tough to find. White is probably the next most available with amethyst in third place, but both are difficult to find. While rare cobalt blue examples do exist, it is the peach opalescent vases that really bring the raves! Most of the known examples exhibit a rich, marigold color, with heavy, near top-to-bottom opalescence. In my opinion, this pattern really has its moment of glory in peach opalescent. A few rare horehound vases are also known. Rumor persist of green examples, but I have yet to see one.

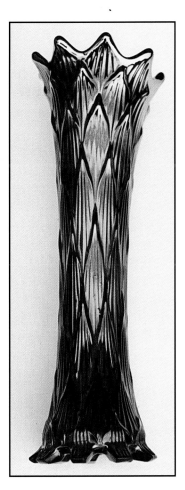

This 12" Lined Lattice vase has the sharply squared feet, and all of them are perfect! This is the rarer of the two versions. The color is amethyst.

This 8" Lined Lattice vase, also in amethyst, has the more rounded, spade-shaped feet. It is somewhat more easily found than the square-footed versions but is still a pretty scarce item.

Shapes & Colors Known
Vase, 5" – 14"   marigold, amethyst, white, peach opalescent, cobalt blue, horehound

Long Leaf

Long Leaf is one of the designs carried over from pre-carnival opalescent glass production. It appears in the 1907 Dugan factory catalog.

Carnival production of the design was limited to use as an exterior pattern on Dogwood Sprays and Stippled Petals pieces. As such, it can be found in all of the known colors for those two patterns.

The Long Leaf pattern shown on the exterior of this peach opalescent Stippled Petals banana bowl.

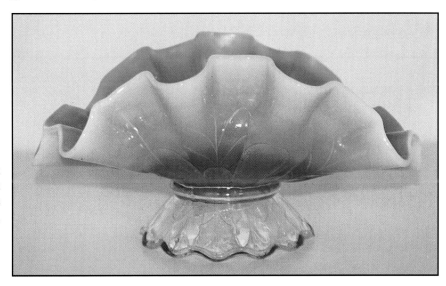

Shapes & Colors Known
Exterior pattern only on Dogwood Sprays & Stippled Petals

101

Malaga

Shards of this pattern were unearthed at the Indiana, Pennsylvania, plant site, so there is virtually no doubt of its origin. Based on design characteristics and the known colors, this is likely a Diamond Glass Company pattern dating from the mid to late 1920s.

Malaga is found only on the interior surface of bowls, plates, and rose bowls. The exterior surface is plain. The 9" bowls have been documented in marigold and amethyst. Either color is very scarce. The plates measure 10" in diameter, which qualifies them as chop plates. They have been reported only in marigold and are very rare. The rose bowls are equally rare. I know of a couple in marigold and only one in amethyst.

Very few examples of this pattern are known, so this design must have had a very short production run. Perhaps it was in production at the time of the 1931 fire, but we just don't know for sure at this point.

The rare amethyst Malaga rose bowl. This is the only example I know of in this color, though I'm sure others must exist.

Shapes & Colors Known	
Bowl, 9"	marigold, amethyst
Chop plate, 10"	marigold
Rose bowl	marigold, amethyst

Many Fruits

The Dugan display at the 1911 annual Pittsburgh Glass Exhibition must have been quite an impressive one. It quite obviously had an impression on at least one of the many glass industry trade journal reporters in attendance. He had this to say about the Dugan display: "Surmounting a solid glass pyramid, in one of their rooms are two samples of punch bowls that radiate the colors of the rainbow in peaches, grapes, and other fruits. The high foot of the punch bowl is reversible."

There seems little doubt that the punch set described in this report is indeed the Many Fruits. Glass houses always featured their newest creations at this annual

The Many Fruits punch bowl and base in amethyst. Note the unique shape of the ruffled base. When not in use with the punch bowl, it could be inverted and used as a compote.

102

event, so we now know that the Many Fruits punch set entered production in 1911. The description given to the high foot, or base as we call it, is interesting because it confirms a theory long held by most collectors. When not in use as a punch set, the base could be reversed and used as a centerpiece or compote. With all that usage, no wonder the bases are in such short supply today. There are probably more collectors searching for Many Fruits punch bases than for any other punch set!

Both the punch bowl and matching base may be found in either one of two styles: a deep, round shape with only slightly flared edges, or quite broadly ruffled edges. The bowls seem to turn up most often in the broadly ruffled version. The matching bases are becoming near impossible to find in either style! The interior of the punch bowl is patterned with cherries and leaves while the exterior carries a pattern of grapes and peaches. The matching base has cherries and leaves and the punch cups have a variation on the Vintage theme, comprising alternating clusters of grapes and grape leaves.

I must admit to having seen more amethyst and oxblood examples over the years than any of the other known colors. While the marigold sets bring fewer raves, I personally feel there are fewer of them around than most collectors realize. The white punch sets are very rare and highly treasured. Comparatively few are known. Rarer still are the cobalt blue examples. I personally know of only one complete cobalt blue set, a couple of bases, and a handful of cups scattered about in various collections. Green punch cups have been rumored to exist for years, but I must admit to never having seen any of them.

I have a personal theory regarding the white and cobalt blue sets that could explain their rarity. From surviving trade journal reports we know that Dugan's white carnival line was introduced in December of 1911. The wholesale catalogs seem to confirm that

Another view of the Many Fruits punch bowl and base, showing the Cherry pattern on the interior and on the base.

The Many Fruits punch cup features only the grapes and grape leaves.

Dugan's cobalt blue carnival first appeared early in 1912. Could the production of the Many Fruits punch set in those two colors have just begun at the time of the February 1912 fire that destroyed so many molds? Could the Many Fruits molds have been among them? I'd be willing to bet on it!

Shapes & Colors Known	
Punch bowl & base	marigold, amethyst, oxblood, cobalt blue, white
Punch cup	marigold, amethyst, oxblood, cobalt blue, white, (green?)

Many Ribs

Found primarily on the exterior surface of two styles of vases and a ruffled hat shape, Dugan's Many Ribs is one of the more easily found patterns. The variety of known colors indicates the design was likely in production during the entire tenure of Thomas Dugan's carnival production at Indiana, Pennsylvania, with continued production by Diamond after 1913.

A beautiful amethyst Many Ribs Jack-in-the-Pulpit style vase. Some of these have a crimped edge while this example has a smooth one.

Ruffled or crimped edge vases, generally in the 5" – 7" size range, are the most often seen shapes. They are quite available in marigold, amethyst, and peach opalescent. White and oxblood examples are much harder to find, but both do exist. Only three known examples in peach opalescent on frosted camphor glass exist, and I'm very pleased to be able to show one here. I have not personally seen a cobalt blue ruffled vase, but the Jack-in-the-Pulpit vase has been confirmed in that color. So the ruffled version likely exists in cobalt blue, but remains unconfirmed. The Jack-in-the-Pulpit-shaped vase is much harder to find. Like all vases in this shape, they are very popular items and eagerly sought. Examples are known in marigold, amethyst, peach opalescent, cobalt blue, and oxblood. Of these, cobalt blue is by far the rarest color. I personally know of only one confirmed example, though others likely exist. No white examples have yet surfaced, but there might well be one out there somewhere.

The only other reported shape is a small, ruffled hat, fashioned from the same mold. They are generally from 3½" to 4" tall, not too difficult to find, and have been reported in marigold, amethyst, and peach opalescent.

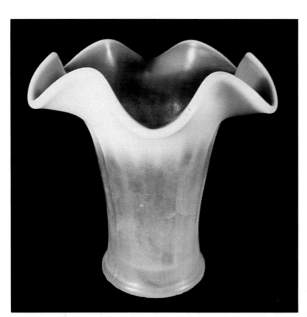

One of three known Many Ribs vases in a most unusual color combination: peach opalescent on a frosted, camphor glass base.

Shapes & Colors Known

Vase, 5" – 7", ruffled or crimped	marigold, amethyst, oxblood, white, peach opalescent, peach opalescent on camphor glass
Vase, JIP shape	marigold, amethyst, peach opalescent, cobalt blue, oxblood
Hat shape	marigold, amethyst, peach opalescent

Maple Leaf

This is one of the patterns at the center of the Dugan/Northwood controversy when the Helman shards were unearthed in the 1970s. Fragments of the design in both carnival and custard glass were found in these diggings. It now appears that the custard glass version was indeed made by Harry Northwood in the late 1890s. A full line was made, including water set, table set, berry set, cruet, jelly compote, toothpick holder, and salt and pepper shakers. The carnival glass version, made in molds left behind by Northwood, first appeared in late 1910, and was definitely made by Dugan. After 1913, Diamond continued limited production of the pattern until as late as 1928.

Carnival production of the design seems to be limited to the berry set, table set, and water set. None of the other shapes mentioned above has ever surfaced in carnival. The variety of colors known is also very limited.

The berry set is unusual in that it is stemmed. The body of the bowl is supported by three

Maple Leaf water set in amethyst.

twig patterned stems that form the leaves on the pedestal foot. The interior surface carries Dugan's version of the Peacock Tail pattern. They are still available in marigold, becoming scarce in amethyst or oxblood, and are actually rather rare in cobalt blue. The same situation applies to the table and water sets. Marigold is available, amethyst and oxblood are harder to find, and the cobalt blue is seen far less often. The oxblood (black amethyst) examples are often found with Dugan's gun metal iridescent treatment. A single example of a small, stemmed berry bowl is also known in green, but I know of no other pieces in that color. Still, they could well exist so it's something to bear in mind.

There are two versions of the Maple Leaf tumbler. One has a wavy line separating the leaf from the band of scalloped panels at the top. The other version has a straight line. The version with the wavy line seems to be the one most frequently found.

Actually, the name Maple Leaf is a misnomer, even though the pattern was originally advertised as such. Whoever named this design, way back when, didn't know their trees and leaves. Look closely, folks. It's actually an oak leaf!

This is another of the author's Dugan pattern drawings done in the late 1970s. It shows the Maple Leaf tumbler variant that has the straight line separating the leaf from the scalloped panels at the top.

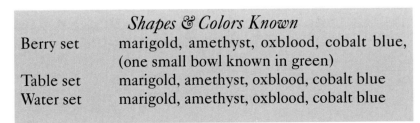

Shapes & Colors Known

Berry set	marigold, amethyst, oxblood, cobalt blue, (one small bowl known in green)
Table set	marigold, amethyst, oxblood, cobalt blue
Water set	marigold, amethyst, oxblood, cobalt blue

105

RICHEST DINING SET ASSORTMENT—Iridescent.

The most exquisite color tones ever possible in this rich ware. The art critic would stamp them "Regal."

1C1690—Full size pieces, heavy embossed maple leaves and jewel effects, rich dark metallic iridescent finish. Comprising:

2 only 7 pc. water sets.
2 " 4 " table sets.
2 " 7 " berry sets—8½ in. footed bowl, 4½ in. nappies.
6 sets in bbl., 68 lbs. Set. **67c**

Caution: Both the water set and table set have been reproduced. L.G. Wright has marketed new water sets in amethyst, cobalt blue, and ice green. There are also new table sets in amethyst and cobalt blue. I recall seeing some of the blue table sets that were marked with the letter "M" in the base, so at least some of the production was done by Mosser.

The mid-spring 1911 Butler Brothers catalog featured this full assortment of Dugan's Maple Leaf in a "rich, dark, metallic iridescent finish." This is probably Dugan's gun metal iridescent treatment. Maple Leaf items are often found with this silvery type of iridescence.

Diamond

Mary Ann

Allegedly, this vase was named after Thomas E. A. Dugan's sister, Fanny Mary Ann Dugan. This may well be the case, but I have one problem with it. The vase does not appear in any of the known wholesale catalogs until 1915, which was two years after Thomas Dugan left Indiana, Pennsylvania. Still, it's possible. Even though Dugan left the firm in 1913, he did retain his stock in the company.

The two-handled version of the Mary Ann vase in marigold.

Two carnival versions of this vase are known. The most often seen version is two handled, has eight scallops on the top edge, and rests on a pedestal foot. Only two colors are known, marigold and amethyst. Marigold is the most often found, but even these are scarce. The amethyst examples rarely surface. A few marigold examples with ten scallops on the top edge are also known. The two-handled version can also be found in non-iridized blue opalescent glass.

The other version of this vase has three handles and is often called a Loving Cup. It has been reported only in marigold, to date, and is far rarer than its two-handled cousin.

Miraculously, the original mold sketch for this vase was unearthed intact at the plant site, ten years after the 1931 fire!

This is the original factory mold drawing for the Mary Ann vase. It was unearthed at the Indiana, Pennsylvania, site ten years after the 1931 fire. Its surviving those years is nothing short of miraculous!

Shapes & Colors Known

Vase, two-handled	marigold, amethyst
Vase, three-handled	marigold

Collectors of custard and opalescent glass call this pattern Argonaut Shell. However, the name Nautilus, used by carnival collectors, is actually the original pattern name. Introduced during Harry Northwood's association with the National Glass Company in 1900, this design was initially produced in non-iridized custard and opalescent colors. A full line of berry set, water set, table set, cruet, jelly compote, toothpick holder, and salt and pepper shakers was made. Many of these pieces bear the Northwood script signature on the base. Harry Northwood actually copied the design from a Worcester porcelain vase owned by his family.

Several carnival glass shards of Nautilus were found in the Helman diggings, and these proved to be key factors in the story of Dugan's carnival production. These iridized Nautilus shards gave us our first real clues to the sequence of events at the Indiana, Pennsylvania, plant. It was from these very shards that we first began to realize an important part of the Northwood/Dugan story. We knew that Harry Northwood had introduced this design in 1900. We knew that he had left this site in 1901, at least seven years before carnival glass was introduced to the market. So,

Carnival glass collectors have labeled this piece a giant compote. It was actually fashioned from the master berry bowl in a mold left behind by Harry Northwood.

what were these carnival glass Nautilus shards doing there? There could only be one answer. When Harry Northwood moved on to Wheeling, West Virginia, he had left the bulk of his molds behind! He probably had no choice! When he joined the National Glass Company in 1899, it seems very likely that his molds became their property. Therefore, when he disassociated himself with National in 1901, he had no choice but to leave his molds at the Indiana, Pennsylvania, factory. When Thomas Dugan purchased the plant from National, the existing molds, including Harry's, were part of the deal.

So, it is very important to realize that even though any carnival glass Nautilus pieces you may have or find bear the Northwood script signature, they were not made by Northwood. They are Dugan products and are no doubt among the very first carnival items produced by Thomas Dugan, ca. 1909 – 1910. During the initial production rush to gain a share of the new iridescent glass market, he simply neglected to remove the Northwood script signature from the mold. Later, as production continued, he eventually did remove it, which accounts for the unsigned examples that exist.

Only three carnival items are known in this design and two of them were fashioned from the same mold. The "classic" Nautilus was probably intended simply as a candy dish. It was made from the spooner mold and can be found in a variety of shapings. Some have two edge surfaces pulled outward in the manner of a double spout, of sorts. Others are found with these ends curled inward. Still others are found with one end pulled out and the other curled in. Any of these may be found with or without the Northwood script signature in the base. They are known in peach opalescent and amethyst, with the latter being far more difficult to find.

A swung vase, also fashioned from the spooner mold, is known in marigold and amethyst. These tend to be in the 8" – 9" size range, but virtually any height is possible. Either color is rare,

with amethyst slightly edging out marigold. Were it not for the distinct pattern on the domed base, these vases would be almost unrecognizable as Nautilus. Because of the "swinging out" process used to make them, the pattern detail on the body of the piece is completely distorted.

The only other carnival shape known is what some have dubbed a giant compote. Actually this is nothing more than a piece fashioned from the mold for the master berry bowl. It is reported only in marigold, and only a couple of examples are known.

Wouldn't it be something if a carnival water pitcher or butter dish were to one day surface? None has ever been reported. But, bear in mind that Thomas Dugan had these molds, so anything is possible.

The "classic" Nautilus shape in peach opalescent. Even though these may bear the Northwood script signature, they were actually made by Dugan using a mold left behind by Harry Northwood.

Shapes & Colors Known	
Candy dish, various shapes	amethyst, peach opalescent
Vase, 8" – 9"	marigold, amethyst
Giant compote (master berry bowl)	marigold

Dugan

Panelled Treetrunk

Very little is known about this beautiful pattern that is found only on vases. Based on the known colors, the shape and especially the stylization of the top edge, I'm convinced it is a Dugan product, likely dating from around 1910. The shaping of the top edge is identical to many other Dugan vases, like Target for example.

Most of the known examples of this very rare vase are in the 6" – 9" size range, but of course, taller examples likely exist. Colors reported include marigold, amethyst, peach opalescent, and at least one extremely rare green example. Any one of them would make a rare and outstanding addition to any collection.

Why so very few examples of this vase are known remains a mystery. Perhaps the mold was yet another casualty of the 1912 fire.

The rare Panelled Treetrunk vase in amethyst. Note the shaping of the top edge, which is identical to several other confirmed Dugan vases.

Shapes & Colors Known	
Vase, 6" – 9"	marigold, amethyst, peach opalescent, green

Peach & Pear

Large collar-based, oval bowls, often called banana bowls by collectors, are the only shapes known in this design. They may vary from 12" to 13" in length and from 7" to as much as 9" in width. Only two carnival colors are reported. Marigold examples seem to be quite plentiful and are easily found, indicating a fairly extensive production. The amethyst bowls are seen far less often. The quality of the iridescence can vary greatly. I have seen some beautifully iridized examples, but a large number of these bowls tend to have rather weak coloring.

Sometimes you have to do a little detective work and a little logical thinking in order to establish a time frame during which a specific piece was made. Such is the case here. The only wholesale ad for this piece that I could locate was undated. But the ad did contain an important clue: the price! The bowl was being offered for 98¢ each wholesale. That's a very high wholesale price! In fact, far too high to date from the early years of carnival production, when large bowls like these were often offered for 25¢ to 50¢ each. So there is little doubt that this pattern dates from the later years of Diamond's carnival production, probably 1925 – 1930.

The Peach & Pear large oval banana bowl in marigold.

Shapes & Colors Known
Banana bowl, large oval   marigold, amethyst

Peacock at the Fountain

Mention Peacock at the Fountain to any carnival glass collector and Harry Northwood immediately comes to mind. It is indeed one of his most well-known and popular iridescent patterns. The discovery of several fragments of this design at the factory site in Indiana, Pennsylvania, was one of the most important finds to emerge from the Helman diggings, proof positive that a version of this design had been made there. But, who made it? Was it Thomas Dugan or had it been made by the Diamond Glass Company? To find the answer we need to examine several factors: the production dates of the Northwood version, the subsequent filing for a patent on the design by Harry Northwood, and the known carnival colors for the version produced at Indiana, Pennsylvania.

Northwood's Peacock at the Fountain first appeared in the wholesale catalogs in mid-spring of 1912 and continued to appear in them through 1917. Thomas Dugan left Indiana, Pennsylvania,

The tumbler on the left is Northwood's Peacock at the Fountain while the example on the right is a Diamond Glass Company version. Note that the Northwood tumbler is slightly fatter. The Northwood tumbler has four mold seams; the Diamond tumbler has only three.

Diamond's Peacock at the Fountain water pitcher in cobalt blue.

at the end of 1912, just a matter of months after the Northwood version of this design first appeared. While few carnival glass producers ever filed exclusive patents on their designs, on February 7, 1914, Harry Northwood did just that for Peacock at the Fountain! The patent was granted on July 7, 1914. Why would he do so, unless of course he was attempting to protect the design from being copied? If it was being copied (and indeed it was), the time frame is all wrong for placing the blame on Thomas Dugan. He had left Indiana, Pennsylvania, over a year earlier. I am convinced that Thomas Dugan had nothing to do with copying this pattern. It was the Diamond Glass Company that was the culprit!

Further evidence for a Diamond Glass Company attribution is found in the known colors in which their version was made. Diamond's Peacock at the Fountain is found only on water sets in marigold, amethyst, and cobalt blue. Dugan produced relatively little cobalt blue carnival. Diamond was much more prolific in the production of that color, and a pretty fair number of cobalt blue examples of the Diamond version do turn up. Also, if Thomas Dugan had made this set, we would surely find examples in oxblood and white, two of his most widely produced iridescent colors. None is known to exist! All the evidence seems to point toward Diamond.

So, how do we tell the difference between the two versions of Peacock at the Fountain? A close examination of both the Northwood tumbler and the Diamond tumbler reveals a surprising number of subtle differences.

The Northwood tumbler has a top diameter of 3" and a base diameter of 2½". Most examples are signed with the N-in-a-circle trademark. There are four mold seams, positioned as follows: through the three plants directly in front of the peacock and directly through the peacock's tail. This same positioning is repeated for the second peacock. One fountain has seven teardrop-shaped beads along the top and the other has eight beads. The smallest of the three plants has a stem that crosses over the stem of the largest plant.

The Diamond tumbler has a top diameter of 2⅞" and a base diameter of 2⁷⁄₁₆". A round plunger mark is often visible on the inside base. There are only three mold seams and they are positioned as follows: through the three plants directly in front of the peacock, directly through the center of the fountain and the spray of water, and through the point of the tail on the second peacock where it joins his body. Both fountains have seven beads along the top edge and the fountains themselves are slightly larger than on the Northwood version. The stem of the smallest plant does not cross that of the largest one.

There are many other small differences in pattern detail, but those mentioned above should provide a fairly easy method of telling the difference between the two. The mold seams are the quickest method. Northwood's tumbler has four and Diamond's has only three. As to the water pitchers, the easiest method to distinguish between the two is to simply check for the presence of a signature. The Diamond version is, of course, unsigned. Virtually all of the Northwood Peacock at the Fountain pitchers bear the N-in-a-circle trademark.

Of the three known colors found on Diamond's versions of Peacock at the Fountain, marigold is the most often seen, followed closely by cobalt blue. The amethyst sets are much harder to find. The Diamond version is found on no shapes other than water sets.

Shapes & Colors Known	
Water pitcher & tumbler	marigold, amethyst, cobalt blue

Peacock Tail

Virtually every major carnival glass producer made a version of this design. Most of them made the pattern in a wide variety of shapes and colors, so it must have been a very popular one with the buying public.

Dugan's version appears only on the interior surface of the Maple Leaf stemmed berry set. As such, it can be found in colors of marigold, amethyst, cobalt blue, and, very rarely, green.

Some have credited a small, ruffled compote to Dugan, but I'm not convinced that it is. Every such example that I have ever seen screamed Fenton! No such item has ever surfaced in any of the Dugan assortments that appear in any of the known wholesale catalogs, nor in any currently known Dugan advertising. Until such time as one does, I will hold off on crediting such an item to Thomas Dugan.

Shapes & Colors Known
Interior design – see Maple Leaf

Dugan's Peacock Tail shown on the interior of Maple Leaf berry bowls.

Persian Garden

This striking, intricate, and very popular Dugan carnival pattern was likely introduced around 1910 – 1911, with at least some production carried over into the Diamond years through mid 1915. This fact, combined with the unusual abundance of white examples, indicates that the molds for this design were among those that survived the 1912 fire. Both Dugan and Diamond certainly got a lot of mileage out of these molds. Of the eight known shapes, seven were produced from the same two molds!

The master berry bowl, master ice cream bowl, chop plate, and the top of the two-piece fruit

Two views of Persian Garden two-piece ruffled fruit bowls in white and lavender. The white examples still turn up on occasion, but the lavender is very rare.

111

Not all known Persian Garden two-piece fruit bowls are ruffled. This is the only known amethyst example that is punch bowl-shaped. I know of two marigold examples that are shaped like this.

Among collectors, peach opalescent is a favorite in the Persian Garden pattern. You can see why with this beautiful 10" ruffled bowl.

bowl were all fashioned from the same mold. Likewise, the small berry bowls, ice cream bowls, and plates were all made from the same mold. Most examples in all shapes carry the Basketweave Variant exterior pattern.

The ruffled master berry bowl may vary from 9" to as much as 11" in diameter, depending on the degree of shaping. Peach opalescent seems to be the most available color, followed by amethyst, white, and marigold, in that order. Green is the scarcest here, with only one confirmed example. The small berry bowls seem to turn up most often in white and peach opalescent. Amethyst and marigold examples are much harder to find.

To say that the large and small ice cream bowls are abundant in white would be a considerable understatement. In fact, they lead the availability list by nearly five to one over all the other known colors! Peach opalescent and amethyst are far more difficult to find. Believe it or not, it is the marigold master ice cream that is by far the rarest color. Since 1983, only a couple have been sold at auction. The small ice cream bowls are most available in white, with the peach opalescent examples in second place. Amethyst and marigold examples are very seldom found.

The rare 11" – 12" chop plates are a sight to behold. The iridescence is often dazzling, especially on the amethyst examples, which are the most often found. Even so, they are highly treasured and always command serious prices. White is the next most available color but is found far less often than its ice cream bowl counterpart. The peach opalescent chop plate is extremely rare, with only a few known. Oddly, no marigold chop plates have yet surfaced. There must be one out there somewhere. The small 6" – 7" plates are really quite available in both white and marigold. Peach opalescent is much harder to find and amethyst examples are rarer still. Cobalt blue takes top honors here. Only one example has been confirmed to date! White examples are sometimes found with a plain exterior or with an exterior design called Pool of Pearls.

The only other reported shape is that of an impressive, two-piece fruit bowl and base. Most examples are ruffled, but a few round unruffled ones are known. The separate pedestal base carries the Big Basketweave pattern. Amethyst is the most often found color, with white a close second. Here again, the marigold fruit bowl and base are actually very rare! Only a few are known. To date, I have not been able to confirm a peach opalescent example, but that is not to say that they could not exist.

Shapes & Colors Known

Bowl, 9" – 11", ruffled	marigold, amethyst, peach opalescent, white, green
Bowl, 5" – 6", ruffled	marigold, amethyst, peach opalescent, white
Bowl, 10", ice cream	marigold, amethyst, peach opalescent, white
Bowl, 5" – 6", ice cream	marigold, amethyst, peach opalescent, white
Chop plate, 11" – 12"	amethyst, peach opalescent, white
Plate, 6" – 7"	marigold, amethyst, peach opalescent, cobalt blue, white
Plate, 6" – 7", Pool of Pearl exterior	white
Plate, 6" – 7", plain exterior	white
Fruit bowl & base	marigold, amethyst, white, lavender

The Persian Garden 7" plate is most often found in marigold or white. Amethyst examples like this beauty are really quite rare.

Petal & Fan

Here we have another early Dugan entry in the carnival glass field. Peach opalescent Petal & Fan bowls appear in the fall 1910 Butler Brothers catalog. The design continued to appear through the spring 1911 issue. This is one of several Dugan carnival patterns that is always accompanied by the Jewelled Heart pattern as an exterior design.

Ruffled berry sets are perhaps the most familiar items here, and peach opalescent is by far the most frequently seen color. Still, they have quietly disappeared over the last few years and are no longer easily found. The amethyst berry sets are very scarce, but well worth the effort it takes to find one. The iridescence on them is usually spectacular. The white berry sets are very rare and underrated. I once owned a complete white set and I'm sorry I ever parted with it. I have yet

Two Petal & Fan 11" ruffled bowls, a six-ruffled version in amethyst and an eight-ruffled in peach opalescent. The exterior carries the Jewelled Heart pattern.

113

to be able to piece together another complete one! Marigold examples do exist, but are really the rarest color here. I have seen only a couple examples.

While the master berry bowl usually measures 10" or more in diameter, there is also a somewhat smaller, 8" – 9" ruffled bowl. They have been documented in peach opalescent, amethyst, white, and marigold. As to the rarity order, it is pretty much the same as the berry set.

On a rare occasion, a small banana-shaped dish with two sides pulled up surfaces. These were shaped from the mold to the small, ruffled berry bowl and are known only in peach opalescent to date.

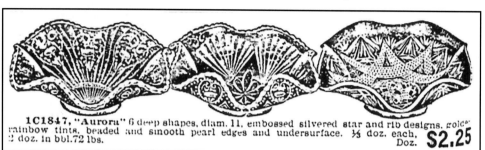

1C1847, "Aurora" 6 deep shapes, diam. 11, embossed silvered star and rib designs, golden rainbow tints, beaded and smooth pearl edges and undersurface. ⅙ doz. each.
2 doz. in bbl.72 lbs.
Doz. $2.25

The only other known shape is a small, 6" – 7" plate, often found with a tightly crimped edge. They are very scarce and have been reported only in amethyst and peach opalescent.

The Petal & Fan 11" ruffled bowl is featured in the center of this assortment of peach opalescent Dugan bowls from the special Christmas 1910 Butler Brothers catalog. The term "aurora" was often used in Butler Brothers catalogs to market Dugan's peach opalescent carnival glass.

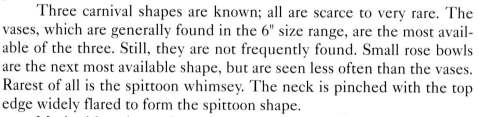

Shapes & Colors Known

Berry set, ruffled	marigold, amethyst, white, peach opalescent
Bowl, 8" – 9", ruffled	marigold, amethyst, white, peach opalescent
Plate, 6" – 7", crimped edge	amethyst, peach opalescent
Banana dish, 5" – 6"	peach opalescent

Pinched Swirl

The influence of Thomas Dugan's pre-carnival Venetian and Japanese art glass lines is very evident here. The style and pinched hand-shaping is very much the same. The Swirl pattern is on the interior surface and the exterior is plain.

Three carnival shapes are known; all are scarce to very rare. The vases, which are generally found in the 6" size range, are the most available of the three. Still, they are not frequently found. Small rose bowls are the next most available shape, but are seen less often than the vases. Rarest of all is the spittoon whimsey. The neck is pinched with the top edge widely flared to form the spittoon shape.

Marigold and peach opalescent are the only reported colors. Marigold is actually seen less often, but it is the peach opalescent examples that are the most popular. Often, the opalescence is rather light and confined to only the very top edge. However, heavily opalized examples do exist, often exhibiting a rich, butterscotch coloring.

This Pinched Swirl vase, in peach opalescent, is one of the earliest Dugan carnival glass items.

114

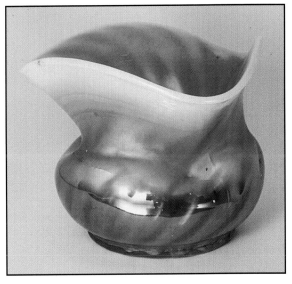

The rare Pinched Swirl Spittoon Whimsey. This example has a most unusual triangular ruffle.

Diamond

Pony

Based on design characteristics and the known carnival colors, it's a pretty safe bet to say this design dates from the Diamond Glass Company era. Thomas Dugan is not known to have produced any ice green carnival, and the Pony bowl is found in that color. Diamond introduced their pastel green iridescent line in 1921, so production of the Pony pattern likely dates from that time and after.

This simple yet attractive pattern is found primarily on 8" – 9" ruffled bowls. They may have six, eight, or very rarely, 10 ruffles. The Pony head in the center is molded in very high relief, with an intaglio effect that can be seen and felt from the underside of the collar base. Marigold is the most often seen color. It may take a little searching, but they are not too difficult to find. Amethyst examples are much harder to find but are not really classified as rare. There are some rarely found colors here. Ice green examples exist and are highly prized. They will usually exhibit the onion-skin stretch effect on the iridescence. A couple of rare examples in aqua with a marigold iridescent overlay are also known. I know at least one in a beautiful, pastel lavender as well. Though not yet confirmed, an example in a delicate shade of iridized pink has been reported. This is well within the realm of possibility. Diamond did make a line of pink glass called After Glow, ca. 1928 – 1929, and some iridized examples of this line do exist. Confirmation of this iridized pink Pony bowl would indeed tend to support my theory that the Pony pattern was among the very last designs created by Diamond for iridescent production.

A beautiful example of a marigold Pony bowl.

Non-ruffled, low ice cream-shaped bowls are also known and this shape is much harder to find. These have been reported in marigold, amethyst, and ice green.

115

A couple of marigold 9" plates, as well as a couple amethyst examples, are also known. These plates are very rare in either color.

Caution: Both the ruffled bowl and the plate were reproduced by L.G. Wright in the early 1980s in both marigold and amethyst. The amethyst examples I have seen were somewhat more mirror-like and gaudy in their iridescent tones. The marigold ones are very nicely done. Be very careful on these!

These two marigold Pony bowls illustrate the variety of shape and iridescent treatment that can be found in this pattern. The six-ruffled bowl has a radium iridescence, while the much scarcer 12-ruffled bowl has a satin iridescence.

Shapes & Colors Known	
Bowl, ruffled	marigold, amethyst, ice green, lavender, aqua w/marigold overlay, (pink?)
Bowl, ice cream shape	marigold, amethyst, ice green
Plate, 9"	marigold, amethyst

Dugan ✧

Pulled Loop

Found only on vases of varying height, Pulled Loop had a long production run. The non-iridized opalescent version appears in the 1907 Dugan factory catalog as Dugan's #1029. Curiously, later Diamond Glass Company advertising lists it as Diamond's #1030. Why two different production numbers remains a mystery. The carnival glass version appeared in the wholesale catalogs from 1912 through 1928. It is known in a surprising variety of colors.

A Pulled Loop squat 6" vase in amethyst, a scarce size for this pattern.

Marigold examples are easily found, with the peach opalescent examples a very close second. Amethyst is also available, but it may take a little searching to find one. The other colors are tough! Cobalt blue and white are very scarce, and only a few celeste blue vases are known. A few rare aqua vases have also surfaced in recent years. Green examples are extremely rare. Like most Dugan/Diamond patterns found in this color, only a few are known. Topping the rarity list is a single known vase in amethyst opalescent, a very rare color for either Dugan or Diamond.

While Pulled Loop vases can likely be found in any size, most known examples tend to be in the 9" – 11" range. There are 5" – 7" squat vases as well. The known colors are somewhat more limited and examples are found far less often than the taller counterparts.

Care should be taken not to confuse this vase with a similar one made by Fenton, sometimes called Boggy Bayou or Reverse Drapery. Pulled Loop has five arched loops between the vertical ribs, while the Fenton vase has eight.

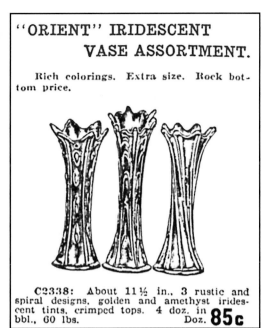
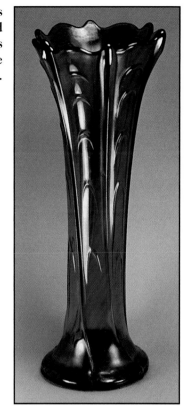

The gorgeous lavender Pulled Loop 9" vase is also a scarce item.

The Pulled Loop vase must have been a very popular seller. It was a regular fixture in the wholesale catalogs for over 14 years! This assortment from the July 1914 Butler Brothers issue offers the Pulled Loop, Target, and Spiralex vases in marigold and amethyst.

Shapes & Colors Known	
Vase, 8" – 14"	marigold, amethyst, peach opalescent, cobalt blue, green, celeste blue, aqua, white, lavender
Vase, 5" – 7", squat	marigold, amethyst, peach opalescent, white, amethyst opalescent

Puzzle

Dugan ✧

This unusual stylized pattern had a long production run. It was likely introduced around 1910 – 1911 and continued to appear in the wholesale catalogs through 1916. However, it was likely still in production well after that date. Diamond introduced its Cerulean blue (what we now call celeste blue) in 1916, and I have seen non-iridized examples of this pattern in that color.

As a primary pattern, Puzzle is found only on the interior surface of stemmed, two-handled bonbons, with Floral & Wheat as the exterior pattern. The usual shape is round, but there are ruffled examples and card tray shapes with two sides pulled up. A fairly extensive variety of colors is known, with marigold, peach opalescent, and white the most often found. Amethyst examples are much harder to find and the cobalt blue bonbons are quite rare. A few examples in a delicate shade of lavender are also known. Green has been reported, but to date remains unconfirmed. I have also seen these bonbons in non-iridized celeste blue, so an iridized example is a strong possibility.

As a secondary pattern, Puzzle is also found on the pedestal foot of compotes and stemmed plates in the Question Marks and Georgia Belle patterns. Information on the known colors for them can be found in the text for those two patterns.

The Puzzle pattern shown on the interior of a Floral & Wheat bonbon in marigold.

Shapes & Colors Known	
Bonbon, stemmed, two-handled	marigold, amethyst, white, peach opalescent, lavender, cobalt blue, (green?), (celeste blue?)

117

Question Marks

Even though this pattern does not appear in any of the known issues of the wholesale catalogs until the early 1920s, I am convinced the design is a Dugan one and likely entered production around 1910. Both peach opalescent and white were colors introduced by Thomas Dugan and this pattern is found frequently in both of them. Question Marks appeared in the wholesale catalogs right up until the plant closed in 1931. So if any carnival glass pattern deserves an award for production longevity, it's surely this one!

A Question Marks stemmed, two-handled bonbon in cobalt blue, a rare color.

The cute little stemmed, two-handled bonbon is the most frequently found shape. They are abundant in marigold and still easily found in peach opalescent as well. White is the next most available color and can still be seen frequently. Amethyst ones are a little harder to find, but are still quite available. The other known colors will present a challenge. The cobalt blue examples are rarely found, but they do indeed exist. Among the rarest of all are the ice green examples, which often have a stretch effect to the iridescence; only a few are known. I can also confirm a couple examples in an unusual smoky/lavender color. Green has been reported, but I have yet to see proof of one.

The other two known shapes are very interesting ones and both were fashioned from the same mold. The pedestal-footed compote actually combines three distinct patterns on the same piece! The interior has the Question Marks pattern. The exterior of the body has an intaglio design of peaches and leaves called Georgia Belle. The pedestal foot carries the Puzzle pattern. No other carnival glass items that combine three distinct patterns on the same piece come to mind. This compote is seen far less often, in any color, than the two-handled bonbon. Marigold is the most available color, followed by peach opalescent, white, and amethyst, in that order.

This compote, in amethyst, actually combines three patterns: Question Marks on the interior, Georgia Belle on the exterior, and Puzzle on the pedestal foot.

The rare pedestal plate was fashioned from the same mold and also combines all three patterns. The top portion is usually flattened out to a diameter of 7" – 8". They are very rarely found in any color, but marigold is probably the most available. The jury is still out as to which is the rarer color, white or amethyst, but I'll stick my neck out and go with amethyst as the rarer of the two. You take your pick; both are very rarely found.

Shapes & Colors Known

Bonbon, stemmed, two-handled	marigold, amethyst, white, cobalt blue, peach opalescent, ice green, smoky/lavender, lime green w/marigold overlay, (green?)
Compote	marigold, amethyst, white, peach opalescent
Stemmed plate	marigold, amethyst, white

Quill

This pattern is another of the carry-over designs from the pre-iridescent era. It was originally part of Dugan's Filigree line which was made ca. 1906 – 1907 in non-iridescent colors of green, blue, custard, and ruby. It appears in the 1907 Dugan factory catalog. The carnival version likely dates early in the iridescent production years, ca. 1909 – 1910.

Extremely rare water sets are the only carnival shapes reported. The water pitchers are mold-blown, with clear, separately applied handles, and measure roughly 10½" tall. The matching tumblers are pressed. Marigold and amethyst are the only carnival colors reported, with the amethyst examples the rarer of the two. But don't sell the marigold sets short! They are near equal in rarity and a pitcher or tumbler in either color is a treasured find. Very few are known and they always bring top dollar.

Shapes & Colors Known

Water pitcher	marigold, amethyst
Tumbler	marigold, amethyst

The rare Dugan's Quill water pitcher in marigold.

Rainbow Lustre

Rainbow Lustre is the original name used by Diamond to market one of their later iridescent lines that dates from the mid to late 1920s. Actually the bulk of this line falls into the category generally called Stretch Glass. However, the candlestick in this line can be found with a true, carnival-like marigold iridescence, so it is included here as part of the carnival family. This candlestick has never been named in carnival collecting circles. Because the name Rainbow Lustre was originally used to market the design, it seems a logical choice.

The candlestick measures 8¾" tall, with a base diameter of 4¼". It has been reported in marigold, white, ice green, celeste blue, and pink. It is not plentiful in any of these colors, but marigold is probably the most available. Celeste blue and pink are the hardest colors to find.

This candlestick is very similar to Imperial's Premium candlestick. In fact, a lot of these are likely sitting in collections, being referred to as such. But, there really are several differences which become more obvious when you compare the two side by side. The photo here should prove helpful in that comparison.

The marigold candlestick on the left is Imperial's Premium. The ice green candlestick is Diamond's Rainbow Lustre.

Shapes & Colors Known

Candlestick	marigold, white, ice green, celeste blue, pink

119

Raindrops

Dugan's African Iridescent line (what we call black amethyst or oxblood) was introduced in March of 1910. The Raindrops pattern is known in this color, so we can safely assume that this design likely dates from that time period. Raindrops is found only on the interior surface of 8" – 9" dome-footed bowls, which are known in a variety of shape variations. The exterior surface carries the Keyhole pattern, one of the designs carried over from pre-carnival opalescent production.

The usual shape encountered is a round, 8" – 9" bowl that is known with a variety of edge treatments. They may be broadly ruffled, tightly crimped, have a three-in-one edge, or have the typical Dugan edge shaping of 10 flat, squared ruffles. The latter version seems to be the most often encountered. Some examples are found in an unusually deep, crimped edge shape that stands nearly 5" high with a top diameter of only 6" – 7". Some collectors refer to these as dome-footed compotes. Peach opalescent is by far the most frequently found color and most examples exhibit a deep, rich color with heavy opalescence. Amethyst examples are seen far less often but are well worth finding. I have never seen a poorly iridized one. Comparatively few oxblood examples are known, but they do exist. I have never seen or heard of a marigold example, nor any other colors.

The only other reported shape is that of a banana bowl, formed by pulling two sides up. These are rarely found and known in peach opalescent, oxblood, and amethyst, with oxblood by far the rarest of the three. These are known only with the flat, square ruffled edge.

An amethyst Raindrops banana bowl shape, not that easily found.

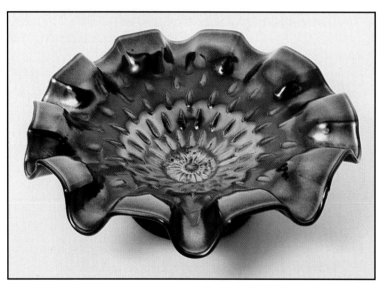

Talk about brilliant, electric iridescence! It just doesn't get any better than on this amethyst Raindrops bowl.

Shapes & Colors Known	
Bowl, 8" – 9", ruffled	peach opalescent, amethyst, oxblood
Compote, dome-footed	peach opalescent, amethyst, oxblood
Banana bowl, 9"	peach opalescent, amethyst, oxblood

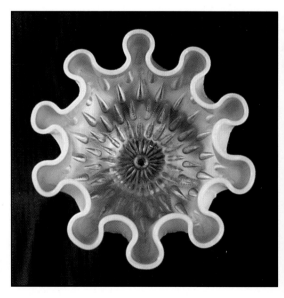

How about this for unusual edge shaping on this peach opalescent Raindrops bowl?

Rambler Rose

Found only on water sets, Rambler Rose was a Diamond Glass Company pattern and was in production during the 1914 – 1915 period. This is a pattern that has quietly disappeared over the last few years. Ten or 15 years ago, these pitchers and tumblers would be seen quite frequently at antique shows and in shops. This is not the case today. An occasional tumbler still turns up here and there, but the pitchers are becoming quite scarce.

The water pitcher is mold-blown with a separately applied handle. Marigold is the most available color. These often tend toward weak iridescence, though there are some very nice ones out there, too. The quality of the iridescence on the amethyst and cobalt blue sets is usually very good, however. Of the two colors, the amethyst is probably the most frequently found, but even they are getting really tough to find. I have seen far fewer cobalt blue sets.

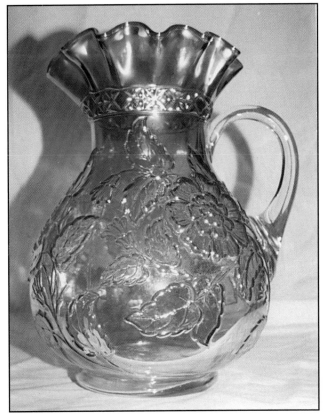

Rambler Rose tumblers were often sold separately, without the matching pitcher. The August 1914 Butler Brothers catalog offered them as part of a general assortment of Diamond carnival novelties. This probably accounts for the fact that these tumblers often turn up individually on today's collector market. Several other Diamond Glass Company tumblers were also marketed in this fashion, and they too are often found on an individual basis today.

Caution: This water set was reproduced by L.G. Wright in purple carnival glass. The tumblers were also reproduced in non-iridized custard glass.

The Rambler Rose water pitcher and tumbler in marigold. The mold-blown pitchers are very delicate and thin. There has no doubt been a lot of breakage over the years, and this has made it one of the tougher carnival pitchers to find.

Shapes & Colors Known	
Water set	marigold, amethyst, cobalt blue

Round-Up

Found only on the interior surface of bowls and plates, Round-Up is one of the most popular Dugan carnival patterns. The design shows striking similarities to Dugan's Fanciful pattern and likely dates from the same period, ca. 1910 – 1912. The range and rarity of the colors and shapes in which it may be found also show striking similarities to the Fanciful pattern, another good indication of a simultaneous production.

Another knockout: an amethyst Round-Up low ruffled bowl with fabulous electric iridescence.

The 8" – 9" bowls are known in several shapes, including ruffled, low ruffled, ice cream, and the three-in-one edge. Like its companion design Fanciful, the three-in-one edged bowls are the least often found. Peach opalescent seems to be the most available color, followed by amethyst and white, in that order. Cobalt blue takes fourth place, with oxblood a close fifth. Like so many Dugan carnival novelty shapes, marigold examples are really much harder to find. A few examples in pastel lavender have also been reported, but only in the ice cream shape to date. No ice cream shape bowls or three-in-one edged bowls have yet been confirmed in cobalt blue.

The 9" plates are a collector's favorite. Like the Fanciful plates, cobalt blue is far and away the most often found color, with peach opalescent and white next in line. Amethyst plates are surprisingly tough to find, with the marigold examples even more so. A few are known in oxblood, but the top spot goes to the decorated peach opalescent plate; I know of only one.

All known examples carry the Big Basketweave exterior pattern. There is currently no evidence to indicate that production of the Round-Up pattern was continued under the Diamond Glass Company management. It is possible that the Round-Up mold may have been among those destroyed in the 1912 fire.

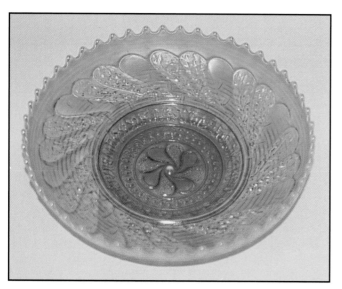

A peach opalescent Round-Up bowl in the low ice cream shape.

Shapes & Colors Known

Bowl, 8" – 9" ruffled	marigold, amethyst, peach opalescent, oxblood, white, cobalt blue
Bowl, 8" – 9", three-in-one edge	marigold, amethyst, peach opalescent, oxblood, white
Bowl, 8" – 9", ice cream	marigold, amethyst, peach opalescent, oxblood, white, lavender
Plate, 9"	marigold, amethyst, peach opalescent, cobalt blue, oxblood, white, decorated peach opalescent

Royal Lustre

A lot of people are going to be very surprised to see these candlesticks and console bowls in this book. For as far back as I can remember, virtually every carnival glass reference source has credited them to Imperial and has called them Imperial Jewels. Well, they never saw the inside of the Imperial factory! They are, in fact, products of the Diamond Glass Company. They were marketed under the name Royal Lustre and were in production ca. 1924 – 1926. They are featured prominently in a Diamond Glass Company ad in the December 18, 1924, issue of *Crockery and Glass Journal*. So we cannot keep calling them Imperial Jewels! As the name Royal Lustre was the original trade name for the line, that seems to me to be the appropriate one.

The trumpet-shaped candlesticks measure 7¼" tall. The matching console bowls may be found in a variety of shapes. Some are very deep, with the edge cupped inward, some are deep with the edge flared outward, and some are very low and almost flat, with the edge cupped inward. I have even seen some that were a deep bell shape. The iridescence on many of these sets is of a brilliant, mirror-like silver lustre, hence Diamond's name for the line, Royal Lustre. They may also be found with a satin, multi-color iridescence, sometimes with the onion-skin effect of stretch glass.

Yes, Diamond did make true red carnival glass! This Royal Lustre three-piece console set, long credited to Imperial, appears in Diamond Glass Company factory advertising from the mid 1920s. Note the unusual shape of the large console bowl.

These console sets may be found in a variety of colors, including marigold, ice green, celeste blue, cobalt blue, and red. Yes, Diamond did make a true red iridized glass! Often, it is the cobalt blue and red examples that have the brilliant silver iridescent lustre. Most of the other known colors are usually found with a satin, multi-color iridescence. Red is by far the rarest of the colors known, but the ice green examples are also quite rare. Celeste blue is very scarce, but the cobalt blue examples seem to turn up from time to time. A little patient searching will likely turn up some marigold examples.

The Royal Lustre console bowl may also be found in a low ice cream shape, like this beautiful blue one.

Shapes & Colors Known	
Candlesticks and console bowl	marigold, ice green, celeste blue, cobalt blue, red

Ruffled Rib

I have considerable reservations concerning a Dugan origin for this design. We have virtually no concrete evidence to place it firmly in the Dugan or Diamond family. Most consider it to be a

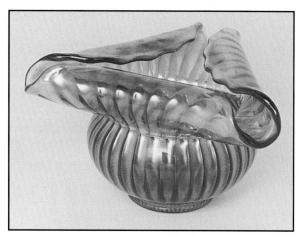

Dugan product, dating from early in the Dugan carnival production era, ca. 1909 – 1910. My only problem with that is the lack of any examples in colors other than marigold, such as peach opalescent or amethyst. Dugan was producing huge quantities of both those colors at that time, so it seems suspicious that no examples of Ruffled Rib have surfaced in them. Still, some of the known Ruffled Rib shapes are styled in similar fashion to many of Dugan's pre-carnival era art glass shapes, so a Dugan origin is possible.

The known Ruffled Rib shapes include round and square topped rose bowls, a spittoon, and ruffled or crimped top vases. The vases are generally found in the 6" – 9" height range, though just about any size is possible. The ribbed design is on the exterior surface and the interior is unpatterned. The design characteristics are quite similar to Imperial's Colonial Lady pattern. Marigold is the only color confirmed to date, and all shapes are seldom found.

Two unusual Ruffled Rib spittoons in marigold, one with a triangular top and the other in a square shape.

Shapes & Colors Known
Rose bowl, spittoon, vases   marigold

Seagull

The Seagull bowl is a late Diamond entry, in production from the late 1920s right up until the plant closed in 1931. It underwent an extensive production in non-iridescent colors of pink and green as part of Diamond's After Glow line and these are still frequently seen in shops and antique malls.

The carnival version is not so easily found. It is known only in marigold, usually with a surprisingly good, dark iridescence that is unusual for such a late carnival item. They don't turn up all that often, so apparently the carnival production was a relatively short one. In fact, the 1931 fire that closed the plant's door forever likely interrupted the production of the Seagull bowl. No colors other than marigold are known.

The Seagull bowl in marigold, often overlooked but not that easily found.

Shapes & Colors Known
Seagull bowl   marigold

Single Flower and Single Flower Framed

Just exactly why these two designs were given pattern names that imply that one is a variant of the other remains a mystery to me. They are actually distinctly different patterns found on distinctly different shapes. They do have some things in common. Both are found primarily in peach opalescent and both date from roughly the same time period, ca. 1909 – 1911, when they appeared in the wholesale catalogs. Both also suspiciously vanished from the wholesale catalogs at about the

time of the 1912 fire. Both are exterior only patterns. Both are here together simply because collectors have come to accept these pattern names.

Single Flower: This is really a very poor name for this pattern. The design actually consists of three groups, each comprising two stemmed flowers. A large leaf spray with flower blossoms fills the center of the base. The interior surface is unpatterned. It has been reported only on ruffled bowls, generally in the 7½" to 8½" size range. In marigold, amethyst, peach opalescent, and enamel decorated peach opalescent, and also on rare baskets with a separately applied, clear glass handle. These baskets are reported only in peach opalescent to date.

Single Flower Framed: This is actually quite an appropriate name for this pattern. It is comprised of three groups, each containing a single, stemmed flower against a stippled, fan-like background device. The center of the base is filled with a faintly molded flower. The interior surface carries the Smooth Rib design. It is found on 7" – 8½" crimped or ruffled bowls, 7" – 8½" crimped edge plates, and on an 8" handgrip plate, also with a crimped edge. Peach opalescent and enamel decorated peach opalescent are the only colors confirmed to date.

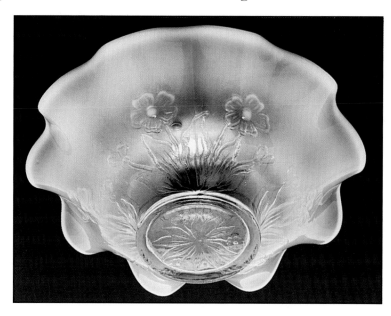

A **Single Flower** 8½" ruffled bowl in peach opalescent.

An interior and exterior view of a Single Flower Framed handgrip plate with the Smooth Ribs interior.

Shapes & Colors Known
Single Flower:

Bowl, 7½" – 8½"	marigold, amethyst, peach opalescent, decorated peach opalescent
Basket, handled	peach opalescent

Single Flower Framed:

Bowl, 7" – 8½"	peach opalescent, decorated peach opalescent
Plate, 7" – 8½"	peach opalescent, decorated peach opalescent
Handgrip plate	peach opalescent, decorated peach opalescent

125

Six Petals

This seems to be one of the more easily found Dugan carnival patterns, and it is still quite available in all known colors. The existence of examples in oxblood tells us that the design was in production in 1910 when that color was introduced, and it was still in production in 1912 when Dugan was making his white carnival line.

Bowls in the 7" – 8" size range are the only confirmed shapes. They may be broadly ruffled,

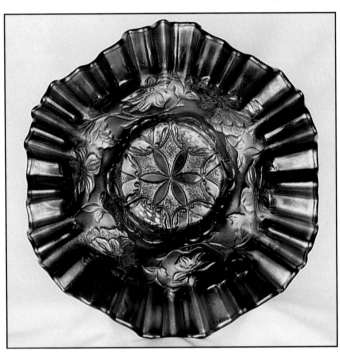

have a tightly crimped edge, or be triangular in shape. The ruffled and crimped edged bowls are seen most often in white and peach opalescent. The amethyst bowls may take a little more searching, but are still quite available. Oxblood examples are rather hard to find, and marigold bowls are actually quite scarce. This bowl has been rumored to exist in green, but remains unconfirmed.

The triangular-shaped bowl is much harder to find, and to date has been confirmed only in amethyst and peach opalescent.

Flat plates have also been rumored to exist, but I cannot, in all honesty, confirm them. In 28 years of collecting, I have neither seen one, nor have I ever spoken with anyone who has. Until such time as one is placed in my hands, or I am presented with a good, clear photo of one, I cannot, in good conscience, acknowledge their existence.

A crimped-edge Six Petals 7½" bowl in amethyst.

Shapes & Colors Known	
Bowl, 7" – 8", ruffled or crimped	marigold, amethyst, oxblood, white, peach opalescent
Bowl, 7" – 8", triangular	amethyst, peach opalescent

Ski-Star

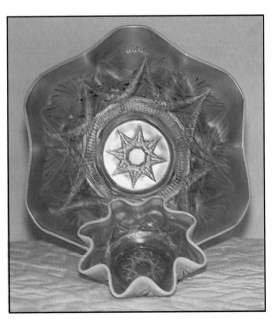

Ski-Star is one of the earlier Dugan carnival efforts. Several items in this pattern line appear in the wholesale catalogs during the 1910 – 1911 period, primarily offered in peach opalescent. All known shapes carry the Compass design on the exterior surface, a pattern carried over from opalescent production in 1907. Ski-Star abruptly disappeared from the wholesale catalogs in 1912. It is possible that the bulk of the molds for this pattern was among those lost to the 1912 fire.

Still, in its relatively short production life, Ski-Star was made in a surprisingly large variety of shapes. It is the variety of available colors that is very limited.

Perhaps the most available and familiar of the shapes are the large 10" – 11" ruffled bowls and the small-

The Ski-Star large and small ruffled berry bowls in peach opalescent are among the more available shapes in this pattern. The large bowls seem to be especially plentiful.

126

er 5" – 6" counterparts, which combine to form a most attractive berry set. Peach opalescent is the most available color. Amethyst examples also exist, but are much harder to find, especially in the large bowl. Rarest of all are the marigold bowls. I have personally seen only two or three in the last 28 years! In addition to the ruffled shape, the small bowl may also be found with a tightly crimped edge or in a triangular shape, the latter of which is very scarce. The same mold was also used to fashion the 6" crimped edge, flat plate. These have been reported only in peach opalescent to date, but I would not be surprised if there are some amethyst ones out there.

Several dome-footed shapes in the 8" – 9" size range also exist, all of which were fashioned from the same mold. These include ruffled bowls found with a variety of edge shapings: ruffled, three-in-one, twelve broad, flat ruffles, or tightly crimped. Here again, peach opalescent is the most often seen color, but very scarce amethyst examples are occasionally found. The same mold was also used to fashion a banana bowl, a deep handgrip bowl, a flat handgrip plate, and an extremely rare rose bowl. Only a couple of the rose bowls are known. All are known in peach opalescent, but only the two handgrip shapes are known in amethyst.

The only other reported shapes are two sizes of handled baskets. The large basket was made from the dome-footed banana bowl shape, with the clear applied handle spanning the two pulled-up sides. They are known only in peach opalescent and are rarely found. The small basket was made from the 6" ruffled bowl and has a clear, applied handle. It is extremely rare, with only a couple examples known. The large basket was a regular production item and appears in several Butler Brothers wholesale catalogs. The small basket was likely a whimsey item.

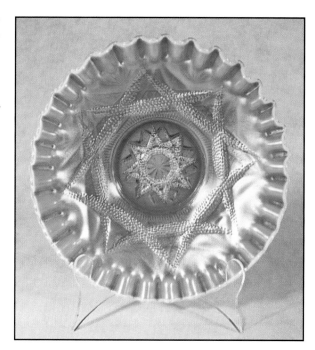

Two variations of Ski-Star plates, both in peach opalescent: the dome-footed handgrip plate and the 6½" collar based crimped plate. Each one is a rare find.

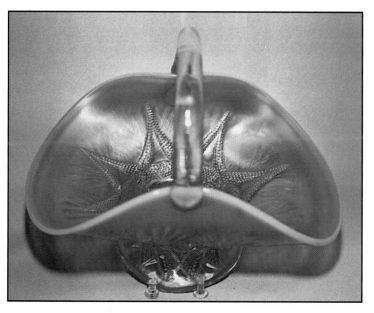

The rare Ski-Star handled basket in peach opalescent.

127

The Ski-Star handled basket was often sold in company with the Stippled Petals handled basket as shown in this ad from the fall 1910 Butler Brothers catalog. The term Mexican Aurora was one of several used by Butler Brothers to market Dugan's peach opalescent.

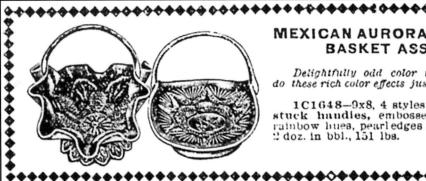

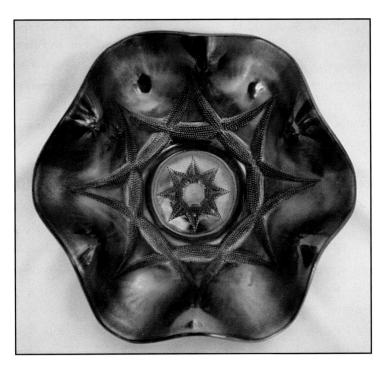

Amethyst examples of the Ski-Star pattern, like this fabulous 11" ruffled bowl, are actually quite scarce and highly treasured.

Shapes & Colors Known

Bowl, 10" – 11", ruffled	marigold, amethyst, peach opalescent
Bowl, 5" – 6", ruffled	marigold, amethyst, peach opalescent
Bowl, 5" – 6", triangular	amethyst, peach opalescent
Bowl, 5" – 6", crimped	amethyst, peach opalescent
Plate, 6", crimped	peach opalescent
Bowl, 8" – 9", dome-footed	amethyst, peach opalescent
Banana bowl, 9", dome-footed	amethyst, peach opalescent
Handgrip plate, 8" – 9", dome-footed	amethyst, peach opalescent
Handgrip plate, 9", dome-footed	amethyst, peach opalescent
Rose bowl, dome-footed	peach opalescent
Basket, large	peach opalescent
Basket, small	peach opalescent

Smooth Rays

Smooth Rays, sometimes called Smooth Ribs, is primarily found on the interior surface of pieces in the following patterns: Caroline, Jewelled Heart, Stippled Flower, and Single Flower Framed. On rare occasion, it can be found on ruffled bowls and small, crimped-edge plates with no exterior design. When so found it is known in marigold, amethyst, peach opalescent, oxblood, and rarely white.

For more information on this design and the shapes and colors known, see the texts for the above listed patterns.

A Smooth Rays crimped-edge plate and bowl in amethyst.

Shapes & Colors Known

Bowls and small plates	marigold, peach opalescent, amethyst, oxblood, white

Soutache

We can say with a fair degree of certainty that this seldom seen carnival design dates from the earlier Dugan carnival years, probably from around 1909 – 1910. The exterior pattern, called Western Daisy, was revived from opalescent glass production and appears in the 1907 Dugan factory catalog. This not only tends to confirm an early carnival production for this design, but also confirms that peach opalescent was one of the first carnival colors produced by Thomas Dugan. It is the only carnival color the Soutache pattern has ever been found in!

Dome-footed, 8" – 9½" bowls are the most often seen shape, but even these are rather hard to find. The edge may be broadly ruffled or tightly crimped. The quality of the marigold color and iridescence is usually very good and the opalescence is often quite heavy, covering a good portion of the exterior.

The same mold was used to fashion the rare dome-footed plates. These are quite flat and the very edge is often tightly crimped. However, I have seen an example or two that were not crimped and completely flat to the edge. These, of course, would likely bring a premium price among plate fanciers. Rarer

Soutache is not the easiest of patterns to find. This is especially true of the beautiful crimped edge plates like this one.

129

still are a couple of known examples with a most unusual edge treatment featuring four prominently fluted points.

How's this for an unusual edge shaping on a Soutache plate? The only other piece I have ever seen this type of edge on is the Western Daisy bowl shown on page 150.

Soutache plates can also
be found with a smooth
edge, like this beauty.

Dugan ✧

Spiralex

This is another of the early Dugan vase patterns that was carried over from the pre-carnival era. It appears in the 1907 Dugan factory catalog in blue, green, and flint opalescent, as well as crystal with ruby stained ribs, and is listed as Dugan's #1028. The carnival glass version appears in the wholesale catalogs from 1910 through the early 1920s, spanning both the Dugan and Diamond production years. It was often sold in assortments that also included the Pulled Loop and Target vases. It can be found in a variety of heights ranging from 8" to 14" tall. Most examples fall into the 9" – 12" size range.

Marigold examples are plentiful and even the amethyst and peach opalescent vases turn up with fair frequency. The white vases are harder to find, but I wouldn't go so far as to call them rare. Scarce, maybe. The only pieces I would give the rare label are the cobalt blue examples. I have seen only a few over the years. Other colors are certainly possible, but I have not been able to confirm any.

The Spiralex
vase in
amethyst.

The original factory pattern name for this unusual design was National, an appropriate one because it was first introduced in non-iridized form when the Indiana plant was still under the ownership of the National Glass Combine. A full line including a water set, table set, berry set, cruet, toothpick holder, syrup jug, wine decanter, stemmed wines, salt and pepper shakers, and a condiment tray was made in blue, amethyst, and light green, usually with fired-on gold decoration.

A far more limited variety of shapes is known in carnival, and with but one controversial exception, all the shapes are known only in amethyst. Headlining these shapes is the massive banquet-size punch set. It is one of only two carnival punch set patterns produced by Dugan. It is interesting to note that this set was apparently created exclusively for iridescent production, as no non-iridized examples have ever surfaced. I have always suspected that the bases to these punch sets were created by adding a different base plate to the mold for the master berry bowl. The two pieces are nearly identical in size and overall configuration, save for the beaded bottom edge on the punch base. This is an extremely rare set with relatively few perfect examples known and they generate very serious prices when they change hands. The punch cups are not all that difficult to find and even the bases turn up from time to time. However, most of the bowls seem to have become casualties of time and use. A single known punch bowl in iridized crystal has recently surfaced. No matching base or cups have yet been found.

Other known carnival shapes include a tiny whimsey creamer fashioned from the punch cup, an extremely rare toothpick holder, and I know of one covered sugar. All are found only in amethyst. The existence of the covered sugar would tend to indicate that the rest of the four-piece table set may one day surface. A handful of very controversial tumblers exist in marigold. Some believe them to be old while others feel they are not. Personally, I feel they are old. The rarity of them is the key factor in my belief. There are only a few known. Were they new, then surely they would be more plentiful.

A variation of the S Repeat pattern, called Seafoam by carnival collectors, is also found as the exterior design on the Constellation compote.

Caution: The toothpick holder has been massively reproduced in just about every iridescent and non-iridescent color imaginable. Amethyst is the only color known for the old ones and examples are extremely rare, with only a few known.

The magnificent S Repeat banquet-size punch set in amethyst, one of the rarest and most eagerly sought of all carnival punch sets. Very few perfect examples are known.

Shapes & Colors Known	
Punch bowl & base, punch cup, whimsey creamer, covered sugar, toothpick holder	amethyst
Punch bowl only	iridized crystal
Tumbler	marigold

Star Fish

This seldom seen and often overlooked carnival pattern likely dates from the early Dugan carnival production era, ca. 1909 – 1912. Strangely, it does not appear in any of the currently known wholesale catalogs. However, based on its relative scarcity and the colors known, a Dugan origin seems likely. Were it a Diamond Glass Company design, there would surely be a greater variety of colors and it would be far more available.

The stemmed, two-handled bonbon is the most frequently found shape, but even these are rather scarce. Peach opalescent is the most available color and they are usually very pretty, often

showing good, rich color and heavy opalescence. They are also known in amethyst and these are really quite rare, with comparatively fewer examples known. As far as the actual numbers known, marigold is by far the rarest color; I have heard of only a few. This is another indication of a Dugan origin for this pattern. Diamond's production of marigold was far more prolific than Dugan's.

The stemmed compote is seen even less often than the two-handled bonbon. Here again, peach opalescent is the most available color. Amethyst is very scarce and the marigold examples are rare.

I have never seen or heard of any Star Fish pieces in any other colors, but I would not be particularly surprised to learn of a white one.

Star Fish pattern on the interior of an amethyst crimped edge compote.

Shapes & Colors Known

Bonbon, two-handled	marigold, amethyst, peach opalescent
Compote	marigold, amethyst, peach opalescent

Stippled Estate

Dating from early in Dugan's carnival production, ca. 1909, Stippled Estate was another carry-over design from Dugan's pre-carnival Japanese, Venetian, and Pompeian art glass lines. These little

mold-blown vases were likely rushed into iridescent production until newer, more suitable patterns could be created later that same year. Hence, the carnival production was likely a very brief one, which would account for their scarcity today. Only a relative handful of examples is known. Most are in peach opalescent, but I also know of at least one example each in marigold and, oddly enough, green.

Standing on average only 3" – 4" tall, most of the examples I have seen had a somewhat triangular ruffled top. However, because they are mold blown, virtually any shape variations are always a possibility. Care should be taken not to confuse this with a somewhat similar pressed carnival design called Estate, also known in peach opalescent, that was made by Westmoreland.

The peach opalescent Stippled Estate vase and its green counterpart. The green example is iridized and lacks the stippled background. The color is close to a lime green, and it glows under a blacklight.

Shapes & Colors Known

Vase, 3" – 4"	peach opalescent, marigold, green

Stippled Flower

This simple but attractive design is found only on the interior surface of 7" – 8" bowls, which are known in a variety of shapes. Round bowls with six broad ruffles are the most often seen and are not too difficult to find. Other shapes are found less often; these include triangular-shaped bowls and even square bowls.

Peach opalescent and amethyst are the only reported colors, and the triangular and square bowls are especially attractive. Often the color is particularly rich and the opalescence covers nearly the entire exterior surface. Some examples are found with enamel painted floral decoration. Decorated peach opalescent pieces appear frequently in the 1910 wholesale catalogs, so Stippled Flower likely dates from that time. Amethyst examples are actually quite scarce.

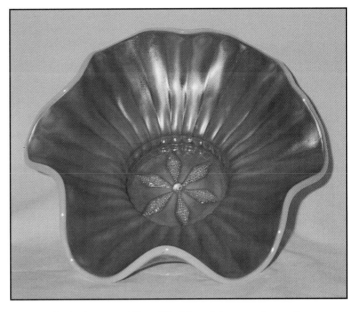

Stippled Flower 7½" ruffled bowl in peach opalescent.

Shapes & Colors Known

All shapes	peach opalescent, decorated peach opalescent, amethyst

Stippled Petals

This simple yet surprisingly attractive design was one of the earliest of Thomas Dugan's carnival creations. Both the dome-footed compote and handled basket appear in the fall 1910 Butler Brothers catalog in peach opalescent. The compote is particularly interesting because it is offered in peach opalescent with painted enamel floral decoration. This proves that the enamel decorated peach opalescent pieces were indeed factory painted.

Four different carnival shapes are known. All were fashioned from the same mold, carry the Long Leaf exterior pattern, and rest on a scalloped dome foot.

The 8" – 9" bowl is the most frequently encountered shape. The smooth edge may be broadly ruffled, have 10 flat square ruffles, or be of the three-in-one crimped style. Peach opalescent is the most available color, but rarely found amethyst examples also exist. Floral decorated examples are also known but are rarely found. Marigold examples also exist and are surprisingly scarce. The banana bowl was made by turning up two sides. These are seen far less often than the usual bowl shape and are known in peach opalescent and amethyst. Of these, the amethyst is the rarer of the two. The compote was fash-

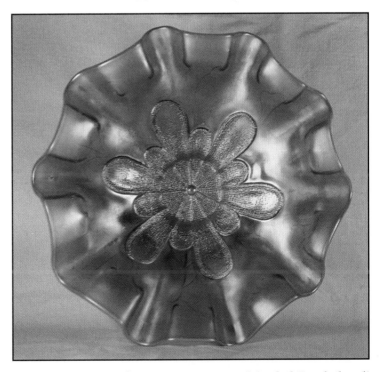

Believe it or not, this is a very scarce Stippled Petals bowl! Dugan produced comparatively little marigold as far as bowls, plates, and other novelty items are concerned.

A Stippled Petals banana bowl, a favorite shape of Thomas Dugan. This same shape was used to fashion the handled basket, which has a clear, applied handle spanning the two high points.

ioned by pulling up the entire body of the piece to a depth of from 4" to as much as 6". The edge may be ruffled or flat and almost plate-like. These have been reported in peach opalescent and floral decorated peach opalescent. Either one is rare.

The only other known shape is that of a handled basket, fashioned from the banana bowl shape described above. A separately applied, clear glass handle spans the two highest points. These rare baskets always attract a great deal of attention whenever shown or offered for sale. Peach opalescent is the only color reported to date.

"PARISIAN ART" COMPORT AND SALAD DISH ASST—(Iridescent)

[Beautiful color tones. Decorations burnt in, will not wash off.]

1C1846—4 shapes and decorations, deep iridescent aurora tints, pearl edges and under surface, enameled lilies of the valley, forget me nots and roses. 2 doz. in bbl. 58 lbs.
Doz. $2.10

The Stippled Petals dome-footed compote is featured in the center of this assortment of Dugan's enamel decorated peach opalescent pieces from the Christmas 1910 Butler Brothers catalog. Note the term Parisian Art. This was the name used by Butler Brothers to market many of Dugan's enamel decorated peach opalescent novelties.

Shapes & Colors Known	
Bowl, 8" – 9"	marigold, peach opalescent, amethyst, decorated peach opalescent
Banana bowl	amethyst, peach opalescent
Compote	peach opalescent, decorate peach opalescent
Handled basket	peach opalescent

Stippled Rambler Rose

This seldom-seen pattern is included here as a possible Diamond Glass Company product. It appears neither in any of the currently known wholesale catalogs nor in any of the known Diamond Glass Company advertising. There is no mention of any design resembling it in any of the period trade journals. In short, all efforts to conclusively tie this pattern to any known carnival manufacturer have led down a dead-end road. The only thing we have to go on is that the shape is vaguely

reminiscent of the Grape Delight nut bowl that is definitely a Diamond Glass Company product. However, attributing any pattern to a specific maker based on shape alone is risky business. So, it is included here with some reservations.

The footed nut bowl is the only shape known. It is not often found. When it is, marigold is the usual color, but a couple of cobalt blue examples have also been reported.

It should perhaps be noted that these two colors were the primary carnival production colors for some of the English and European carnival producers, so the possibility of an origin outside the United States is always there. We just don't know for certain at this point.

The Stippled Rambler Rose nut bowl in marigold.

Shapes & Colors Known
Footed nut bowl   marigold, cobalt blue

Stork in the Rushes

This pattern first appeared in the wholesale catalogs in 1915 and continued to appear through 1922. From these dates we know this design was a Diamond Glass creation. It was by far the most extensive of Diamond's carnival lines, with 16 different items documented to date. Many of them are still quite available, but a few are surprisingly rare. It is the known colors that are very limited here. Most pieces are known in only two or three colors.

This pattern is found on berry sets, table sets, punch sets, mugs, ruffled hat shapes, handled baskets, a two-piece ruffled fruit bowl and base, and two different water set variations.

The berry sets and table sets are found in marigold and amethyst. The berry sets turn up from time to time. The table set is quite scarce, even in marigold, and actually very rare in amethyst. The punch sets are tough in marigold and extremely so in amethyst, primarily due to a shortage of the bases. The base is unusually tall and carries a floral motif with a band of ribs encircling it just

An extremely rare Lattice Band Stork in the Rushes water pitcher in cobalt blue.

135

above the scalloped bottom and again just below the top. Because of this unusual shape, these bases were often likely used as vases and may have even been marketed as such. Some collectors refer to them as "Summer Days" vases, and you will find an example of this, illustrated under that name, on page 139. They are extremely difficult to find. Strangely, the Stork in the Rushes punch cups are fairly easy to find in either color. The punch bowl and base molds were used to fashion a ruffled fruit bowl and base. There is no doubt that these were intended to be used as such. They are far too widely flared and ruffled to hold any amount of liquid. These have been reported only in marigold to date.

Ruffled hat shapes made from the tumbler mold exist in both marigold and amethyst. By adding a separately applied, clear handle, the very scarce basket was created. These have been reported only in marigold.

There are two distinct versions of the water set. The beaded water set has rows of beads encircling the pitchers and tumblers at the base and near the top. It is the most frequently found of the two styles. The tumblers are quite plentiful in both marigold and cobalt blue but very rarely found in

Even though they are somewhat more available than the Lattice Band version, this cobalt blue beaded Stork in the Rushes pitcher is seldom seen.

amethyst. The water pitchers are, in my opinion, very hard to find in any color and are much underrated. Marigold ones do surface on occasion, but the cobalt blue and amethyst pitchers are very seldom found. The other version of the water set is called the Lattice Band. On this variant, the two rows of beads are replaced by bands of criss-crossed lattice. The marigold lattice band tum-

blers are much harder to find than their beaded cousins. The cobalt blue examples are quite scarce and the amethyst ones are rare. To say that the matching water pitcher is rare is a considerable understatement. I know of a few in cobalt blue and have received an unconfirmed report of one in marigold. To the best of my knowledge, no amethyst examples have ever surfaced, but there must surely be some out there somewhere.

There has been some speculation that only the Lattice Band version of the water set was made by Diamond and that the beaded version is Northwood. Sorry to burst anyone's bubble, but both versions appear in the same assortment of several 1915 Butler Brothers issues, so there is virtually no doubt that both are Diamond Glass Company products.

The Stork in the Rushes mug is probably the most familiar of all the shapes in

Stork in the Rushes small berry bowl, mug, and a beaded version of the tumbler, all in marigold.

this design. They have the lattice bands at the top and base and are abundant in marigold. Surprisingly, they are found in several other colors as well, and here the situation is very different. They are very scarce in amethyst and more so in lavender. The cobalt blue examples can be classified as rare. A couple of very rare examples in aqua with a marigold iridescent overlay, and light blue with a marigold iridescent overlay is also known. It seems strange that this mug was produced in such a variety of colors, while all the other items in this design are found in so few.

Caution: The beaded version of the water set, as well as the creamer, spooner, and covered sugar have been reproduced in marigold by L.G. Wright. They are very nicely done! The master berry bowl has also been reproduced in purple.

Believe it or not, this is the proper base to the Stork in the Rushes punch bowl! When not in use with the punch set, it could be inverted and used as a vase. Collectors call it Summer Days.

This Stork in the Rushes whimsey basket was fashioned from the Lattice Band tumbler mold.

Shapes & Colors Known

Berry set, table set, punch set	marigold, amethyst
Ruffled fruit bowl & base	marigold
Hat shape	marigold, amethyst
Handled basket	marigold
Water pitcher, beaded	marigold, amethyst, cobalt blue
Tumbler, beaded	marigold, amethyst, cobalt blue
Water pitcher, Lattice Band	cobalt blue, (marigold?)
Tumbler, Lattice Band	marigold, amethyst, cobalt blue
Mug	marigold, amethyst, lavender, cobalt blue, aqua w/marigold overlay, light blue w/marigold overlay

Strawberry Epergne

Remember the old riddle, "Which came first: the chicken or the egg?" That could well be applied here. For years, carnival collectors have been puzzled by the existence of the non-iridized opalescent version of this epergne because it incorporates a completely different lily combined with the same dome footed base. It was assumed that this version pre-dates the carnival version and that the use of a different lily on the carnival version was merely cosmetic. Research has now proven that quite the opposite is true.

The carnival glass version of the Strawberry Epergne shows all the characteristics of a Dugan Glass Company design and predates the opalescent version by several years! It likely was made 1909 – 1911. The opalescent glass version, with its different lily, does not appear in the wholesale catalogs until 1916, which definitely places it in the Diamond Glass Company family! The lily on the opalescent version is patterned with a spiral stem and a floral wreath at the top. Some opalescent glass collectors call this version Strawberry & Dahlia Twist.

Knowing that the opalescent version of this epergne came after the carnival version also provides us with a possible answer to the mystery of the two lilies. The mold for the lily used on the carnival version may have been lost to the 1912 fire. The base mold was saved, and later, a new lily mold was fashioned for the 1916 opalescent production.

The lily used for carnival production is patterned on the top half by a design of criss-crossed diamonds. The lower portion is patterned with rows of raised studs that show a striking similarity to the design used on the formal vase.

The dome-footed base of this epergne is, of course, patterned with strawberries and leaves. The only color known to date is amethyst, usually with a rich, multi-color lustre. These epergnes are eagerly sought, rarely found, and, like all carnival epergnes, command a good deal of attention when offered for sale.

Two views of the Strawberry Epergne in amethyst, showing the unusual pattern detail of the lily and the strawberry and leaf design on the interior of the base.

Shapes & Colors Known
Single lily epergne   amethyst

Summer Days

This vase was named Summer Days way back in the early days of the carnival collecting hobby. In many ways, it's a shame it was, because this still causes considerable confusion today, especially for the collector just starting out. With the limited resources available to the hobby 30 years ago, we had no idea that this piece served another purpose.

The Summer Days vase, when inverted, is actually the proper base to the Stork in the Rushes punch bowl. This practice of having dual purpose punch bowl bases was one used by both Dugan and Diamond on virtually all their carnival punch sets. When inverted, the base to the Many Fruits punch bowl can be used as a compote. Likewise, the base to the S Repeat punch bowl can be inverted to be a very nice centerpiece bowl.

The Summer Days vase is known in marigold and amethyst, and neither color is all that easily found. I suspect there are a fair number of these sitting in vase collections, the owners unaware of their original purpose.

When inverted, this beautiful amethyst Summer Days vase is the proper base to the Stork in the Rushes punch bowl.

Shapes & Colors Known	
Vase/punch bowl base, 6"	marigold, amethyst

Swan

Both Fenton and Dugan made carnival glass versions of this little novelty. The Dugan version was first made in non-iridized opalescent colors around 1906 and was one of the earliest Dugan carry-overs into iridescent production. The Diamond Glass Company continued to produce them well into the late teens. Many collectors and most reference sources call this piece Pastel Swan. I have never liked that name because it implies that all are found in pastel colors and such is not the case. It is the Fenton version that is primarily found in the pastel, iridized colors of ice green, ice blue, celeste blue, pink, etc. Not so with the Dugan version. The Dugan Swan also differs from the Fenton Swan in that the neck of the swan emerges from the body near the base, leaving a large portion of the body above the neck open. On the Fenton version, the emerging neck covers nearly the entire front portion of the body.

Dugan/Diamond's Swan novelty in amethyst.

The Dugan/Diamond carnival Swan is featured in this assortment from the mid-spring 1915 Butler Brothers catalog. Note also the Mary Ann vase on the left and the ruffled bowl next to it. To the best of my knowledge, this bowl is a completely unknown and unidentified pattern in carnival glass! More research will have to be done on this bowl. It appears to be a variation of the Folding Fan pattern, combined with a flower blossom design in the center.

Dugan's Swan is far more difficult to find than the Fenton version. The variety of colors known is also much more limited. The celeste blue examples, which were made by Diamond ca. 1916, are actually the most available color. The marigold examples, also Diamond-made ca. 1914, are harder to find. It is the amethyst and peach opalescent swans, which are Dugan-made ca. 1909 – 1910, that are the most difficult to find and the most popular with collectors. They always command a great deal of attention and will not linger for long when offered in a shop or antique mall.

I have never seen a Dugan Swan in any other colors, but they could well exist. A white one would come as no surprise.

Shapes & Colors Known	
Swan novelty	marigold, amethyst, peach opalescent, celeste blue

Target

Found only on vases of varying height, this design must have been an extremely popular one with the buying public. The non-iridized opalescent version appears in the 1907 Dugan factory catalog. The carnival version appeared in the earliest documented Dugan carnival assortment in the mid-spring 1909 Butler Brothers wholesale catalog. It continued to appear through 1924, spanning both the Dugan and Diamond production era. It is known in a fairly wide variety of iridescent colors. Known sizes range from a squat, widely flared, 5" – 6" version, to a tall, 13" – 14" swung version.

Marigold, peach opalescent, and white seem to be the most available colors. The squat 5" – 6" version seems to turn up particularly often in white. Amethyst Target vases are much harder to find, and they are rarely found in cobalt blue. Rarer still are the vaseline examples, usually found with a marigold iridescent overlay, and a few very rare green examples are also known. We have a two-way tie for the top honors in rarity. I know of one example in lime green opalescent and one in vaseline opalescent. Take your pick! With such a wide variety of carnival colors already known, others

Three sizes of Target vases in three colors: a 12" vase in amethyst, a squat vase in peach opalescent, and a rare green 9" vase.

could well exist but are unconfirmed to date. This vase enjoyed an extremely long production time span, so I wouldn't be surprised if celeste blue or sapphire blue examples also existed.

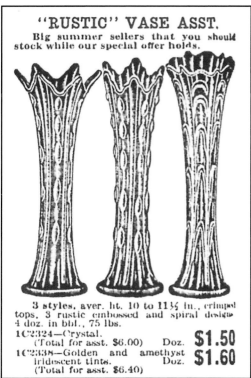

"RUSTIC" VASE ASST.
Big summer sellers that you should stock while our special offer holds.

3 styles, aver. ht. 10 to 11½ in., crimped tops, 3 rustic embossed and spiral design 4 doz. in bbl., 75 lbs.
1C2324—Crystal.   Doz. **$1.50**
    (Total for asst. $6.00)
1C2338—Golden and amethyst   Doz. **$1.60**
    iridescent tints.
    (Total for asst. $6.40)

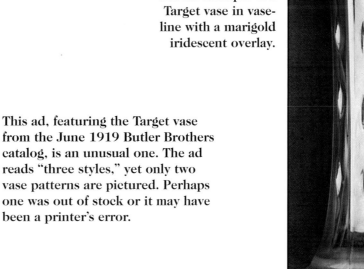

This is the only known example of a Target vase in vase-line with a marigold iridescent overlay.

This ad, featuring the Target vase from the June 1919 Butler Brothers catalog, is an unusual one. The ad reads "three styles," yet only two vase patterns are pictured. Perhaps one was out of stock or it may have been a printer's error.

Shapes & Colors Known	
Vase, 5" – 14"	marigold, amethyst, white, peach opalescent, cobalt blue, vaseline, green, lime green opalescent, vaseline opalescent

Three Fruits

The question mark after the Dugan/Diamond attribution is a big one. I have more reservations about including this design here than I do for any of the other questionable patterns presented in this book. Most collectors consider this version of the Three Fruits pattern, which does differ from the well-known Northwood version, to be a Dugan product. I am not one of them!

This version of the design is found only on 9" flat plates. The edge is usually fluted and has a 12-sided effect to the shape. The exterior surface is unpatterned. It is known in marigold, amethyst, cobalt blue, and green, with the amethyst examples found most often. The cobalt blue and green examples turn up in pretty fair numbers as well, and herein lies the basis for one of the reasons I tend to doubt a Dugan or Diamond origin.

Actually there are a number of reasons why I doubt a Dugan or Diamond origin for these plates and I think it is important to note them.

Known colors: The four known colors are not typical of either Dugan's or Diamond's carnival production. Both of these firms produced only moderate amounts of cobalt blue and precious little green. Far too many examples turn up in both of those colors! Fenton was far more prolific in the production of cobalt blue and green carnival. In fact, even the amethyst examples, which are usually of a fairly light, more violet-like color tone, more closely match Fenton's amethyst color. In addition, all four known colors — marigold, amethyst, cobalt blue, and green — match the bulk of Fenton's carnival production scheme. They do not match either Dugan's or Diamond's!

Shape: The 12-sided effect is very typical of Fenton's plates. Many Fenton carnival plates have this characteristic while I know of none from either Dugan or Diamond that do.

141

The Three Fruits 12-sided plate in amethyst. Is it Dugan? Diamond? Fenton?

Iridescent quality: To me, it simply screams Fenton on most examples. It is a satiny, multi-color effect, usually with a strong metallic tone, and often of only average quality, though I have seen some beautifully iridized examples. It is also interesting that both the interior and exterior surfaces are usually iridized. This is typical of Fenton pieces. Ever notice that relatively few Dugan bowls and plates are iridized on the exterior?

Still, I will not discount the possibility that this version of Three Fruits could be a Dugan or Diamond product. The L.G. Wright Glass Company did reproduce it in purple carnival glass, and they do own many Dugan/Diamond molds. However, there is a "fly in the ointment" here as well. Wright does not manufacture their own glass. A large portion of it has been made for them by Fenton. It is possible that Fenton could have made this reproduction for Wright, using one of their own molds.

Further research is definitely needed here. If this version of the Three Fruits pattern did indeed come out of Indiana, Pennsylvania, it likely came from Diamond rather than Dugan, but we just don't know for sure. For now, you'll have to make up your own mind on this one.

Tiny Twigs

Dugan

Don't mistake this very rare Dugan pattern for the similar, but far more common Twigs bud vase, made later by Diamond! They are a world apart in rarity, desirability, and value. The Tiny Twigs vase was a carry-over from earlier opalescent production. The opalescent version appears in the April 1906 Butler Brothers catalog and in the 1907 Dugan factory catalog. The carnival version likely dates early in Dugan's iridescent production, ca. 1909 – 1910. Their rarity indicates that they were probably not in production for very long. With their open twig base design, there were likely molding problems and a lot of breakage.

Depending upon the shaping, most Tiny Twigs vases stand from 3½" to 5" tall. They are known with a ruffled edge, a tightly crimped edge, and a crimped Jack-in-the-Pulpit shape. The Jack-in-the-Pulpit shape is considered the rarest and most desirable, but virtually any shape is a rare treasure. Marigold and amethyst are the only reported colors. Amethyst receives all the raves and attention, but there are probably fewer marigold examples known. Still, the amethyst examples rightfully deserve the praise bestowed upon them. The quality of the iridescence is often quite stunning, exhibiting brilliant, electric highlights.

A very rare crimped Jack-in-the-Pulpit Tiny Twigs vase.

142

There is no evidence to indicate that production of the Tiny Twigs vase was continued after the Diamond takeover. I can't help but wonder if the mold may have been another casualty of the 1912 fire.

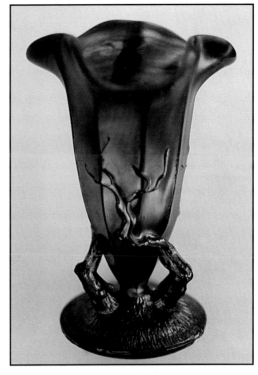

The ruffled top version of the amethyst Tiny Twigs vase is really equal in rarity to the Jack-in-the-Pulpit style.

Shapes & Colors Known
Vase, 3½" – 5", all shapes   marigold, amethyst

Tree of Life (Soda Gold)

Some collectors refer to this design as Soda Gold, and this causes confusion with a similar pattern of the same name that was made by Imperial. By using the name Tree of Life, which is a very old and commonly used name for this type of design, this confusion could be eliminated, but most still insist on calling it Soda Gold.

As a primary pattern, it is found on small handled baskets. These are rather late entries in the carnival field, likely dating from the 1920s. Marigold is the usual color, often rather light in tone, but examples with a dark, rich iridescence are found on occasion. Amethyst examples also exist but are seen far less often. The few that I have seen were of a very light, weak amethyst color and were poorly iridized.

This design is occasionally found on the exterior surface of bowls and plates in the Four Flowers and Garden Path patterns. I have seen only marigold and amethyst examples, both of which are likely the result of a continued production of Four Flowers and Garden Path by Diamond.

The Tree of Life (Soda Gold) pattern shown on the exterior surface of an amethyst Garden Path plate

The Tree of Life (Soda Gold) small basket in marigold.

Shapes & Colors Known
Small handled basket   marigold, amethyst
Exterior pattern on some Four Flowers and Garden Path pieces

143

Dugan

Triplets

This simple, naturalistic design is actually not often found and is frequently bypassed by the majority of collectors. The pattern detail is of minimal quality, so I guess I would have to classify it not one of Dugan's best efforts. Its general scarcity, along with the limited variety of known colors, would tend to indicate a rather brief production period, likely around the 1910 period. The design shows strong similarities to the Daisy Dear on page 56, but there really are differences between the two. Triplets has only three stemmed flowers equally spaced around the exterior surface, while

Daisy Dear has four. The leaves on the stem are somewhat larger and the flower in the center of the design is less rounded with more pointed petals.

Triplets is most often seen on the exterior surface of small, ruffled bowls in the 7" diameter size range. Marigold and peach opalescent are the most frequently encountered colors, although amethyst examples are sometimes seen as well. Green has been reported, but remains unconfirmed. Often the color and iridescence tend to be rather weak.

A more deeply ruffled hat shape, known in the same colors and fashioned from the same mold, is the only other reported shape.

Exterior view of a Triplets bowl in marigold.

Shapes & Colors Known
Bowl, 7", ruffled	marigold, amethyst, peach opalescent, (green?)
Hat shape	marigold, amethyst, peach opalescent

Diamond

Twig Bud Vase

The Twig Bud Vase was a near-permanent fixture in the wholesale catalogs from its initial appearance in 1916 right up until the Diamond factory closed in 1931. With such a lengthy production, it must have been a very popular item with consumers. No wonder they are still found in such abundance today.

Generally standing from 7" to 9" tall and found in the colors of marigold and amethyst, an example or two can be found in just about every antique mall. At least, this seems to be true of the marigold examples. Often the marigold color fades to clear from top to bottom, and the iridescence may be rather weak. The amethyst examples are actually quite scarce and will often sell at eight or 10 times the price of the marigold. Here too, the color and iridescence are often weak, but I have seen some beautifully iridized ones.

While the design is very similar to the Tiny Twigs Vase shown on page 142, the Twig Bud Vase was not made from the same mold. There are considerable differences in the design and, more importantly, the base diameter.

Shapes & Colors Known
Bud vase, 7" – 9"	marigold, amethyst

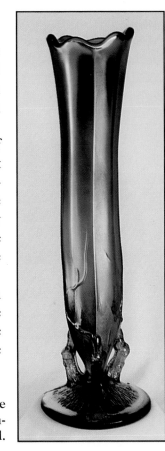

While the marigold Twig Bud Vase may be among the most easily found of all carnival vases, examples in amethyst like this one are quite hard to find.

144

This bold, stylized design is among the most impressive ones to come out of the Dugan Glass Company. It is found only on the interior surface of large, 10" – 12" ruffled bowls, and on a single known 10½" low, ice cream-shaped bowl. The concentric rings form a flower-like center design. The pattern is bordered by six sprigs of three leaves. This three-leaf sprig is a border device found frequently on Dugan carnival bowl patterns.

Almost all the known examples are in amethyst. The base glass color is usually of a striking, deep purple shade. The iridescent quality is often astounding and some examples are known with a brilliant electric blue iridescence. These are very scarce bowls and they always command very respectable prices.

The only other color reported is peach opalescent and to call them rare is a considerable understatement! I know of two examples and only one of these is perfect. No other colors have ever surfaced, but of course, it's always possible. Wouldn't a white one be something?

Most examples of the Victorian bowl are ruffled. This round, low ice cream-shaped example is the only one confirmed as of this writing.

Shapes & Colors Known

Bowl, ruffled, 10" – 12"	amethyst, peach opalescent
Bowl, 10½", ice cream shape	amethyst

Here we have another pattern that Dugan made from a mold Harry Northwood left behind. It was made in opaque, non-iridized green and decorated milk glass prior to the carnival era in a wide variety of shapes. Pattern glass collectors call these earlier pieces Grape & Leaf. The carnival version was definitely made by Dugan and dates early in the carnival era, about 1910, with production continuing for several years.

Water sets are the only carnival shapes reported to date, and the number of colors known is also quite limited. The marigold pitchers and tumblers are quite available and it shouldn't take too much time or money to come up with them. The amethyst tumblers also still turn up in fair numbers, but the pitchers are getting tough. Peach opalescent is the only other color reported and only in the water pitcher; they are quite rare. Strangely, no matching peach opalescent tumblers have ever been found.

Shapes & Colors Known

Water pitcher	marigold, amethyst, peach opalescent
Tumbler	marigold, amethyst

While marigold Vineyard water sets are still quite available, amethyst sets with iridescence of this caliber are very hard to come by.

145

Vintage Banded

While the grape and leaf portion of this design shows many strong similarities to that found on Dugan's Vintage perfume bottle and powder jar, Vintage Banded is a much later pattern that dates from the Diamond production years. It did not appear in the wholesale catalogs until 1922, but it does continue to do so through 1930, so the production period was still a long one.

I'm sure just about everyone reading this has likely seen a marigold Vintage Banded mug. Along with Fenton's marigold Orange Tree mugs, they must be the most common and easily found of all carnival mugs. This is one of the very few Diamond carnival pieces that is known in smoke. It is interesting to note that the production dates for this mug just happen to coincide with the time frame in which the bulk of Imperial's smoke carnival was made. These smoke Vintage Banded mugs are really quite scarce. A few examples are also known in light green with a marigold iridescent overlay. Topping the rarity list is the amethyst Vintage Banded mug. While there may be more of them out there, I personally know of only one confirmed example!

It is the water set in this design that is the rare bird indeed. The water pitcher is one of the few pedestal-footed pitchers made in carnival. Both pitcher and tumbler are known in marigold. Oddly, there are more pitchers known than there are tumblers. Only a very few tumblers exist. Stranger still, the water pitcher is known in amethyst, but to date, no amethyst tumblers are known. Where are they?

Caution: The Vintage Banded water set has been reproduced in purple carnival glass by L.G. Wright.

The marigold Vintage Banded water pitcher is quite scarce but still surfaces from time to time. The matching tumbler is extremely rare, with relatively few examples known.

This is the only amethyst example of the Vintage Banded mug that I have ever seen or heard of.

Shapes & Colors Known	
Mug	marigold, smoke, light green w/marigold overlay, amethyst
Water pitcher	marigold, amethyst
Tumbler	marigold

Vintage Perfume & Powder Jar

I'm sure that my decision to list these items together under this name will raise a few eyebrows and cause some controversy. So be it. But facts are facts and it's time we all accepted them and cleared up the confusion surrounding these two items, especially in the case of the perfume.

For many years this perfume bottle was considered to be a part of Northwood's Grape & Cable dresser set. When the first copies of the Butler Brothers wholesale catalog began to surface in the 1970s, things began to change. Northwood's Grape & Cable dresser set appeared in several of them and the perfume bottle was conspicuously absent. Then, several shards of this perfume, including a complete stopper, turned up in the Helman diggings. It became clear that this perfume bottle was not made by Northwood and therefore not part of the Grape & Cable dresser set. However, collectors continued to refer to it as the Grape & Cable perfume bottle. Most still do, and this is not correct! It is now time to take this a step further and look at this perfume bottle for what it really is.

The pattern on this perfume bottle is not Grape & Cable! There are several important differences between the two designs:

1. All Grape & Cable items have a distinct cable either surrounding the pattern or encircling the piece. This perfume bottle has no cable.

2. The main feature of the Grape & Cable pattern is, of course, the alternating bunches of grapes separated by the grape leaves. This is also true of this perfume bottle, but with one important difference. If you examine this piece closely, you will notice that the bunches of grapes are super-imposed over a grape leaf, which can be clearly seen protruding from under the bunch of grapes. The Grape & Cable pattern does not have this.

3. A close comparison of this perfume bottle with the Vintage Powder Jar will reveal that the patterns on each are identical. The Vintage Powder Jar also has the grape leaf protruding from beneath the bunches of grapes, and both pieces have a row of raised beads encircling the piece, in place of a cable.

Bearing this in mind, the picture becomes much clearer. If this perfume bottle was meant to accompany anything at all, it likely was intended as a companion piece to the Vintage Powder Jar. It is time that we all stopped calling it Grape & Cable!

This is also important for another reason. It is because of this persistence in calling this piece Grape & Cable that Dugan and Diamond have been credited with producing their own version of the Grape & Cable pattern. There is virtually no evidence whatsoever that either firm ever copied or produced the Grape & Cable pattern! No Dugan or Diamond advertising, or any wholesale catalog advertising linking these two firms with the Grape & Cable pattern, has ever been found. The entire myth of Dugan or Dia-

The Vintage Powder Jar and Perfume Bottle in marigold. Note how a grape leaf protrudes from under the bunch of grapes. This does not occur on the Grape & Cable pattern. Note also that there is no cable on the perfume. It is time we stopped calling this a Grape & Cable Perfume simply because it is not.

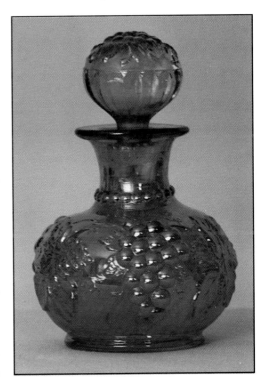

147

mond making a version of the Grape & Cable design stems from the shards of this perfume bottle from the Helman diggings being misidentified as Grape & Cable!

The Dugan Vintage perfume bottle has surfaced in only two carnival colors, to date: marigold and amethyst. While the amethyst perfumes usually get the most attention, it is the marigold examples that are actually the harder of the two colors to find. The delicate, hollow stoppers are highly prone to damage, so a perfect example in either color is really a rare find.

The matching powder jar is much easier to find, but still, there seems to be a shortage of lids. These lids are much thinner glass and lighter in weight than the base of the jar, so many of them have become casualties of time and use. Marigold is the most often found color, but even these are usually missing the lids. Amethyst is much harder to find, but they do turn up on occasion. Cobalt blue is a rare color for these, but examples do exist. Topping the list are the very rare white examples. Only a few are known.

Shapes & Colors Known

Perfume bottle	marigold, amethyst
Powder jar	marigold, amethyst, cobalt blue, white

No perfume bottle has yet been confirmed in cobalt blue or white, but I would not be too surprised if either of them were to turn up.

Diamond

Vintage Variant

Most reference sources list this pattern as Dugan's Vintage Variant. However, examples of this design are found in celeste blue. This color was not introduced until the 1916 – 1917 period, so this firmly places the production of Vintage Variant in the Diamond years, long after Thomas Dugan's departure. Examples are not plentiful, so the design apparently had a rather short production.

The pattern is often confused with a similar one made by Fenton. Actually, it's really not difficult to tell them apart. Both versions have a grape leaf center, but there the similarities end. Fenton's Vintage has five grape clusters that are interspaced with seven grape leaves. Diamond's Vintage Variant has six grape clusters and only five grape leaves. There is also a gap in the pattern on the Diamond version. The grapes and leaves are larger on the Fenton version and cover a larger area of the interior surface. The pattern is more confined towards the center area on the Diamond version and there is a broader, unpatterned area toward the edge.

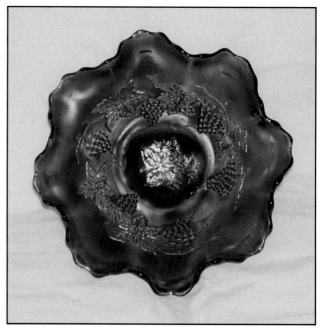

A marigold Vintage Variant plate and a ruffled bowl in amethyst. Note the "break" in the continuation of the pattern. This is a good way to tell the difference between the Diamond version and Fenton's Vintage.

Diamond's Vintage Variant is found on the interior surface of 8" – 9" dome-footed bowls, collar-based bowls, and on dome-footed plates. Collar-based plates may well exist, but I have yet to see one.

The dome-footed bowls are rather scarce in any color, but marigold examples are the most often found. Amethyst ones are seen far less often. Only a few examples of each are known in white, cobalt blue, green, and celeste blue. Collar-based bowls have been confirmed only in marigold and amethyst, to date, but other colors likely exist.

Plates are very rare, with marigold the usual color. I do know of one example in amethyst. No other colors have been confirmed. However, with the variety of colors known in the bowl shape, others likely exist. Be on the lookout for them. You might just find a real "sleeper."

Shapes & Colors Known	
Bowl, 8" – 9", dome-footed	marigold, amethyst, cobalt blue, green, white, celeste blue
Bowl, 8" – 9", collar-based	marigold, amethyst
Plate, 9", dome-footed	marigold, amethyst

Weeping Cherry

Based on the relative scarcity of this pattern, the known colors, and the general mold characteristics, Weeping Cherry likely dates from fairly late in the Diamond Glass Company production era, probably from the early 1920s. It does bear some similarities in basic concept to Dugan's Cherry, but I'm convinced it is a much later Diamond pattern.

It is found only on the interior surface of 8" – 9½" dome-footed bowls. Only three colors have been reported to date. Marigold Weeping Cherry bowls are really quite scarce. Over the years I have only seen a relative handful of them. The cobalt blue examples would have to be classed as rare. In fact, I'd be surprised to learn of more than a dozen or two known! Rarer still are the amethyst Weeping Cherry bowls. I only know of four or five examples. In the rush to find examples of the highly promoted rarities, we often overlook a handful of patterns that truly are rare, and I believe that Weeping Cherry is a case in point.

Weeping Cherry dome-footed bowl in marigold. This pattern is not easily found and is terribly underrated in any color.

Shapes & Colors Known	
Bowl, dome-footed	marigold, cobalt blue, amethyst

Western Daisy

This design is often found on the exterior of unusually shaped 8" – 9" dome-footed bowls. The shape is so unusual that it is a miracle that any of these bowls has survived the years at all. The edge of the bowl is turned up. The normal edge fluting is interrupted at four equally spaced points by a single fluted point standing nearly one inch higher than the rest of the edge of the bowl. The interior of the bowl is unpatterned. Equally unusual is the fact that these bowls have been found only in peach opalescent to date. They are actually quite rare, with only a relatively few examples known.

Some reference sources have listed a ruffled hat shape in this design. I have neither seen one nor have I ever spoken with anyone who has. This pattern is so similar to Triplets and Daisy Dear that I cannot help but wonder if perhaps someone, at some point, misidentified a Triplets or Daisy Dear ruffled hat shape bowl as Western Daisy. Until such time as a Western Daisy hat shape is placed in my hands, or I see a good, clear photo of one, I will hold off on listing it as a known shape.

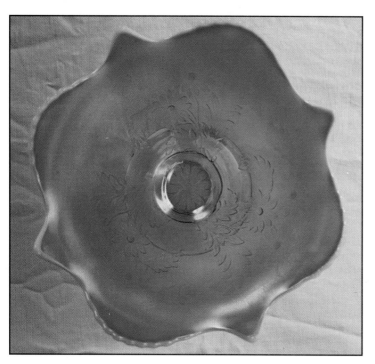

The Western Daisy square ruffled bowl in peach opalescent. This design can also be found on the exterior of some Soutache pieces.

Shapes & Colors Known

Bowl, dome-footed   peach opalescent

Wide Rib & Pinched Rib

There are so many rib patterned vases in carnival glass that you could get dizzy trying to sort them all out! Just about every major carnival glass manufacturer produced a version of this design. It must have been extremely popular with the consumers of the era. Dugan's version of Wide Rib had the longest production run of them all. It first appeared in 1909; production continued through the Diamond years with examples still appearing in the wholesale catalogs as late as 1931. No wonder there are so many of them still around!

Nearly identical versions of this vase were produced by Northwood, Westmoreland and Dugan. So, how do you tell them apart? Actually, it's fairly easy. The Northwood version has a raised ridge along the top and the wide ribs end just shy of this. The ribs go all the way up on the Dugan version, ending in a slightly ball-shaped bulge at

The Wide Rib squat vase in peach opalescent.

the very top. On the Westmoreland version, called Corinth, the ribs are slightly wider and more bulging toward the base.

Dugan's Wide Rib vases are found in heights varying from a 4" – 5" squat version to a tall, 14" size. They are known in a fairly wide variety of colors. Marigold and peach opalescent are the most available, followed by amethyst and white. Much harder to find are the examples in cobalt blue, green, aqua, and vaseline with marigold overlay, but all of them do exist.

A scarce spittoon-shaped vase fashioned from the same mold is also known and is commonly called Pinched Rib. It stands roughly 5" tall. It has a pinched neck with the very top of the vase flattened out to form the spittoon shape. It has been reported only in peach opalescent, to date. Some have labeled these as whimsies, but I have seen far too many of them over the years to agree with that designation.

Collectors call this version of the Wide Rib vase Pinched Rib for obvious reasons.

Shapes & Colors Known

Vase, 4" – 14"	marigold, amethyst, peach opalescent, cobalt blue, green, aqua, vaseline w/marigold overlay
Vase, spittoon shape	peach opalescent

Windflower

Windflower made its debut in the spring 1915 Butler Brothers wholesale catalog as part of Butler's Etruscan iridescent novelty assortment. At least one item in this pattern is known in ice green. From this we know that the design was still in production in 1921 when Diamond first introduced its pastel green iridescent line, so Windflower had quite a long run. It must have been a popular pattern as many examples are still quite easily found.

Three carnival shapes are known. Collar-based 7½" – 9" bowls abound in marigold. They are probably one of the most frequently seen of all Diamond Glass carnival pieces. The amethyst examples are harder to find, but a little patience will prove fruitful. Cobalt blue is harder still to find, but I would still not class them as rare. Most of these bowls are ruffled, but I have seen ice cream-shaped examples as well.

The 8" – 9" flat plate is seen far less often, but the marigold examples can still be found with a little patience. The amethyst plates are much more difficult to find and I would list them as becoming scarce. Like the bowls, cobalt blue is the rarest color here.

The only other known shape is that of a large, single-handled nappy that is usually spade-shaped. Strangely, these are found in a much wider variety of colors. Marigold examples are very easily found, with

This original factory mold drawing was found at the Indiana, Pennsylvania, site 10 years after the 1931 fire that closed the plant.

151

Windflower ruffled bowl and nappy in marigold.

the amethyst nappies a little tougher, but most of the other colors range from scarce to very rare. Some very light pastel lavender examples are seldom seen, and I would definitely class the cobalt blue nappies as rare. Two other colors are known and both are very rare. A relative handful of beautiful, frosty ice green examples is known but rarely ever found. Rarest of all are the peach opalescent nappies. I have only heard of a few examples.

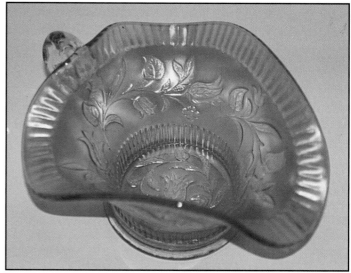

Shapes & Colors Known

Bowl, 7½" – 9"	marigold, amethyst, cobalt blue, amber
Plate, 8" – 9"	marigold, amethyst, cobalt blue
Nappy	marigold, amethyst, cobalt blue, lavender, ice green, peach opalescent

Winterlily

It's always exciting to learn of the existence of a previously undocumented carnival glass pattern and I'm pleased to be able to present this one. I had heard rumors about the existence of this piece for several years, but I was not able to offer any confirmation until now. To the best of my knowledge, it is shown here for the very first time.

The late William Heacock named this pattern way back in the mid 1970s, and he chose a most appropriate one. Dugan's Winterlily vase has previously been documented only in non-iridescent colors of blue and flint opalescent. It appears in Dugan assortments of opalescent novelties in several Butler Brothers catalogs from the 1906 – 1907 period. It seems likely that the carnival glass example presented here dates from early in Dugan's iridescent production, ca. 1909 – 1910.

Standing just 5½" tall, this most unusual vase rests on four log-like feet. The body of the vase forms the lily and is patterned with the open bud leaves swirling upward from the base. There are eight vertical rows of tiny beads running from the base to the top edge, which is round and smooth on the carnival glass version. All of the known opalescent examples feature an additional ½" tall pinched fold on the top edge.

The marigold carnival example shown here is the only one confirmed at present. As you can see, the marigold color is a light to medium tone, shading to a clear base. An amethyst or a peach opalescent example would be an exciting find, but none has yet been reported. Still, it's a very strong possibility, as both of those colors were in production during the 1909 – 1910 period. So, keep your eyes open for additional carnival examples and colors. You just might discover a real treasure!

Even the non-iridized opalescent examples of the Winterlily vase are rarely found and I suspect there were considerable molding difficulties. Removing this vase from the mold with its unusual footed base intact must have given the glassworkers nightmares! There was likely a lot of breakage during the manufacturing process and even more during use over the years. Perfect examples of the Winterlily vase, in any form, are likely few and far between.

The only known carnival example of the Winterlily vase is shown here in company with its blue and flint opalescent counterparts. Note the difference in the shaping of the top between the marigold vase and the opalescent examples.

Wishbone & Spades

One of the most popular Dugan designs, Wishbone & Spades dates from 1911 when it appeared in the wholesale catalogs in company with the Four Flowers pattern. It is not easily found in any shape, and its production run was likely a very brief one. The design abruptly vanished from the wholesale catalogs early in 1912, so it may well have been a casualty of the February, 1912 fire. The variety of shapes and colors known is quite limited.

Large, 10" – 11" chop plates, along with their smaller 6" – 7" companions, are among the most treasured and eagerly sought items. They were originally advertised as seven-piece cake sets. The large plates are found almost exclusively in amethyst and most tend to be of a deep, rich purple shade. They are usually heavily iridized with a brilliant, near electric multi-color blend. They are rarely found and always command serious attention when they are. As rare as these are, they are completely overwhelmed by the peach opalescent Wishbone & Spades chop plate. To date, only one perfect example has been confirmed! The small, 6" – 7" plates are somewhat easier to find but are still very scarce and desirable items. Here again, amethyst examples are found more often than the peach opalescent, on about a 6:1 ratio.

The Wishbone & Spades chop plate and small plate in amethyst. Both are very rare and highly treasured. The chop plate, in company with six small plates, was sold as a seven-piece cake set in a 1911 Butler Brothers wholesale catalog.

153

A **Wishbone & Spades** ruffled bowl in amethyst, also a scarce and desirable item.

Ruffled berry sets, fashioned from the same molds, are also known. While they may not command the same degree of attention paid to the plates, they are still very scarce items and often beautifully iridized. In this case, it is the peach opalescent bowls that seem to turn up most often, with the amethyst examples far more difficult to find. The large bowls have also been documented in a true, low ice cream shape and in an unusual triangular shape. The ice cream-shaped bowls are known in peach opalescent and amethyst, but both are very rare. The triangular-shaped bowl has been reported only in peach opalescent.

The only other reported shape is that of a banana bowl, fashioned from the mold used for the large bowls and plates. Only a few are known and only in peach opalescent.

Many collectors have wondered why no white Wishbone & Spades pieces have ever surfaced. This is another strong indication that the Wishbone & Spades molds may have been lost in the February, 1912 fire. Dugan's white carnival line had only been in production for a little over a month when this fire occurred. So, it seems doubtful that any white examples will ever surface. Still, we can always hope.

Shapes & Colors Known	
Chop plate, 10" – 11"	amethyst, peach opalescent
Plate, 6" – 7"	amethyst, peach opalescent
Ruffled bowl, 9" – 10"	amethyst, peach opalescent
Ruffled bowl, 5" – 6"	amethyst, peach opalescent
Ice cream bowl, 10"	amethyst, peach opalescent
Triangular bowl, 9" – 10"	peach opalescent
Banana bowl, 9" – 10"	peach opalescent

Diamond

Woodpecker

Fragments of this design, found only on a cone-shaped wall vase, were found in the Helman diggings, so there is virtually no doubt that it was made at Indiana, Pennsylvania. It is a late pattern, dating from the early to mid 1920s, so this firmly places it in the Diamond Glass Company family.

Marigold is the only color reported, often rather light in tone. However, an example with good, dark, rich marigold color will surface from time to time.

Shapes & Colors Known	
Wall vase	marigold

The Woodpecker cone-shaped wall vase.

154

Wreathed Cherry

This popular carnival design dates from the Dugan years, with production carried over well into the Diamond Glass Company era. It appeared frequently in the wholesale catalogs during the 1911 – 1913 period. A full line, including berry set, table set, water set, and a rare toothpick holder, was made. The water set was often sold as part of an assortment that included the Maple Leaf water set. The full line also appears in a 1912 Charles Broadway Rouss catalog as the "Cherry-land" dining assortment. This is one of the very few patterns that on rare occasion is found with the Dugan D-in-a-diamond trademark, primarily on the butter dish.

The berry set is unusual in that it is oval-shaped, rather than round. Because of this, some collectors refer to the master berry bowl as a banana bowl. Amethyst, oxblood, and white are the most often found colors here, with marigold examples really much harder to find. Peach opalescent examples are quite scarce. Both the master and small bowls have also been documented in cobalt blue and these are extremely rare. It is interesting to note that the berry set is the only shape in this pattern known in peach opalescent and cobalt blue. None of the other shapes has ever been found in those two colors. It is also interesting that the small bowls are so much scarcer than are the large, in any of the known colors.

The Wreathed Cherry water pitcher and tumbler in amethyst.

The table sets and water sets are known in marigold, amethyst, oxblood, and white. Marigold is the most available color, but even these are not easily found. As to the other three colors, it's a pretty close call as to which is the rarest, but I must admit that over the years I have probably seen more white examples than amethyst or oxblood. A table set or water set in any color is really a rare find.

The white Wreathed Cherry pieces are often found with a fired-on gold and red decoration on the cherries and leaves. I have also seen a marigold water set that had this.

The only other shape known is the toothpick holder,

Shapes & Colors Known

Berry set, oval	marigold, amethyst, white, peach opalescent, cobalt blue, oxblood
Table set	marigold, amethyst, white, oxblood
Water set	marigold, amethyst, white, oxblood
Toothpick holder	amethyst (old only)

"DAZZLING IRIDESCENT" WATER SET ASST.

The richest sets ever shown. Will be reliable business makers.

1C1962—Asst. shapes, heavy ½ gal. jugs, heavily embossed maple leaves and cherries, pressed tumblers. 2 golden, 4 violet iridescent finish. 6 sets in bbl., 7½ lbs. Set. **69c**

The Wreathed Cherry water set was offered in company with the Maple Leaf water set in the mid-spring 1911 Butler Brothers catalog.

Note the fired-on gold and red decoration on this white Wreathed Cherry covered sugar and spooner.

and extreme caution should be observed on this. This toothpick was reproduced by St. Clair in the late 1960s, primarily in cobalt blue. They were not trademarked, and a lot of people have been fooled by them. The iridescent quality of these reproductions is first rate and they could easily pass for old. Since then, they have also been reproduced in just about every iridescent and non-iridescent color imaginable! The only color documented for the old ones in amethyst. All others are reproductions!

It should be noted that the creamer, spooner, and water set have also been reproduced in non-iridized blue and vaseline opalescent. The new spooners often have a ruffled top. No old opalescent glass examples of this pattern have ever been found.

Dugan ✧

Wreath of Roses

Care should be taken to avoid confusing this pattern with Fenton's carnival design of the same name. In the early days of the carnival hobby it was assumed that both patterns were the same and came from the same maker. Of course, we now know that this is not the case.

Dugan/Diamond's Wreath of Roses is found on only three shapes, and the variety of colors known is also very limited. All three shapes were fashioned from the same mold. The most frequently seen of these is the small, collar-based rose bowl. It is very easily found in marigold, but the amethyst ones are really very scarce. Small, ruffled whimsey bowls are much harder to find. Often they are ruffled in a somewhat triangular configuration. They are scarce in marigold and very rarely found in amethyst. The only other reported shape is the extremely rare whimsey spittoon. Only one example in marigold has been found to date.

Dugan/Diamond's Wreath of Roses rose bowl in marigold.

Shapes & Colors Known	
Rose bowl	marigold, amethyst
Tri-shaped whimsey bowl	marigold, amethyst
Spittoon	marigold

Additional Dugan/Diamond Possibilities

In addition to all the patterns presented in this book, there are at least two others that I strongly suspect are either Dugan or Diamond creations. I have not included or illustrated them in the main body of the text because I have nothing conclusive to prove their origins as of this writing. But I do feel that both likely came from Indiana, Pennsylvania. There is some circumstantial evidence to support my theories and I present that here. Illustrations of both of these patterns will be found in Bill Edward's *Standard Encyclopedia of Carnival Glass, 5th Edition.*

Martha: You will find this pattern on page 169 of the aforementioned book. It has long been believed to be of English origin. Look at it closely and compare it to the Intaglio Daisy pattern illustrated in this book. Note the ribbed band around the top of both patterns; it appears to be identical. The intaglio stylization of the vines and leaves also appears strikingly similar. I am really convinced that Martha is a Diamond Glass Company pattern, dating from the same time frame as Intaglio Daisy, ca. 1928 – 1930. I simply have no proof … yet!

Grape & Cherry: You will find this pattern on page 120 of the aforementioned book. It has long been credited to Sowerby of England. I have always been suspicious of this attribution and the L.G. Wright Glass Company has reinforced these suspicions. Wright has reproduced this bowl in non-iridized opalescent colors. Wright owns many Dugan/Diamond molds. They are not known to have ever owned any molds from foreign manufacturers, so there is little doubt that this mold for the Grape & Cherry pattern was purchased from an American company. Here again, I strongly suspect a Diamond Glass Company origin, ca. late 1920s.

The Waterlily & Cattails Controversy

It is an established fact that both Northwood and Fenton produced a carnival glass version of the Waterlily & Cattails pattern. Northwood produced a water set and Fenton made a full line including a water set, table set, berry set, and assorted novelty items. Did Dugan or Diamond also produce a carnival glass version of this popular design? Reportedly, small fragments of marigold Waterlily & Cattails tumblers were unearthed at the Indiana, Pennsylvania, site. At least, the late William Heacock identified them as such. But were they really Waterlily & Cattails? Maybe … or maybe not!

There are four known tumbler variations in this pattern. The Northwood tumblers are signed with the N-in-a-circle trademark, so we can eliminate those from Dugan/Diamond contention straight away. The other three versions differ primarily in the positioning of the cattails. They are as follows:

Version 1: The cattails are apart, angled at approximately 45 degrees.

Version 2: The cattails are just slightly apart with one overlapping the other, positioned just slightly above it.

Version 3: The cattails meet, almost touching tip to tip.

A check of early Fenton factory catalog reprints reveals that pieces of Waterlily & Cattails showing the characteristics of both versions one and two are definitely Fenton products. This is not surprising as more than one tumbler mold for the production of water sets is necessary in order to meet demand. I have owned Fenton Waterlily & Cattails water sets in both carnival and opalescent colors that contained both version one and two tumblers.

Now, what about version three? Could this be a Dugan or Diamond product? Possibly, but there's a problem with that, at least in my mind. You see, I have also owned Fenton Waterlily & Cattails water sets that contained all three versions of the tumbler! I will concede that it is always possible that someone could have pieced together these sets prior to my purchase of them and unknowingly included some version three tumblers in the process. If so, it is entirely possible that the version three tumbler could be a Dugan or Diamond product. But there is another possibility that nags at me and I feel it is important to make note of it, if for no other reason than food for thought.

The Waterlily & Cattails tumbler fragments from the Indiana, Pennsylvania, diggings were described by William Heacock as being of a light, transparent marigold color and having far less detail in the molding than the Fenton version. At the time that he examined these fragments, Mr. Heacock was, by his own admission, very much a novice when it came to carnival research. I cannot help but wonder if he may have unintentionally misidentified these shards! You see, the Fisherman's mug, a confirmed Dugan/Diamond pattern, also contains both a waterlily and cattails in the design, and they are positioned in a very similar fashion. The marigold examples are often a light, transparent color and there is far less detail in the Waterlily & Cattails than there is on the Fenton tumblers! Could these Waterlily & Cattails fragments have actually been shards of a marigold Fisherman's mug? This possibility simply cannot be discounted.

No Dugan or Diamond assortments in any of the currently known wholesale catalogs feature any form of the Waterlily & Cattails pattern. Likewise, no known factory advertising from either firm shows this pattern and there appears to be no mention of it in any of the fragmentary, surviving factory records. So, did Dugan or Diamond make a version of the Waterlily & Cattails pattern? The jury is still out on this one. Perhaps future research will one day provide something more conclusive, but until such time all we can say with any certainty is … maybe!

Carnival Glass Collectors' Clubs

There are probably more clubs and associations devoted to carnival glass collecting than there are for just about any other form of collectible glassware. They offer many benefits for both the beginner and the more advanced collector. In addition to regular meetings, many publish bulletins on a monthly, bi-monthly, or quarterly basis. These bulletins contain not only club news, but also educational articles, glass for sale, auction reports, and calendars of carnival glass-related events. Club members also have access to purchasing many reference books and videos not generally available elsewhere. Many hold annual conventions. Lifelong friendships are made through these clubs. Let's face it. Collecting is a lot more fun when you can share experiences. No matter where you live, there is a club somewhere near you. You will never regret joining one!

Further information can be obtained by writing to the addresses given here.

Carnival Glass Clubs in the United States

Air Capital Carnival Glass Club
Donald Kime, Secretary
15201 E. 47th S.
Derby, KS 67037

American Carnival Glass Assoc.
Dolores Wagner, Secretary
5951 Fredricksburg Rd., Rt. 4
Wooster, OH 44691

Dakota Territory Carnival Glass Club
Kathy Evans, Secretary
1400 Edgewater Dr., Apt. #207
Pierre, SD 57501

Gateway Carnival Glass Club
Karen Skinner, Treasurer
108 Riverwoods Cove
East Alton, IL 62024

Great Lakes Carnival Glass Club
Maxine Burkhardt, Secretary
612 White Pine Blvd.
Lansing, MI 48917

Heart of America Carnival Glass Association (HOAC-GA)
Ed Kramer, Secretary
4305 W. 78th St.
Prairie Village, KS 66208

Hoosier Carnival Glass Assoc.
Eunice E. Booker, Secretary
944 W. Pine St.
Griffith, IN 46319

International Carnival Glass
   Assoc. (ICGA)
Lee Markley, Secretary
Box 306
Mentone, IN 46539

Keystone Carnival Glass Club
Mary Sharp, Secretary
719 W. Brubaker-Valley Rd.
Lititz, PA 17543

Lincoln-Land Carnival Glass
   Club
Ellen Hemm, Secretary
N. 951. Hwy. 27
Conrath, WI 54731

New England Carnival Glass
   Assoc.
Lynn & Harold March,
   Sec./Treas.
10 Seminole Rd.
Canton, MA 02021

Northern California Carnival
   Glass Club
June McCarter, Treasurer
1205 Clinton Dr.
Modesto, CA 95355

Pacific Northwest Carnival
   Glass Club
Bev Osbon, Secretary
34931 S E Dodge Park Blvd.
Gresham, OR 97080

San Diego County Carnival
   Glass Club
Diane Fry, Secretary
5395 Middleton Rd.
San Diego, CA 92109-1525

San Joaquin Valley Carnival
   Glass Club
Joan Steskal, Treasurer
PO Box 389
Ahwahnee, CA 93601

Southern California Carnival
   Glass Club
Betty Robertson, Treasurer
1430 Kendall Ave.
Camarillo, CA 93010-3606

Sunshine State Carnival Glass
   Assoc.
Jackie Poucher, Secretary
9087 Baywood Park Dr.
Seminole, FL 33777

Tampa Bay Carnival Glass
   Club
Naomi Calkins, President
120 Woodlant Court
Safety Harbor, FL 34695

Texas Carnival Glass Club
Matzi Thrasher, Treasurer
611 W. Main St.
Tomball, TX 77375

Western New York Carnival
   Glass Club
Linda Matties, Secretary
1246 Flynn Rd.
Rochester, NY 14612

Carnival Glass Clubs outside the United States

Australian Carnival Enthusi-
   asts Assoc., Inc.
M. Dickinson, Secretary
RSD Fryerstown, Victoria
Australia 3451

Canadian Carnival Glass Assoc.
Carol Cressman, Secretary
107 Montcalm Dr.
Ketchener, Ontario N2B 2R4
   Canada

Carnival Companions
Nigel Gamble, Secretary
24 Crabtree Ave.
London, Ontario N6G 8EJ
   Canada

L'Association Du Verre Car-
   naval Du Quebec
J. Leo Richer, Secretary
3250 Leon Brisebois
Ile Bizard, Quebec H9C 1T6
   Canada

The Carnival Glass Society
   (UK) Ltd.
Vernon Kelvin, Secretary
162 Green Lane
Edgware, Middx, HA8 8EJ
   England

Bibliography

Burns, Carl O. *The Collector's Guide To Northwood's Carnival Glass.* L. W. Books, 1994.

Burns Auction Service. "Carnival Glass Auction Brochures," 1981 – 1997.

Butler Brothers Wholesale Catalogs, "Our Drummer." Various issues, 1900 – 1931.

Carnival Glass Pattern Notebook; published by The Heart of American Carnival Glass Association.

Charles Broadway Rouss Wholesale Catalogs. Various issues, 1912 – 1919.

Edwards, Bill. *The Standard Encyclopedia Of Carnival Glass, 5th Edition.* Collector Books, 1996.

G. Sommers & Co. Wholesale Catalogs. Various issues, 1916 – 1929.

Hartung, Marion. *Carnival Glass Pattern Books, Volumes 1 – 10.* 1968 – 1973 (Now published by The Heart of America Carnival Glass Association).

Heacock, William. *Encyclopedia of Victorian Colored Pattern Glass, Volumes 1 – 7.* Antique Publications, 1974 – 1986.

Heacock, William. *Pattern Glass Preview, Volumes 1 – 6.* Peacock Publications & Antique Publications, 1980.

Heacock, William. *The Glass Collector, Volumes 1 – 6.* Antique Publications, 1982 – 1985.

Heacock, William. *Collecting Glass, Volumes 1 – 3.* Antique Publications, 1985 – 1986.

Heacock, William; Measell, James; Wiggins, Berry. *Harry Northwood — The Early Years 1881 – 1900.* Antique Publications, 1990.

Heacock, William; Measell, James; Wiggins, Berry. *Harry Northwood — The Wheeling Years 1901 – 1925.* Antique Publications 1991.

Heacock, William; Measell, James; Wiggins, Berry. *Dugan/Diamond — The Story of Indiana, Pennsylvania, Glass.* Antique Publications, 1993.

Heart of America Carnival Glass Association Bulletins. Various issues, 1971 – 1997.

Jennings, Steve. *"A Catalog Reprint of Dugan Glass Company and H. Northwood Co., Glass Manufacturers."* 1988.

Lincoln-Land Carnival Glass Club Bulletins. Various issues, 1988 – 1997.

Madeley, John, and Dave Shetlar. *American Iridescent Stretch Glass.* Collector Books, 1998

Measell, James; Roetteis, W.C. *The L.G. Wright Glass Company.* Antique Publications, 1997.

Moore, Donald E. *The Complete Guide To Carnival Glass Rarities.* Published by Donald E. Moore.

Mordini, Tom & Sharon. "Carnival Glass Auction Price Reports." 1984 – 1996.

Owens, Richard E. *Carnival Glass Tumblers.* Published by Richard Owens, 1973.

Pottery and Glass Salesman. Various issues, 1918 – 1941.

San Diego Carnival Glass Club Bulletins. Various issues, 1990 – 1997.

Wholesale Catalogs Selling Carnival Glass. Published by The San Diego Carnival Glass Club and The Southern California Carnival Glass Club, 1994.

No values are ever written in stone. Nowhere else is this more apparent than in the field of carnival glass collecting. There are more factors to be considered here than for any other type of collectible glassware. Not only must we consider condition, pattern, color, and shape, but also quality of iridescence, sharpness and clarity of the mold strike, and the symmetry of any hand shaping. In addition, we must also consider geographic location, for values vary from one area to another. Patterns and shapes easily found in Pennsylvania, for example, might be considered scarce by collectors in Oregon, for they may be rarely found there. Prices also tend to be much higher at carnival glass specialty auctions than those that can be realized outside the auction circuit on the open market. Carnival glass specialty auctions are the top of the food chain, so to speak. If you have but two bidders at such an auction, both of whom have made up their minds that they simply have to have a piece, regardless of cost, then a very unrealistic price is often the result. So, carnival glass auction prices have been factored in here, but with a "healthy dose of salt."

The values listed in this guide represent an average price range of the actual prices paid at auctions, antique shows, antique shops, and private sales by collectors. These values are for pieces in absolutely perfect condition, with top quality iridescence, molding, and shaping. Pieces of only average or below iridescent quality, below average molding clarity, or misshapen pieces will bring nowhere near these prices. Damaged pieces will usually sell for only a fraction of the values listed in this guide.

The author and the publisher assume no responsibility for any transactions made as a result of using this guide.

The colors known by collectors as purple and amethyst were intended to be the same color at the time of manufacture. They are listed together under the price column AME. Oxblood was Dugan's version of the color known as black amethyst, which he marketed under the name African Iridescent; this has been given a separate column. Because of the large quantity of this color produced by Dugan, the values for it are generally not much higher than those listed for amethyst.

The following abbreviations have been used in the column "Others:"

AME/OP – amethyst opalescent
AQ – aqua
AQ/M – aqua w/marigold overlay
BO – cobalt blue opalescent
CEL – celeste blue
DEC/PO – decorated peach opalescent
HORE – horehound
IB – ice blue
IG – ice green
IRID – iridescent
LAV – lavender
LGO – lime green opalescent
LIME/MAR – lime green w/marigold overlay
LT. B/M – light blue w/marigold overlay
LT. G/M – light green w/marigold overlay
MMG – marigold on milk glass
PINK/M – pink w/marigold overlay
PO/CAMPHOR – peach opalescent w/camphor overlay
SAPH – sapphire blue
VAS – vaseline
VAS/OP – vaseline opalescent

	MARI	AME	OX-BLOOD	PEACH OPAL	WHITE	BLUE	GREEN	OTHERS
ADAM'S RIB								
Candlesticks, pressed	90							120 IG 120 CEL
Candlesticks, blown	90							135 CEL
Console, ped. ftd.								175 CEL 450 MMG
Compote								100 IG 100 CEL
Covered candy jar								100 IG
Fan vase	55							75 IG 85 CEL
Lemonade pitcher								325 IG 500 CEL
Mug								80 IG 100 VAS
Open sugar, 2-hdld.								45 IG
Vase, 9¾"								200 CEL
AMARYLLIS								
Compote, deep round	475							
Compote, ruffled	300	400			500	600		
Compote, triangular	325	425			525			
Whimsey plate	400	475			450			
APPLE BLOSSOM								
Bowl, 6" – 7"	25	55		90	75	100	125	
Rose bowl	100							
APPLE BLOSSOM TWIGS								
Banana bowl		475		350				
Bowl, 8" – 9", fluted edge	85	255		185	135	250		300 LAV 425 SMOKE
Bowl, 8" – 9", smooth edge		195		250				
Plate, 9", fluted edge	195	350		375	250	325		3,000 IB 375 LAV
Plate, 9", smooth edge		395		400				
BAND								
Basket	75							
Hat shape	20	35						
BEADED BASKET								
Basket, 2-hdld.	40	175			150	200		450 AQ 235 LIME 175 PINK/M
BEADED PANELS								
Compote	75	250		125		325		
BEADED SHELL								
Berry bowl, lg.	90	135						
Berry bowl, sm.	25	35						
Butter dish	175	250						
Covered sugar	100	150						
Creamer or spooner	65	95						
Mug	140	95			650	175		165 LAV
Water pitcher	400	700						
Tumbler	50	80				165		135 LAV
Whimsey mug, flared					800			

	MARI	AME	OX-BLOOD	PEACH OPAL	WHITE	BLUE	GREEN	OTHERS
BEAUTY BUD								
Bud vase, 7" – 9"	15							
BELLS & BEADS								
Bowl, 7", ruffled	45	175	225	100			400	
Bowl, 7", triangular		175		100				
Card tray		200		145				
Compote	100	175						
Nappy, hdld.	75	135	165	120				
Plate 7" – 8", round		275		225				
Plate, 7" – 8", triangular		350		300				
BIG BASKETWEAVE								
Basket, lg.	100	175						
Basket, sm.	25	65						
Vase, squat, 5" – 6"	150	225	275	375	160			
Vase, swung, 8" – 14"	75	125	200	300	130	375		500 CEL 575 SAPH 600 IB 475 LAV 275 HORE
BLOSSOMS & BAND								
Car vase	45							
BORDER PLANTS								
Bowl, 8" – 9", dome-ftd.	200	500	600	275				
Bowl, 8" – 9", handgrip		350		300				
Plate, 9", handgrip		550		375				
Rose bowl		750		500				
BROOKLYN BRIDGE								
Bowl, 8" – 9", lettered	300							400 PINK/M
Bowl, 8" – 9", unlettered	1,200							
BUTTERFLY & TULIP								
Bowl, round deep	375	1,850						
Bowl, square ruffled	750	2,350						
CAROLINE								
Banana bowl				100				
Bowl, 8" – 9"	45			70				150 DEC/PO
Handled basket				350				575 LAV/OPAL
Plate, handgrip				100				
CHERRY, DUGAN'S:								
Collar-Based Version								
Bowl, 8" – 10", ruffled	110	325	375	275	500			
Bowl, 5" – 6", ruffled	25	70	65	45	100			
Bowl, 8" – 9", round deep		350		300				
Bowl, 5", round deep		50		50				
Bowl, 9", ice cream		475		375				
Plate, 6" – 7" crimped		250	275	200				

	MARI	AME	OX-BLOOD	PEACH OPAL	WHITE	BLUE	GREEN	OTHERS
Ftd. Version, Plain Int.								
Bowl, 8" – 9"	45	90		100				225 DEC/PO
Ftd. Version, Patt. Int.								
Bowl, 8" – 9"	65	335	275	165	500	550		850 VAS/M
Banana bowl shape		275	300	225				
CHRISTMAS COMPOTE								
Large compote	3,250	4,850						
CIRCLE SCROLL								
Berry bowl, lg.	100	150						
Berry bowl, sm.	25	30						
Butter dish	325	450						
Covered sugar	125	175						
Creamer or spooner	80	125						
Hat shape, ruffled	75	125						
Hat shape, JIP	125	175						
Jelly compote		300						
Vase, swung, 7" – 9"	100	300						
Water pitcher	1,500	2,500						
Tumbler	175	500						
COIN SPOT								
Compote	45	150		90		325		750 CEL 400 IG
Goblet								600 IG
COMPASS								
Exterior pattern only								
CONSTELLATION								
Compote	150	375		475	125			400 WHITE/M. STEM
								500 LAV
CORN VASE								
Husk-handled vase	6,500							
COSMOS VARIANT								
Bowl, 9" – 10", ruffled	30	60			100			225 VAS
Bowl, 9" – 10", ice cream	40	75			125			
Chop plate, 10" – 11"	165	245			375			
DAHLIA								
Berry bowl, lg.	100	150			200			
Berry bowl, sm.	25	40			80			
Butter dish	185	275			350			
Covered sugar	100	135			165			
Creamer or spooner	75	100			125			
Water pitcher	425	675			850			
Tumbler	75	135			175			

	MARI	AME	OX-BLOOD	PEACH OPAL	WHITE	BLUE	GREEN	OTHERS
DAISY DEAR								
Bowl, 7" – 8"	30	45		65	75			
Bowl, 8", JIP shape	200							
DAISY & PLUME								
Candy dish, ftd.	75	150		225				300 LIME/M
Ftd. bowl, cherry int.		500						
DAISY WEB								
Basket, hdld.	300	450						
Hat shape, crimped	275	380			775			
Hat shape, JIP		600						
DOGWOOD SPRAYS								
Bowl, 8" – 9", dome-ftd.	125	145	175	125		225		350 BLUE OPAL 200 MMG
Compote, dome-ftd.		155		135				
DOUBLE STEMMED ROSE								
Bowl, 8" – 9", dome-ftd.	45	75	175	150	110	125	500	425 AQ 550 CEL 525 OLIVE 2,000 IG 750 BLUE OPAL 185 LAV
Plate, 9", dome-ftd	200	375		235	175			
ELKS NAPPY								
Nappy, spade or ruffled		7,500						
FAN								
Breakfast creamer		175		145				
Open sugar		100		65				
FANCIFUL								
Bowl, 8" – 9", ruffled	95	250	325	235	125	300		475 LAV
Bowl, 8" – 9", ice cream	100	260	350	175	125			
Bowl, 8" – 9", 3-in-1 edge	75	275		200	165	375		450 LAV
Plate, 9"	200	450	550	400	250	575	2,000	
FARMYARD								
Bowl, 10" – 11", ruffled		5,500		15,000+				
Bowl, 10" – 11", square		6,500						
Bowl, 10" – 11", 3-in-1 edge		7,000					10,000+	
Plate, 12"		25,000+						
FEATHER SCROLL								
Covered sugar	350							
Tumbler	50							
FILIGREE								
Vase		6,000						

	MARI	AME	OX-BLOOD	PEACH OPAL	WHITE	BLUE	GREEN	OTHERS
FISHERMAN'S MUG								
Mug	275	135		1,100		1,500		
FISHNET EPERGNE								
Single lily epergne		275		250				
FISHSCALE & BEADS								
Bowl, 5" – 7", ruffled	25	35	65	125	90	175		
Bowl, 5" – 7", triangular	45	75		150				
Bride's bowl w/holder				275				
Card tray	55	125		85	135			
Plate, 6½" – 7"	75	250		150	145			
FIVE HEARTS								
Bowl, 8" – 9", dome-ftd.	150	255		275				
Rose bowl, dome-ftd.	900							
Whimsey flared bowl	500							
FLORAL & GRAPE								
Water pitcher	150	225			275	325		600 LIME
Tumbler	18	40			50	65		
Hat shape, ruffled	20	45						
Hat shape, JIP	75							
FLORAL & WHEAT								
Bon bon, stemmed	45	100		75	150	225		
FLOWERS & BEADS								
Bowl, 6" – 7"	35	55	65	80				
Plate, 7" – 8", hexagonal	80	100	120	150				
FLOWERS & FRAMES								
Bowl, 8" – 9", ruffled		300	350	200				
Bowl, 8" – 9", triangular		425	275	175				
Compote, dome ftd.		225	250	150				
FLOWERS & SPADES								
Bowl, 10", ruffled		275		250				
Bowl, 5" – 6", ruffled		65		50				
Bowl, 10", ice cream		425						
FLUTED SCROLLS								
Rose bowl, ftd.	3,000	3,500						
FOLDING FAN								
Compote	55	200		95				
FORMAL								
Hatpin holder (bud vase)	800	950						
Vase, JIP	475	900						
Vase, ruffled top	450	750						

	MARI	AME	OX-BLOOD	PEACH OPAL	WHITE	BLUE	GREEN	OTHERS
FOUR FLOWERS								
Banana bowl, 8" – 9"		450		375				
Bowl, 9" – 10", ruffled	80	400		200		275	600	450 AMB 575 VAS
Bowl, 5" – 6", ruffled		50		45				
Bowl, 9" – 10", ice cream		700		575				
Bowl, 8" – 9", triangular				245				
Plate, 10"	400	3,000		450				
Plate, 6½"		400		175				
Rose bowl	675	1,000						
GARDEN PATH & VARIANT								
Bowl, 8" – 9", ruffled	85	700		425	475			
Bowl, 8" – 9", round, deep	70	475		300	325			
Bowl, 10", ice cream	475	1,350		1,000	1,100			
Bowl, 6" – 7"	45	125		170	90			
Compote	350	525			750			
Chop plate, 11"	5,000	5,500		8,500				
Plate, 6" – 7"	500	800		650	450			
Rose bowl	175							
GEORGIA BELLE								
Exterior pattern only								
GOD & HOME								
Water pitcher						1,200		
Tumbler						225		
GOLDEN GRAPE								
Bowl, 6" – 7"	35	50						
Rose bowl	85							
GOLDEN HARVEST								
Wine decanter & stopper	100	375						
Stemmed wine	20	40						
GRAPE ARBOR								
Bowl, large ftd.	150	220		1,400		275		
GRAPE DELIGHT								
Nut bowl, 6 ftd.	55	145			110	95		400 HORE 235 LAV
Rose bowl, 6 ftd.	100	175			85	110		325 HORE 275 LAV
GRAPEVINE LATTICE								
Bowl, 6" – 7", ruffled	30	55			50			
Hat, ruffled	65	90						
Hat, JIP		135						
Plate, 7"	125	175		475	150			300 LAV
Water pitcher, tankard	275	750			1,100	1,350		
Tumbler	60	80			185	200		110 SMOKE BLUE

	MARI	AME	OX-BLOOD	PEACH OPAL	WHITE	BLUE	GREEN	OTHERS
HARVEST FLOWER								
Water pitcher	3,000							
Tumbler	175	1200						125 LIME
HEAVY GRAPE, DUGAN'S								
Bowl, 10" – 11", ruffled	1,000	700		425				
Bowl, 10" – 11", ice cream		1,200						
Bowl, 5" – 6", ruffled	150	125		200				
HEAVY IRIS								
Tankard pitcher, ruffled	375	1,100		1,000	1,200			
Tankard pitcher, straight					1,350			
Tumbler	65	100			200			
Hat shape, JIP	400				500			
HEAVY WEB								
Bowl, lg. ruffled				600				
Bowl, lg. banana shape				1,000				
Bowl, lg. square				1,750				
Chop plate				3,500				
HERON								
Mug	3,000	325						
HOLLY & BERRY								
Bowl, 6" – 7½"	65	120	140	95				
Nappy, hdld.	80	135	155	95		275		
HOLLY & POINSETTIA								
Compote, dome-ftd.	500							
HONEYCOMB								
Bowl, 5" – 7"	30	55	65	50				
Plate, 7", crimped	65	125	140	90				
Rose bowl	550			265				
HYACINTH								
Vase				225				
INTAGLIO DAISY								
Bowl, round deep	75	325						
Bowl, flared	75							
Rose bowl, angular	150							
Rose bowl, round	175							
JEWELLED HEART								
Lg. berry (smooth rays)	80	240	250	150	275			
Sm. berry (smooth rays)	20	40	45	35	50			
Plate, 6" – 7" (smooth rays)		135	150	140				
Water pitcher	550							
Tumbler	80				650			

168

	MARI	AME	OX-BLOOD	PEACH OPAL	WHITE	BLUE	GREEN	OTHERS
Whimsey basket				700				
KEYHOLE								
Exterior pattern only								
LATTICE & DAISY								
Berry bowl, lg.	100							
Berry bowl, sm.	45				125			
Water pitcher	185	1,200				1,700		
Tumbler	30	120			325	175		
Whimsey vase		200						
LATTICE & POINTS								
(VINING TWIGS)								
Bowl, 6" – 7"	40	75			100			65 CLAMBROTH
Hat shape	45	135		225	175			
Plate, 7" – 8"					750			
Vase, 7" – 9"	55	120		200	155	195		
Shot glass (Dugan?)	250							
LATTICE HEARTS								
Bowl, 6" – 7½"		185						
Plate/salver, 7" – 8"		250						
LEAF RAYS								
Nappy, ruffled	35	110		75				
Nappy, spade shape	25	65		45	50	150		
LINED LATTICE								
Vase, 5" – 7", squat	150	265	295	300	175	475		325 HORE
Vase, 8" – 14", swung	95	185	225	250	110	400		200 HORE
LONG LEAF								
Exterior pattern only								
MALAGA								
Bowl, 8" – 9"	55	85						
Chop plate, 10"	500							
Rose bowl	100	325						
MANY FRUITS								
Punch bowl & base	375	625	750		1,850	2,800		
Punch cup	30	40	50		75	125		
MANY RIBS								
Hat shape	25	35		45				
Vase, 5" – 7"	25	45	50	55	75			300 PO/CAMPHOR
Vase, JIP shape	75	135	150	125		200		
MAPLE LEAF								
Large berry, ped.-ftd.	60	100	110			145		
Small berry, ped.-ftd.	20	30	35			45	75	

	MARI	AME	OX-BLOOD	PEACH OPAL	WHITE	BLUE	GREEN	OTHERS
Butter dish	135	175	200			165		
Covered sugar	75	100	110			75		
Creamer or spooner	50	65	75			60		
Water pitcher	165	275	285			300		
Tumbler	35	45	50			60		
MARY ANN								
Vase, 2-hdld.	120	225						
Vase, 3-hdld.	800							
NAUTILUS								
Candy dish		265	300	175				
Giant compote	700							
Vase, 8" – 9"	125	275						
PANELLED TREETRUNK								
Vase, 6" – 9"	200	300		375			450	
PEACH & PEAR								
Banana bowl, lg. oval	100	185						
PEACOCK AT THE FOUNTAIN								
Water pitcher	225	400				325		
Tumbler	35	50				45		
PEACOCK TAIL								
Maple Leaf interior								
PERSIAN GARDEN								
Bowl, 9" – 11", ruffled	250	375		335	225		1,500	
Bowl, 5" – 6", ruffled	45	65		75	50			
Bowl, 10" – 11", ice cream	375	750		450	200			
Bowl, 5" – 6", ice cream	40	85		60	45			
Chop plate, 11" – 12"		11,000		7,500	3,000			
Fruit bowl & base	300	750			425			850 LAV
Plate, 6" – 7", basket. ext	125	450		300	175	850		
Plate, 6" – 7", plain ext.					165			
Plate, 6" – 7", Pool of Pearl ext.					135			
Punch bowl & base (not ruffled)	675	1,000						
PETAL & FAN								
Bowl, 10" – 11", ruffled	125	375		185	275			
Bowl, 8" – 9", ruffled	100	275		165	250			
Bowl, 5" – 6", ruffled	35	75		55	65			
Plate, 6" – 7", crimped		475		225				
Banana dish whimsey				200				
PINCHED SWIRL								
Rose bowl	125			175				

	MARI	AME	OX-BLOOD	PEACH OPAL	WHITE	BLUE	GREEN	OTHERS
Spittoon whimsey	150			225				
Vase, 5" – 6"	60			85				
PONY								
Bowl, 8" – 9", ruffled	90	165						1,200 IG 325 LAV 1,100 AQUA
Bowl, 8" – 9", ice cream	135	225						950 IG
Plate, 9"	500	750						
PULLED LOOP								
Vase, 5" – 7", squat	100	175		225	500			750 AME/OPAL
Vase, 8" – 14", swung	30	90		60	100	250	350	700 CEL 325 AQUA
PUZZLE								
See Floral & Wheat								
QUESTION MARKS								
Bon bon, stemmed	30	55	65	50	55	275		500 IG 200 SMOKE/LAV
Compote	45	75		145	110			
Plate, stemmed	225	275			225			
QUILL								
Water pitcher	1,250	3,000						
Tumbler	225	375						
RAINBOW LUSTRE								
Candlesticks, pair	50				80			100 CEL 90 IG 125 PINK
RAINDROPS								
Bowl, 8" – 9", ruffled		175	200	85				
Banana bowl, 9"		425	500	175				
Compote, dome-ftd.		150	175	100				
RAMBLER ROSE								
Water pitcher	225	600				375		
Tumbler	35	100				55		
ROUND UP								
Bowl, 8" – 9", ruffled	135	365	350	265	175	285		
Bowl, 8" – 9", 3-in-1 edge	125	195	200	325	200			
Bowl, 8" – 9", ice cream	140	550	700	200	140			600 LAV
Plate, 9"	300	575	750	825	225	425		800 DEC/PO
ROYAL LUSTRE								
Candlesticks, pair	100					150		300 RED 175 CEL 150 IG
Console bowl	45					80		200 RED 90 CEL 75 IG

	MARI	AME	OX-BLOOD	PEACH OPAL	WHITE	BLUE	GREEN	OTHERS
RUFFLED RIB								
Rose bowl	125							
Spittoon whimsey	250							
Vase	75							
SEAGULL								
Bowl	150							
SINGLE FLOWER								
Bowl, 7½" – 8½"	40	175		55				100 DEC/PO
Handled basket				300				
SINGLE FLOWER FRAMED								
Bowl, 7" – 8½"				50				100 DEC/PO
Handgrip plate				75				125 DEC/PO
Plate, 7" – 8½", crimped				90				110 DEC/PO
SIX PETALS								
Bowl, 7" – 8", ruffled	50	125	200	95	60			
Bowl, 7" – 8", triangular		225	250	100				
SKI-STAR								
Bowl, 10" – 11", ruffled	100	375		125				
Bowl, 5" – 6", ruffled	40	90		50				
Bowl, 5" – 6", crimped edge		150		70				
Bowl, 5" – 6", triangular		200		95				
Bowl, 8" – 9", dome-ftd.		235		145				
Banana bowl, dome-ftd.		300		185				
Handgrip bowl, dome-ftd.		325		200				
Handgrip plate, dome-ftd.		450		300				
Plate, 6", crimped				170				
Basket, lg. hdld.				725				
Basket, sm. hdld.				275				
Rose bowl, dome-ftd.				600				
SMOOTH RAYS (Plain Ext.)								
Bowl, 6" – 7½"	30	45	50	65	100			
Plate, 7" – 8"	50	75	85	100	125			
SOUTACHE								
Bowl, 8" – 9", dome-ftd.				135				
Plate, 9" dome-ftd.				275				
SPIRALEX								
Vase, 8" – 14", swung	35	75		85	100	175		
S REPEAT								
Covered sugar		250						
Punch bowl & base		6,500						500 IRID CRYSTAL
Punch cup		60						
Toothpick holder		200						

	MARI	AME	OX-BLOOD	PEACH OPAL	WHITE	BLUE	GREEN	OTHERS
Tumbler	300							
Whimsey creamer		75						
STAR FISH								
Bon bon, 2-hdld.	75	150		100				
Compote	95	225		135				
STIPPLED ESTATE								
Vase, 3" – 4"	125			175			150	
STIPPLED FLOWER								
Bowl, 7" – 8", ruffled				50				
Bowl, 7" – 8", square				75				
Bowl, 7" – 8", triangular				75				
STIPPLED PETALS								
Bowl, 8" – 9", dome-ftd.	75	135	150	100				150 DEC/PO
Banana bowl, dome-ftd		275		175				
Compote, dome-ftd.		165		125				
Handled basket				375				
STIPPLED RAMBLER ROSE								
Nut bowl, ftd.	60					100		
STORK IN THE RUSHES								
Berry bowl, lg.	50	90						
Berry bowl, sm.	15	25						
Butter dish	165	300						
Covered sugar	65	100						
Creamer or spooner	50	75						
Handled basket	125							
Hat shape	50	90						
Mug	40	150				1,250		750 AQUA 350 LAV 225 LT B/M
Punch bowl & base	200	600						
Punch cup	25	45						
Ruffled fruit bowl, 2 pc.	375							
Water pitcher, beaded	195	625				550		
Water pitcher, lattice	265					850		
Tumbler, beaded	30	65				40		
Tumbler, lattice	45	100				65		
STRAWBERRY EPERGNE								
Single lily epergne		800						
SUMMER DAYS								
Vase/punch base	60	100						
SWAN								
Swan novelty	285	225		250				45 CEL

	MARI	AME	OX-BLOOD	PEACH OPAL	WHITE	BLUE	GREEN	OTHERS
TARGET								
Vase, 5" – 7", squat	50	90	100	125	75	225		
Vase, 8" – 14", swung	30	75	125	100	100	165		350 VAS 400 LGO 475 VAS/OPAL
THREE FRUITS								
Plate, 9", 12-sided	135	225				200	265	
TINY TWIGS								
Vase, ruffled or crimped	1,000	800						
Vase, JIP shape	1,500	1,100						
TREE OF LIFE (SODA GOLD)								
Basket, sm.	30	75						
TRIPLETS								
Bowl, 7", ruffled	25	35		45				
Hat shape	20	30		50				
TWIG BUD VASE								
Vase, 7" – 9"	25	140						
VICTORIAN								
Bowl, 10" – 12", ruffled		500		2,000				
Bowl, 10" – 11", ice cream		1,200						
VINEYARD								
Water pitcher	150	600		1,100				
Tumbler	35	75						
VINTAGE BANDED								
Mug	35	1,000						250 SMOKE 175 LT G/M
Water pitcher	350	750						
Tumbler	475							
VINTAGE PERFUME								
Perfume bottle	475	575						
VINTAGE POWDER JAR								
Covered powder jar	75	195			325	265		
VINTAGE VARIANT								
Bowl, 8" – 9", dome-ftd.	75	165				220	275	1,000 CEL
Bowl, 8" – 9", collar base	100	200						
Plate, 9", dome-ftd.	400	700						
WEEPING CHERRY								
Bowl, 8" – 9", dome-ftd.	125	200				275		

	MARI	AME	OX-BLOOD	PEACH OPAL	WHITE	BLUE	GREEN	OTHERS
WESTERN DAISY								
Bowl, 8" – 9", dome-ftd.				325				
WIDE RIB								
Vase, 4" – 7" squat	40	85		65				
Vase, 8" – 14" swung	30	55		75		100	175	200 AQUA 250 VAS
Vase, pinched rib				175				
WINDFLOWER								
Bowl, 7½" – 9"	35	65				100		125 AMBER
Nappy, single hdld.	35	85		175		275		275 IG 125 LAV
Plate, 8" – 9"	145	375				225		
WINTERLILY								
Vase, 5½"	1,000							
WISHBONE & SPADES								
Banana bowl, 9" – 10"				575				
Bowl, 9" – 10", ruffled		575		275				
Bowl, 5" – 6", ruffled		75		50				
Bowl, 10", ice cream		900		350				
Bowl, 9" – 10", triangular				300				
Chop plate, 10" – 11"		1,500		4,500				
Plate, 6" – 7"		475		275				
WOODPECKER								
Wall vase	75							
WREATHED CHERRY								
Berry bowl, lg. oval	100	150	165	375	200	325		
Berry bowl, sm. oval	30	50	60	85	55	100		
Butter dish	165	275	295		300			
Covered sugar	80	110	125		150			
Creamer or spooner	50	75	85		100			
Toothpick holder		225						
Water pitcher	300	475	500		825			
Tumbler	45	70	75		110			
WREATH OF ROSES								
Rose bowl	45	75						85 LIME/M
Tri-shaped whimsey	60	100						
Spittoon	950							

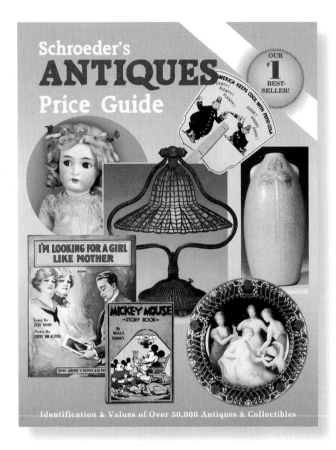